Fleeting Memories

MIT Press/Bradford Books Series in Cognitive Psychology
Stephen E. Palmer, editor

A Dynamic Systems Approach to Development: Applications, edited by Linda B. Smith and Esther Thelen (1993)

A Dynamic Systems Approach to the Development of Cognition and Action, edited by Esther Thelen and Linda B. Smith (1994)

Cognition and the Visual Arts, by Robert L. Solso (1994)

Indirect Perception, edited by Irvin Rock (1996)

Perceiving Talking Faces: From Speech Perception to a Behavioral Principle, by Dominic W. Massaro (1997)

Inattentional Blindness, by Arien Mack and Irvin Rock (1998)

Fleeting Memories: Cognition of Brief Visual Stimuli, edited by Veronika Coltheart (1999)

Fleeting Memories

Cognition of Brief Visual Stimuli

edited by *Veronika Coltheart*

© 1999 Massachusetts Institute of Technology

All rights reserved. No part of this book may be reproduced in any form by any electronic or mechanical means (including photocopying, recording, or information storage and retrieval) without permission in writing from the publisher.

This book was set in Palatino by Crane Composition, Inc.

Printed and bound in the United States of America.

Library of Congress Cataloging-in-Publication Data

Fleeting memories : cognition of brief visual stimuli / edited by Veronika Coltheart.
    p.   cm.—(MIT Press/Bradford Books series in cognitive psychology)
    "A Bradford book."
    Includes bibliographical references and index.
    ISBN 0-262-03261-9 (hardcover : alk. paper)
    1. Visual perception.   2. Short-term memory.   3. Cognition.
   I. Coltheart, Veronika.   II. Series.
   BF241.F57   1999
   153.1'32—dc21   98-36547
                                                               CIP

Contents

Series Foreword

This series presents definitive works on cognition viewed from a psychological perspective, including undergraduate and graduate textbooks, reference works, research monographs, and edited volumes. Among the wide variety of topics addressed are perception, attention, imagery, memory, learning, categorization, language, problem solving, thinking, and cognitive development. Although the primary emphasis is on presenting psychological theories and findings, most volumes in the series are interdisciplinary, attempting to develop important connections between cognitive psychology and the related fields of anthropology, computer science, education, linguistics, neuroscience, and philosophy.

Stephen E. Palmer

Acknowledgments

This book on fleeting memories profited from comments made by a number of colleagues who read some of the draft chapters. I thank Molly Potter, who read and commented on many of the chapters, and the following people, who read one or more chapters: Timothy Bates, Eugene Chekaluk, Max Coltheart, Robyn Langdon, Steve Mondy, and Jeremy Wolfe. I am also grateful for editorial assistance provided by Max Coltheart, Tonia Corner, Robyn Langdon, Steve Mondy, and Judy Vago and the staff at The MIT Press: Amy Brand, Katherine Almeida, and Ann Rae Jonas. The research reported in chapter 8 was supported by Australian Research Council funding and Macquarie University Research Grants, and the assistance of Robyn Langdon and Jo Millar is gratefully acknowledged.

Fleeting Memories

Chapter 1

Introduction: Perceiving and Remembering Brief Visual Stimuli

Veronika Coltheart

There is a long history of research investigating people's ability to perceive and remember briefly presented visual stimuli. This work began in the latter part of the nineteenth century, after the development of the tachistoscope. That device made it possible to study the amount of information that can be reported by an observer as a function of exposure duration, which could be accurately manipulated. The research from that period of Cattell (1885–1886) and of Erdman and Dodge (1898) is still cited in many textbooks of visual information-processing and cognitive psychology.

Early investigations by Javal (1878) showed that the process of reading involves periods during which the eye is motionless, fixed on part of the text, alternating with rapid eye movements referred to as saccades. Information is taken in by the visual system only when the eye is still, as during a saccade the information is blurred across the retina. Research on the nature of eye movements in reading and on the information acquired during fixation has been conducted in a number of laboratories in France, Britain, Germany, and the United States; reviews of this research have been written by Rayner and his colleagues (e.g., Rayner & Pollatsek 1987; 1989). These studies show that adult readers fixate on nearly every word of a text, skipping over only short, function words such as *the, of,* and *in,* and that longer words may be fixated more than once. Fixation durations vary, but typically last for 250–350 msec; that interval includes decision-making about where and when to move the eye next, as well as the motor programming required for the next saccade. The latency of an eye movement exceeds a tenth of a second (100 msec); thus stimulus exposure durations under 100 msec provide information about what is perceived and remembered from a single fixation in the absence of eye movements.

The question of what is perceived and retained from a single brief fixation was systematically studied by Sperling (1960) and by Averbach and Coriell (1961). These investigators devised an ingenious method for studying what is immediately perceived in brief displays of alphanumeric characters shown for intervals as short as 50 msec. Sperling noted that people say they saw more letters than the three or four they typically can report after a brief exposure. He considered the possibility that the limit on *recall* was produced by a limit on processes available to encode items for oral or written report. Perhaps more information was initially available, but it suffered rapid decay or was replaced by subsequent visual input. Sperling therefore devised a *partial report technique* that allowed the subject to limit report to three or four items from the display. However, the subjects did not know until *after* the display went off which items had to be reported. They were required to report one row only from a 3 × 3 or a 3 × 4 matrix of letters cued by a tone. Their high level of accuracy indicated that all, or most, of the display letters were available immediately after the display offset. Cue delay reduced accuracy, and Sperling concluded that visual recognition occurred in parallel for a large array, and that a rapidly fading high-capacity visual memory was available for a short period after the display was turned off. This was termed "iconic memory" by Neisser (1967).

Visual Masking and Metacontrast

Experiments by Sperling (1960) and by Averbach and Coriell (1961) demonstrated that the visual stimuli preceding and following the display were critical in determining what subjects were able to report. A visual stimulus preceding or following the display could reduce target display report: such stimuli are termed "visual masks." If a dark field follows the display, the partial report superiority can last up to 5 sec, suggesting that iconic memory can last for several seconds. However, if a bright light field follows, the partial report superiority lasts only 0.3–0.5 sec. Other visual displays also reduce report of the letter array, and we can distinguish homogeneous light masks from pattern masks. A stimulus functions as a mask if it reduces target detection. Masks can precede (forward masking) or follow targets (backward masking).

In one experiment, Averbach and Coriell (1961) used a circle around the designated letter's position as the cue. When the circle is presented at a certain time after stimulus offset, this can result in complete loss of the letter's identity, through what has become known as *metacontrast masking*. Contour proximity is a necessary condition for metacontrast masking. A large body of experiments was subsequently conducted to investigate the nature of iconic memory and masking. Turvey (1973) demonstrated that a mask that is a bright unpatterned field functions only monocularly, whereas some pattern masks show interocular transfer. This suggests that masking by a bright homogeneous field and masking by a patterned stimulus represent different mechanisms of masking. The reader interested in this topic is referred to a comprehensive review of the literature on iconic memory and visual persistence by M. Coltheart (1980).

On the face of it, these phenomena might appear to have little bearing on the way we view and extract information in "the real world." I argue that, on the contrary, the phenomena described above have an integral role in seeing and remembering in the wider sense, in naturally occurring settings. However, this issue has been controversial; for example, Haber (1983) suggested that the study of iconic memory was relevant only to the way we perceive visual stimuli during lightning storms, whereas M. Coltheart (1983) and others who commented on Haber's paper challenged his view. As I noted earlier, skilled reading involves intake of information during discrete fixations of 250–350 msec, and the content of prior fixations is likely to exert some masking effect on the processing of the current fixation.

Furthermore, the processes of scene perception also involve extraction of detailed information during fixations. When we look at scenes, the subjective experience is that we see the entire visual field clearly. This, however, is an illusion: we see in detail only information that falls on the fovea. This is an area about 1 mm square on the retina that is very densely packed with photoreceptive cells, the cones. Scene perception consists of periods of fixations when the eye is still and we gaze at objects of interest, having moved our eyes so that the image of the objects lies on the fovea. The duration of fixations during scene perception varies, but averages about 200–300 msec, and the eye movements are the rapid ballistic movements, saccades, that also occur during reading. Information outside the fovea is far less clearly perceived; acuity falls off rapidly beyond the fovea because the density of cones is sharply reduced and, although the density of rods is high immediately beyond the fovea (parafovea), rod vision has lower acuity.

A single glimpse corresponding to an eye fixation is sufficient for comprehending the gist (and main objects) of most scenes. However, the perception and comprehension of detailed features is built up from discrete views of parts of the scene, as only parts of the scene fall on the fovea on any fixation. In reading, perception of detail is essential for accurate word recognition. Again, the subjective impression is that all of the information on a page is continuously perceived. But, in fact, we see in detail only the segment of text that is fixated on the fovea; parafoveal information is seen less clearly; and only gross, fuzzy information is available from the periphery of vision. Readers can, of course, make regressive eye movements back to earlier words in the text they are reading. Consequently, much visual information is acquired in discrete, brief intervals in the real world and not just in laboratory settings; thus, reading can be viewed as an example of the intake of information from rapid sequences of briefly viewed stimuli.

The investigation of what is understood and remembered from rapidly presented *sequences* of visual stimuli began with the research of Potter and Levy (1969) and Forster (1970), using a technique of rapid presentation of sequences of visual stimuli, termed RSVP (rapid serial visual presentation) by Forster, who developed the paradigm using 16 mm motion pictures. Forster (1997, personal communication) thought of using this technique after hearing Potter's seminar on her research with rapidly presented pictures at MIT in 1968. His interests were in the processes underlying sentence comprehension, and his sequences consisted of written sentences, some of them scrambled, presented one word at a time.

Rapidly Presented Visual Sequences of Words

As Potter (1984) noted, Forster's technique can be used to study text-reading in the absence of eye movements. Forster (1970) presented words one at a time on film, using a fast exposure rate of 16 words per sec (62.5 msec per word). The subject's task was to report exactly what had been seen. Various types of 6-word sequences were shown: random word lists or sentences differing in syntactic structure. There were simple sentences with one underlying proposition (predicate constructions, transitives, and adverbials) and complex sentences with two underlying propositions (reduced relatives, unreduced relatives, complements, and time or manner adverbials). Most words were recalled from simple sentences (64.5%), followed by complex sentences (58.5%); recall of random word lists was lowest (39%). Recall was characterized by frequent omissions (80% of errors) with a few intrusions and order errors.

Subjects typically said that they failed to see words not reported, rather than that the words were unclear or illegible. However, these subjective reports of conscious experience were not reliable indices of what was "seen" or comprehended. Some subjects reported feeling that they "knew" what was in a sentence without having "seen" some of the words. This occurred despite the fact that the words were not always very predictable from the context (e.g., the word *shabby*, in the sentence "Both priests wore shabby sandals").

Forster (1970) suggested that failure of identification could be partly attributable to visual masking, forward and backward, which affects all but first and last words (they are better reported than other words).

Long words experience less masking than do short words because they are less likely to be overlaid at their ends, and the results showed that the likelihood of recall increased with word length: from 43% for 2-letter words to 82% for 8-letter and longer words. Another possible explanation was that word identification occurred, but the masking reduced processing time (of single words and syntax) and attention. Finally, the rate of presentation did not permit transfer to STM (short-term memory) and so the information was forgotten. Subsequent experiments (Forster 1970) suggested that all three factors, along with syntactic complexity, affected recall in RSVP tasks.

Potter's Research and the Theory of Conceptual STM

Potter (1984) provided a comprehensive review of RSVP methods and findings with lists and sentences, and subsequently (Potter 1993) proposed the existence of a very short-term conceptual memory system. Her chapter in this volume (chapter 2) presents a more detailed and elaborated account of this form of memory. Potter reviews her more recent research with sentences along with other paradigms using RSVP, and she presents a theoretical account of the memories established at fast rates of presentation.

The postulation of a very short-term conceptual memory can be found in Potter and Levy's (1969) report of experiments that studied comprehension and memory of rapidly presented photographs of scenes. These and subsequent experiments by Potter (1975, 1976) and by Intraub (1981) showed that pictures can be recognized and comprehended by RSVP rates of 10 pictures per sec, but that memory for the pictures immediately afterward is quite poor.

Scene Recognition and Memory

In chapter 3, Intraub reviews research suggesting that abstract representations of scenes are used in the interpretation of pictures of scenes. She discusses her earlier studies using rapidly presented series of pictures, as well as the studies of single brief presentations of pictures by Biederman (1981) and others.

Potter (1976) distinguished between perceptual and conceptual masking. Perceptual masking interrupts or degrades early forms of visual processing, and includes masking by light fields, pattern, and metacontrast, as discussed earlier. Conceptual masking interrupts later higher-level processing required for long-term storage of picture information. Subsequent research by Intraub (1980, 1984) and by Loftus and

Ginn (1984) extended the findings and demonstrated the importance of the attentional demands of the mask. New and meaningful pictures interfere with processing of their predecessors.

Intraub's chapter reports her recent investigations of the phenomenon of "boundary extension." *Boundary extension* refers to the finding that people tend to remember information that was not shown but is likely to have been present outside the picture's boundaries. She reports that this phenomenon can be found with briefly presented stimuli, which indicates early involvement of higher-order knowledge about scenes.

Detection of Scene Changes

While the gist of a scene may indeed be extracted in the first glance, Wolfe's chapter 4 reports that there are some quite remarkable failures in people's ability to detect large changes to currently viewed scenes. Such failures occur even when subjects have been inspecting the scene for up to 20 sec. The essential feature in the experiments seems to be that the change is effected during a saccade, or after a brief blank field, or when unrelated transients occur (e.g., "mud splashes"). Some impressive examples from Rensink, Clark, and O'Regan can be viewed at the following Web addresses:

> http://pathfinder.cbr.com/people/rensink/flicker/
> flickDescr.html
> http://pathfinder.cbr.com/people/clark/java/mudsplash.html
> http://pathfinder.cbr.com/people/oregan/traffic.movie4.mov.

Rensink also has Macintosh examples that can be downloaded: type "download/macExamples.html" after "rensink/" in the first address above.

Stephen Mondy (1997) has kindly provided an example for this book, shown in figure 1.1. The altered version is shown in figure 1.2. Mondy (reported in Mondy & Coltheart 1998) presented picture pairs such as those in figures 1.1 and 1.2, as well as identical picture pairs, for 10 sec each, separated by a 1 sec blue masking field. Subjects were asked to report whether or not the picture changed, and if something had changed, what it was. Very few of the 80 subjects detected the difference between figures 1.1 and figure 1.2, regardless of which picture was shown first. In his review of results such as these in chapter 4, Wolfe concludes that the failures to detect scene changes arise through *inattentional amnesia* rather than *inattentional blindness*.

Wolfe's research (discussed in chapter 4) has shown that postattentive representations are not remembered. The visual representation of

Figure 1.1
Version 1 of a picture presented to subjects in a scene-change detection experiment
(Mondy 1997).

an object seems to lapse into its preattentive state. Evidence for this
comes from performance in a repeated search task in which the stimuli
have been letters, curves, pictures, and geometrical figures conjoined
from simple features.

The Attentional Blink

There are limits on conceptual processing and on the establishment of
reportable episodic memory traces. One of these is the demonstration
of difficulty in reporting the second target in a dual target detection
task: this difficulty is termed the *attentional blink*. Raymond, Shapiro,
and Arnell (1992) presented lists of 16–24 letters at 11 letters per sec.
Subjects had to identify a white target letter and report the presence
of a subsequently presented designated probe letter (What was the
white letter, and was there a black X in the list?). Probe detection was
impaired following target identification for up to about half a second.
In chapter 5, Shapiro and Luck report their research on the attentional
blink, which includes ERP (evoked response potential) and neuropsychological data. They discuss how the attentional blink might be
explained in terms of the interference model of Shapiro, Raymond, and
Arnell (1994).

Figure 1.2
Version 2 of a picture presented to subjects in a scene-change detection experiment
(Mondy 1997).

Chapter 5 reports the results of dual target report tasks with "neglect" patients who cannot report visual stimuli in half the visual field after brain injuries. These patients exhibited a substantially more prolonged attentional blink than did control patients with other forms of right hemisphere lesions or elderly intact control subjects.

They also report neurophysiological data (ERP recordings) in experiments using normal subjects performing the dual target detection task. The results showed that semantic information about the second target was available despite the fact that subjects demonstrated an attentional blink manifested by impaired accuracy in deciding whether or not the probe word was semantically related to a context word at the beginning of the trial. Their N400 responses showed no corresponding drop in magnitude, suggesting that detection of the semantic match or mismatch had occurred at the time the probe word was presented. This finding is consistent with an alternative model of the attentional blink, the two-stage model of Chun and Potter (1995), described in chapter 2.

Repetition Blindness

The attentional blink is one example of a limit on establishing reportable explicit memory codes for rapidly presented visual stimuli. Another striking instance is provided by the repetition blindness phenomenon: subjects are less able to detect and report the second occurrence of a repeated word, letter, or digit in a rapidly presented visual sequence, which can consist of unrelated words or a sentence (Kanwisher 1987). The difficulty in reporting both items is confined to rapid presentation rates of 100–180 msec per item and an interstimulus interval (between the critical stimuli) of no more than 400–500 msec. Repetition blindness is not confined to pairs of identical items: it also occurs for orthographically similar words such as barn/bar, sort/ressort/ baguette/bague. It has been found for a number of languages: English (Kanwisher 1987), French (Bavelier 1992), Spanish (Altarriba and Soltano 1996), and Chinese (Chen and Wong 1997; Coltheart and Ling 1997, unpublished data).

Kanwisher (1987) proposed a token individuation model to account for repetition blindness. The model assumes that two stages occur during the registration of an event in episodic memory. The first recognition stage, type activation, involves activation of representations in long-term semantic memory. The second, token individuation, involves the establishment of links between the activated types and tokens. A variant of this model was proposed by Bavelier and Potter (1992), and Bavelier reviews her more recent account in chapter 7.

Repetition Blindness for Pictures

Chapter 6, by Kanwisher, Yin, and Wojciulik, reports a program of research studying repetition blindness for pictures. Their aim was to investigate the nature of intermediate representations extracted during scene and object recognition. They argue that the identity of the repeated item must be extracted at some level, and hence is an example of recognition without awareness. The experiments investigated recall of lists of three pictures interspersed with two masks, presented at a 100 msec rate. They found that repetition blindness for pictures is unaffected by changes in size, position, orientation in the picture plane, and viewpoint. A reduced level of repetition blindness was obtained with different exemplars of the same type of object (upright piano/ grand piano), and a further reduced but significant repetition blindness occurred with conceptually or semantically related pictures (helicopter/fixed-wing plane). Repetition blindness did not occur for pictures sharing a name only (baseball bat/flying bat), suggesting that phonological codes do not contribute to *picture* repetition blindness. Another difference between picture repetition blindness and word repetition blindness is that the conceptually related *picture names* did not show repetition blindness; instead, they showed a repetition *benefit* or *advan-*

tage. Thus, picture repetition blindness differs in important ways from written word repetition blindness. The results indicate perception and extraction of viewpoint-invariant representations and semantic information about pictures outside of awareness.

Repetition Blindness for Written Words

Bavelier's chapter 7 presents further research on the establishment of object-specific STM representations (token instantiation). She argues that token instantiation is initiated by spatiotemporal discontinuity in the visual environment. Repetition blindness demonstrates a failure of this process. Bavelier hypothesized that token instantiation is a graded process during which information from various perceptual levels is integrated into a common episodic representation. These ideas are developed in the light of her research on the parameters determining repetition blindness for written words.

Phonological Codes in Reading Comprehension and Memory

My chapter 8 reviews evidence concerning the involvement of phonological codes in reading and memory tasks. Phonologically based memory errors and reduced recall of phonologically similar lists (Baddeley 1966; Conrad 1994) led to the assumption that visually presented items were registered in a phonological short-term store after phonological recoding or name retrieval (Baddeley 1986). The chapter reports the results of several experiments that used RSVP list presentation rates up to 10 times as fast as those used in STM research. These experiments, like STM studies, demonstrated reduced recall for phonologically similar and long words, and the removal of these effects when subjects had to engage in irrelevant concurrent articulation. The results demonstrated a continuity between processes supporting recall at fast RSVP rates and those of the much slower standard STM tasks.

Sentence Repetition by Patients with STM Deficit

Saffran and Martin's chapter 9 considers the unusual form of sentence repetition by patients with left parietal lesions and a verbal STM deficit. These patients have abnormally low digit span but relatively intact language functioning. Their ability to recall lists of unrelated words is poor, as is their verbatim recall of sentences more than 5–6 words long. However, sentence recall often preserves the meaning of the sentence, expressed as a paraphrase. Saffran and Martin consider the question of whether the performance of these patients can be interpreted in terms of the presence of a defective auditory-verbal STM along with an intact conceptual STM.

The chapters of this book report a considerable body of empirical data concerning the characteristics of fleeting memories. The evidence includes experimental, neuropsychological, and electrophysiological data. Chapter 10 draws attention to some of the convergent findings that have emerged. For example, different paradigms indicate that visual and orthographic codes are extracted early in processing and phonological codes emerge later. This difference is more marked in the case of pictures than of words. In fact, for pictures, semantic and conceptual information is available before phonological picture name codes. Evidence of implicit semantic activation of words that cannot be reported has been obtained under conditions of the attentional blink and of repetition blindness.

References

Altarriba, J., & Soltano, E. G. (1996). Repetition blindness and bilingual memory: Token individuation for translation equivalents. *Memory & Cognition, 24*, 700–711.

Averbach, E., & Coriell, A. S. (1961). Short-term memory in vision. *Bell System Technical Journal, 40,* 309–328.

Baddeley, A. D. (1966). Short-term memory for word sequences as a function of acoustic, semantic and formal similarity. *Quarterly Journal of Experimental Psychology, 18,* 362–365.

Baddeley, A. D. (1986). *Working memory.* Oxford: Clarendon Press.

Bavelier, D. (1992). Phonological repetition blindness. Ph.D. dissertation, Massachusetts Institute of Technology.

Bavelier, D. (1994). Repetition blindness between visually different items: The case of pictures and words. *Cognition, 51,* 199–236.

Bavelier, D., & Potter, M. C. (1992). Visual and phonological codes in repetition blindness. *Journal of Experimental Psychology: Human Perception and Performance, 18,* 134–147.

Biederman, I. (1981). On the semantics of a glance at a scene. In M. Kubovy & J. R. Pomerantz (eds.), *Perceptual organization* (pp. 213–253). Hillsdale, NJ: Lawrence Erlbaum Associates.

Cattell, J. McK. (1885–1886). The inertia of the eye and brain. *Brain, 8,* 295–312.

Chen, H. C., & Wong, K. F. E. (1997). Reaction time analyses of repetition blindness. In M. G. Shafto and P. Langley (eds.), *Proceedings of the 19th annual conference of the cognitive science society* (pp. 102–106). Hillsdale, NJ: Lawrence Erlbaum Associates.

Chun, M. M., & Potter, M. C. (1995). A two-stage model for multiple target detection in rapid serial visual presentation. *Journal of Experimental Psychology: Human Perception and Performance, 21,* 109–127.

Coltheart, M. (1972). Visual information processing. In P. C. Dodwell (ed.), *New horizons in psychology* (vol. 2, pp. 62–85). London: Penguin.

Coltheart, M. (1980). Iconic memory and visual persistence. *Perception & Psychophysics, 27,* 183–228.

Coltheart, M. (1983). Ecological necessity of iconic memory. *The Behavioral and Brain Sciences, 6,* 17–18.

Conrad, R. (1964). Acoustic confusion in immediate memory. *British Journal of Psychology, 55,* 75–84.

Erdman, B., & Dodge, R. (1898). Cited in K. T. Spoehr & S. W. Lehmkuhle, *Visual information processing*. San Francisco: W. H. Freeman, 1982.

Forster, K. I. (1970). Visual perception of rapidly presented word sequences of varying complexity. *Perception & Psychophysics, 8,* 215–221.

Haber, R. N. (1983). The impending demise of the icon: A critique of the concept of iconic storage in visual information processing. *The Behavioral and Brain Sciences, 6,* 1–11.

Intraub, H. (1980). Presentation rate and the representation of briefly glimpsed pictures in memory. *Journal of Experimental Psychology: Human Learning and Memory, 6,* 1–12.

Intraub, H. (1981). Rapid conceptual identification of sequentially presented pictures. *Journal of Experimental Psychology: Human Perception and Performance, 7,* 604–610.

Intraub, H. (1984). Conceptual masking: The effects of subsequent visual events on memory for pictures. *Journal of Experimental Psychology: Learning, Memory and Cognition, 10,* 115–125.

Javal, L. E. (1878). Cited in R. L. Solso, *Cognitive psychology.* (3rd ed.). Boston: Allyn and Bacon, 1991.

Kanwisher, N. G. (1987). Repetition blindness: Type recognition without token individuation. *Cognition, 27,* 117–143.

Loftus, G. R., & Ginn, M. (1984). Perceptual and conceptual masking of pictures. *Journal of Experimental Psychology: Learning, Memory and Cognition, 10,* 435–441.

Mondy, S. (1997) Unpublished PhD experiments. Macquaine University, NSW Australia

Mondy, S., & Coltheart, V. (1998). Change blindness. Paper presented at the *Twenty-fifth Annual Australian Experimental Psychology Conference,* April 1998, University of Tasmania, Hobart.

Neisser, U. (1967). *Cognitive psychology.* New York: Appleton-Century-Crofts.

Potter, M. C. (1975). Meaning in visual search. *Science, 187,* 965–966.

Potter, M. C. (1976). Short-term conceptual memory for pictures. *Journal of Experimental Psychology: Human Learning and Memory, 2,* 509–522.

Potter, M. C. (1984). Rapid serial visual presentation (RSVP): A method for studying language processing. In D. E. Kieras & M. A. Just (eds.), *New methods in reading comprehension research* (pp. 91–118). Hillsdale, NJ: Lawrence Erlbaum Associates.

Potter, M. C. (1993). Very short-term conceptual memory. *Memory & Cognition, 21,* 156–161.

Potter, M. C., & Levy, E. I. (1969). Recognition memory for a rapid sequence of pictures. *Journal of Experimental Psychology, 81,* 10–15.

Raymond, J. E., Shapiro, K. L., & Arnell, K. M. (1992). Temporary suppression of visual processing in an RSVP task: An attentional blink? *Journal of Experimental Psychology: Human Perception and Performance, 18,* 849–860.

Rayner, K., & Pollatsek, A. (1987). Eye movements in reading: A tutorial review. In M. Coltheart (ed.), *Attention and performance.* Vol. 12, *The psychology of reading* (pp. 327–362). London: Lawrence Erlbaum Associates.

Rayner, K., & Pollatsek, A. (1989). *The psychology of reading.* London: Prentice-Hall.

Shapiro, K. L., Raymond, J. E., & Arnell, K. M. (1994). Attention to visual pattern information produces the attentional blink in RSVP. *Journal of Experimental Psychology: Human Perception and Performance, 20,* 357–371.

Sperling, G. (1960). The information available in brief visual presentations. *Psychological Monographs, 74,* 1–29.

Turvey, M. T. (1973). On peripheral and central processes in vision: Inferences from an information-processing analysis of masking with patterned stimuli. *Psychological Review, 80,* 1–52.

Chapter 2

Understanding Sentences and Scenes: The Role of Conceptual Short-Term Memory

Mary C. Potter

In this chapter I summarize a thesis concerning a very brief form of memory that I have termed conceptual short-term memory (CSTM). I then consider the role of this form of working memory in attending selectively, understanding language, and recognizing and remembering scenes. Finally, I discuss some issues relevant to CSTM, including the question of whether CSTM is conscious.

When people view or listen to continuous sequences of scenes or words, as they do when they look around, read, listen, or watch TV, a series of conceptual representations is activated. These rapidly activated and equally rapidly forgotten representations are the raw material for identification and comprehension of words, pictures, and sequences such as a sentence, and indeed for intelligent thought more generally. The normal ease with which we understand what we read and see around us is based on selective processing that takes place much faster than has been supposed in many theories of working and short-term memory, leading to the CSTM hypothesis (Potter 1993).

The CSTM hypothesis proposes that when a stimulus is identified, its meaning is rapidly activated and maintained briefly in CSTM. CSTM is a processing and memory system different from early visual (iconic) memory, conventional short-term memory (STM), and longer-term memory (LTM) in three important respects: (1) the rapidity with which stimuli reach a postcategorical, meaningful level of representation, (2) the rapid structuring of these representations, and (3) the lack of awareness (or immediate forgetting) of information that is not structured or otherwise consolidated. Structure-building in CSTM ranges from spontaneous grouping of words in lists on the basis of meaning (one of the simplest forms of conceptual structuring) to linguistic parsing and semantic interpretation of sentences and more extended texts (examples of highly skilled structuring). Organization or structuring of new stimuli enhances memory for them.

The idea here is that most cognitive processing occurs on the fly, without review of material in standard short-term memory and with little or no conscious reasoning. Yet, these rapid processes are flexible, not fixed: new sentences are processed, new scenes are comprehended, important items are selected for attention even though they cannot be explicitly anticipated, novel sentences are formulated to express an idea, and appropriate actions are taken. I propose that CSTM plays an essential role in these processes. The working of CSTM is best revealed when two or more stimuli are presented together or in a rapid sequence, as in rapid serial visual presentation (RSVP), or when a rich stimulus is presented, such as a picture of a scene.

> Unlike STM, CSTM is central to cognitive processing. Recognition of meaningful stimuli such as words or objects rapidly activates conceptual information and leads to the retrieval of additional relevant information from LTM. New links among concurrently active concepts are formed, guided by parsing mechanisms of language or scene perception and by higher-level knowledge. When these new links result in well-connected structures, the structures are likely to be consolidated into LTM. Information that is not incorporated into such structures is rapidly forgotten. This whole cycle—identification of stimuli, memory recruitment, structuring, consolidation, and forgetting of nonstructured material—may occur in less than 1 sec when viewing a pictured scene or reading a sentence. (Potter 1993, p. 156)

The proposal that CSTM is a memory system distinct from STM and LTM is based on evidence for high-level processes that occur within a second of the onset of a stimulus, processes that depend on at least brief retention of stimuli at a conceptual level, together with associations that these conceptual representations activate from LTM. Standard short-term or working memory, such as Baddeley's articulatory loop and visuospatial sketchpad (e.g., Baddeley 1986), focuses on memory systems that support cognitive processes that take place over several seconds or minutes. A memory system such as the articulatory loop is unsuited for conceptual processing that takes place within a second of the onset of a stream of stimuli: it takes too long to be set up, and it does not represent semantic and conceptual information directly. Instead, STM directly represents articulatory and phonological information (the articulatory loop system) or visuospatial properties (the visuospatial sketchpad): these representations must be reinterpreted conceptually before further meaning-based processing can occur.

That approach neglects the evidence (some of it reviewed in the present chapter and elsewhere in this volume) that stimuli in almost any cognitive task rapidly activate a large amount of potentially pertinent information, followed by rapid selection and then decay or deactivation of the rest. That can happen an order of magnitude faster than the setting up of a standard, rehearsable STM representation, permitting the seemingly effortless processing of experience that is typical of cognition. Of course, not all cognitive processing is effortless: our ability to engage in slower, more effortful reasoning, recollection, and planning may well draw on conventional short-term memory representations. I return to this point later.

The proposed architecture is similar in spirit to such contemporary models of processing as Anderson's ACT* (1983; see also Anderson 1993), Kintsch's (1988) construction–integration model of discourse comprehension, Ericsson and Kintsch's (1995) theory of long-term working memory (LT-WM), and Just and Carpenter's model of reading comprehension (1992). While these models differ from each other in many respects, all assume some form of processing that relies on activation or memory buffers other than standard STM. Thus, the idea of immediacy of processing (with a brief memory buffer) is not new, although it tends to be neglected in favor of the slower processes of conventional working memory.

Evidence for CSTM—An Overview

The CSTM hypothesis consists of several interrelated claims. First, presentation of a sequence of meaningful stimuli gives rapid access to semantic information about each stimulus, including its associations. Second, this information is used in various ways, depending on the viewer's current goal: if the viewer is trying to understand the whole sequence (e.g., a sentence), the information is used to discover or build a comprehensive structured representation, but if the viewer is trying to locate and identify a particular kind of information (as in target search), then only a subset of the information is selected. Third, whatever information has not been incorporated in such a structure, or selected as a target of interest, is highly likely to be forgotten, often before it enters awareness. A brief review of evidence for each of these assumptions of the model follows. A more detailed discussion of some of this work follows this overview.

> 1. *There is rapid access to semantic information about a stimulus.* As recently as the early 1970s it was still unclear whether semantic information was retrieved as part of STM or only subsequent to phonemic encoding (e.g., Shulman 1971), even when words to be remembered were each presented for 1 sec or longer. Since that time it has become evident that conceptual information about a

stimulus such as a word or a picture is available within 100–300 msec. Among the experimental paradigms that have shown such rapid availability are semantic priming (Neely 1991), including masked priming and so-called fast priming (Sereno & Rayner 1992); eye tracking of reading (Rayner 1983) and of scene perception (Loftus 1983); measurement of event-related potentials during reading (Kutas & Hillyard 1980); and target detection in rapidly presented sequences of pictures (Potter 1976), words (Lawrence 1971b), and letters and digits (Chun & Potter 1995; Sperling, Budiansky, Spivak, & Johnson 1971). These and other studies, some of which are discussed in more detail later in this chapter, show that semantic or conceptual factors have an effect on performance within a few hundred msec of the onset of the critical stimulus.

2. *This activated conceptual information can be used to discover or build a structured representation of the information, or to select certain stimuli at the expense of others.* A major source of evidence for this claim comes from rapid serial visual presentation (RSVP; Forster 1970) of words of a sentence, compared with scrambled sentences or lists of unrelated words. Studies by Forster (1970) and Potter (1984a; 1993; Potter, Kroll, & Harris 1980; Potter, Kroll, Yachzel, Carpenter, & Sherman 1986) show that it is possible to process the structure in a sentence and hence to recall it subsequently, at a rate such as 12 words/sec. In contrast, when short lists of unrelated words are presented at that rate, only 2 or 3 words can be recalled (see also Lawrence 1971a). For sentences, not only the syntactic structure but also the meaning and plausibility of the sentence are recovered as the sentence is processed (Potter et al. 1986). Because almost all sentences one normally encounters (and all the sentences in these experiments) include new combinations of ideas, structure-building is not simply a matter of locating a previously encountered pattern in long-term memory: it involves the instantiation of a new relationship among existing concepts. Structure-building presumably takes advantage of as much old structure as possible, using any preexisting associations and chunks of information to bind elements (such as individual words in a list) together.

Selective processing based on rapid access to information about the identity and meaning of stimuli is shown in serial search for targets that are specified by category (e.g., "an animal," "a letter"), as in recent work on the attentional blink (e.g., Chun & Potter 1995; Raymond, Shapiro, & Arnell 1992; Potter, Chun, Banks, & Muckenhoupt 1998) and in older picture search (e.g., Intraub 1981;

Potter 1975, 1976) and word search (Lawrence 1971b) studies. To detect a target defined by its category, the target must first be identified. The finding in all these experiments that targets can be detected at rates of 8–10 items/sec or higher shows that categorical information about a stimulus is activated and then selected extremely rapidly.

3. *There is rapid loss of information that does not become structured or that is not selected for further processing.* The CSTM hypothesis is not only that conceptual information is activated rapidly, but also that the initial activation is highly unstable, such that the information is deactivated or forgotten within a few hundred msec if it is not incorporated into a structure (or selected for further processing). (Note the similarity between this assumption and that of rapid decay of iconic memory; however, precategorical iconic memory is clearly distinct from CSTM. Theories such as that of M. Coltheart [e.g., 1983] include a postcategorical stage in iconic memory, which may be identified with CSTM.) The assumption is that as a structure is built—for example, as a sentence is being parsed and interpreted—the resulting interpretation can be held in memory and ultimately stabilized or consolidated in longer-term memory as a unit, whereas only a small part of an unstructured sequence such as a string of unrelated words can be consolidated in the same time period.

I use the term "consolidation" descriptively; the nature of the process that results in a more stable representation, in either STM or LTM, is not yet known. Consolidation of information from CSTM into a more stable representation such as STM appears to operate serially on single items, chunks, or connected structures, and to require time, as shown in studies of picture memory and studies of the attentional blink already cited. The importance of structuring and of study time in converting a short-term memory into a long-term memory is well recognized; as a rule of thumb, it has been suggested that it takes 5 sec per item to establish a long-term memory. However, a single item in CSTM appears to take an order of magnitude less time to become stabilized in STM: 500 msec or less. When a sequence of items such as the words in a sentence can be structured rapidly in CSTM, stabilization in reportable memory seems to occur simply as a consequence of structuring, just as comprehension of a conversation or story results in a long-term memory representation. Evidence for rapid forgetting of material that is not well-structured is discussed below.

Rapid Processing Followed by Rapid Forgetting: Case Studies Using RSVP

The original motivation for presenting static stimuli such as still photographs in a continuous sequence was to simulate normal visual perception, in which the eye fixates briefly on a succession of points and thus processes a continuous sequence of snapshots (Potter & Levy 1969). Similarly, in reading or in listening to speech there is a steady flow of new information: events do not occur in single, isolated trials. In these circumstances rapid conceptual activation is often followed by rapid forgetting of some of the material. In this section I discuss a number of studies using RSVP as a tool to investigate rapid comprehension and rapid forgetting in CSTM.

Selective Search and the Attentional Blink

In brief, the attentional blink (AB) is a phenomenon that occurs in RSVP search tasks in which two targets are presented among distractors. When the rate of presentation is high but still compatible with accurate report of a single target (e.g., a presentation rate of 10/sec when detecting a letter among digit distractors), two targets are also likely to be reported accurately—except when the second target appears within 200–500 msec of the onset of the first target. This interval during which second-target detection drops dramatically was termed an attentional blink by Raymond et al. (1992). Shapiro and Luck's chapter in this volume provides a comprehensive review of the literature on AB, so in the following I focus on Chun's and my research as it pertains to CSTM (Chun 1997a, 1997b; Chun, Bromberg, & Potter 1994; Chun & Potter 1995; Potter, Chun, et al. 1998).

The attentional blink is relevant to CSTM because it provides evidence for rapid access to categorical information about rapidly presented items and at the same time shows that selective processing of specified targets has a cost. AB experiments suggest that there is a difference in time course between two stages of processing, a first stage that results in identification of a stimulus (CSTM) and a second stage required to consolidate that information in a reportable form, when the task is to pick out targets from among distractors (Chun & Potter 1995).

Consider a task in which targets are any letter of the alphabet, presented in an RSVP sequence of digit distractors. Presumably a target letter must be identified in order to be classified as a target (see Sperling et al. 1971). At rates as high as 11 items/sec the first letter target (T1) is detected quite accurately, consistent with evidence that a letter can be identified in less than 100 msec. We term this initial identification

Stage 1 processing, which constitutes activation of a conceptual but short-lasting representation, a CSTM representation.

A second target letter (T2) that arrives soon after the first one is likely to be missed, suggesting that a selected target requires additional processing beyond identification: Stage 2 processing. It is Stage 2 processing of T1 that interferes with the processing of T2. Stage 2 processing is necessary to consolidate a selected item into some form of short-term memory that is more stable than CSTM. We further hypothesized that the items following the first target (T1) continue to be processed successfully in Stage 1 and remain for a short time in CSTM; the problem is that as long as Stage 2 is tied up with T1, a second target may be identified but must wait, and thus may be lost from CSTM before Stage 2 is available. When this happens, T2 is missed, producing an attentional blink. Although the duration of the AB varies, it is marked at 200 msec after the onset of the first target and diminishes over the next 300 msecs; it is usually gone by 500 msec.

Recently, several findings have supported the Chun–Potter hypothesis that T2 does receive Stage 1 processing, even if it is subsequently unavailable for report because it is "blinked." Luck, Vogel, and Shapiro (1996) found that an unreported T2 word (falling in the AB interval) nonetheless resulted in a significant N400 cortical evoked potential based on its meaning. Maki, Frigen, and Paulson (1997) found that an unattended distractor falling in the AB interval could semantically prime a second target also falling in that interval, and the size of the priming effect was as great as that between the prime-target pairs outside the blink interval. They interpreted this result as consistent with the claim of the Chun–Potter two-stage model that all (or most) items are processed to a conceptual level, whether or not they can be reported. Shapiro, Driver, Ward, and Sorenson (1997) also obtained evidence for semantic activation of targets that appear in the attentional blink window and fail to be reported.

In Chun and Potter's model, Stage 1 identification of the first target initiates the Stage 2 process of attention and consolidation. However, the attentional process that selects the target for second-stage processing is temporally inexact, so that frequently the target and the following item are both passed to Stage 2 (Raymond et al. 1992 proposed a similar hypothesis). When a distractor that is confusable with a target (e.g., a digit distractor with a letter target) is processed together with the target in Stage 2, sorting out and consolidating the target is slower than it would be with no following distractor, or with a dissimilar distractor such as an asterisk (Chun & Potter 1995; see also Maki, Couture, Frigen, & Lien 1997). When the immediately following item is the second target, then the inexact attentional process is likely to pick up both T1 and T2 for processing in Stage 2, and both targets are likely to be successfully processed, producing the lag 1 sparing (the check mark profile as a function of lag) that is frequently observed in AB experiments. But if even a single distractor intervenes between T1 and T2, then T2 waits: thus, the AB effect is reduced or absent at lag 1 and maximal at lag 2, when the wait for Stage 2 processing is longest on average.

Is There a Cross-Modal Attentional Blink?   Potter, Chun, et al. (1998; see also Potter, Chun, & Muckenhoupt 1995) reported a series of experiments in which compressed speech was used to create an auditory equivalent of RSVP. Subjects listened to a rapid series of spoken digit distractors and two letter targets. In this condition we found some deficit for the second letter, but critically there was no effect of the lag between the two spoken letters, and thus no indication of a transient auditory "blink." Similarly, when the sequence started out in one modality and then switched to the other modality, with one target in each modality, there was again no evidence for a blink. However, Arnell and Jolicoeur (1995, 1997) did find evidence for a lag-dependent deficit in auditory and cross-modal conditions that they considered to be an attentional blink. To attempt to resolve this difference in results, Potter, Chun, et al. (1998) differentiated the visual attentional blink from another attentional deficit in serial search tasks that we believe to be the consequence of task-switching.

Costs of switching between one task and another are standardly studied by comparing performance on the first trial of the new task with performance on the second or subsequent trials. In many conditions, the first trial after a task switch is slower or less accurate than subsequent trials, even though the task is highly practiced and the participant is informed that a switch is about to occur (Allport, Styles, & Hsieh 1994; Meiran 1996; Monsell 1996; Rogers & Monsell 1995). These experiments (with one exception) used single trials in which the subject responded to each stimulus before seeing the next one.

Consider, however, what one might expect in the case of serial search, if the second of two targets requires a switch in perceptual set. Potter, Chun, et al. (1998) noted that in some AB studies (e.g., Chun & Potter 1995) the two targets are defined in the same way (two letters among digits), whereas in other studies the two targets are defined differently. In a typical procedure of the latter type, the first target is a white letter among black letter distractors and the second target is a black letter X among other letters: the X is present on a random half of the trials (Raymond et al. 1992). The viewer has to report the identity of the

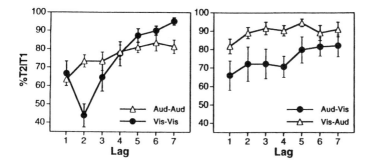

Figure 2.1
Correct report of T2 (given correct report of T1) as a function of lag, with 2 simultaneous sequences of visual and auditory items (SOA = 120 msec) and instructions to identify T1 and detect "X" (T2) in specified modalities, for the groups with 2 visual or 2 auditory targets (panel at left), and the groups with 1 visual and 1 auditory target (panel at right). Only trials on which an "X" was presented are included. Vertical bars show standard error of the mean. (Potter, Chun, et al. 1998, experiment 4.)

white letter (T1) and then report the presence or absence of T2 (the X). Thus, there is a switch from a set to pick out and identify the white letter, ignoring black letters, to a set to make a presence–absence decision as to a black X. Even though subjects do not make an overt response until after both targets have been presented, such a switch in perceptual and (covert) response set could take time, during which T2 might be missed. The covert task switch would produce a lag-dependent deficit that is maximal at lag 1, the immediately following stimulus (in contrast to the attentional blink, which shows sparing at lag 1).

In most of Arnell and Jolicoeur's experiments showing cross-modal and auditory attentional deficits (1995, 1997), they used different tasks for T1 and T2. Potter, Chun, et al. (1998) hypothesized that the deficits Arnell and Jolicoeur observed in the cross-modal and auditory conditions were actually task-switch deficits; one cue was that in the cross-modal conditions the largest deficit was at lag 1. We replicated their findings when we adopted their task-switch procedure (figure 2.1), but when we used the same letter-detection task (or digit-detection task) for both T1 and T2, we attenuated or eliminated the lag-dependent deficit—except for the all-visual condition (figure 2.2). Significantly, in the task-switch condition the greatest deficit was at lag 1—except for the all-visual condition, in which lag 1 reflected a combination of the visual AB pattern of sparing and the task-switch deficit. The lag 1 benefit reflects the properties of visual stimuli, which are unstable in visual STM or CSTM and must be stabilized by further processing in Stage 2. In contrast, auditory stimuli appear to enter an auditory buffer

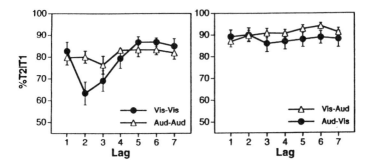

Figure 2.2
Correct report of T2 (given correct report of T1) as a function of lag, with 2 simultaneous sequences of visual and auditory items (SOA = 120 msec), when the task was to report 2 letters among digit distractors. The results are shown separately for each of the 4 conditions, VV, AA, VA, and AV. Vertical bars show standard error of the mean. (Potter, Chun, et al. 1998, experiment 5.)

that has a longer time course, reducing or eliminating lag effects as long as the task is consistent from T1 to T2. Task-switching costs, however, have to do with central set and presumably are not modality-dependent, which is why they show up in auditory and cross-modal conditions. When a task-switching procedure is combined with all-visual presentations, then both the standard AB effects and task-switching effects are observed; lag 1 benefits may or may not be found.

Summary: CSTM and AB   Studies of the visual attentional blink demonstrate a dissociation between an early stage of processing sufficient to identify letters or words presented at a rate of about 10/sec, and a subsequent stage of variable duration (up to about 400 msec) required to stabilize a selected item in reportable STM. The attentional blink thus provides evidence for the central claims of CSTM.

Repetition Blindness and Token Failure
Helene Intraub was the first person to discover the repetition blindness phenomenon, when she was investigating conceptual short-term memory for pictures in the late 1970s as a postdoctoral fellow in my lab. She noted that the repeated picture she had placed in a sequence seemed to disappear when she ran the film, even though there were other pictures intervening between the two presentations: she had to check the film slowly to confirm that the picture had indeed appeared twice. She called me into the lab to observe this surprising illusion. Kanwisher (1987) investigated this illusion with sequences of words, in lists and sentences; she dubbed the effect "repetition blindness"

(RB). She confirmed that the second of two identical visual stimuli is often not noticed when it appears in an RSVP sequence shortly after the first stimulus. What is remarkable is that items that intervene between the first instance (C1) and the second one (C2) may be perceived and reported accurately. Like the attentional blink, RB shows a lag effect, although Chun (1997a) has found that, unlike visual AB, RB is maximal at lag 1.[1] Using the AB target-search procedure, Chun showed that AB and RB are doubly dissociable: RB is found for second identical targets (or for targets identical except for letter case) even when the distractors are keyboard symbols and there is no AB, and RB turns into a repetition benefit when the targets (letters among digits) are redundantly signaled by being colored rather than black, whereas AB is substantial in this condition.

Kanwisher (1987) proposed that repetition blindness occurs when the viewer fails to set up a token (or object file; Kahneman & Treisman 1984) of the second stimulus. Tokens are contrasted with types: types are the long-term representations of types or categories of objects, including words, that are used in the recognition of objects. When an object or word is viewed, recognition requires not only that the appropriate type representation be activated, but also that a representation or token of the object's presence be set up in this particular episode (see Kanwisher's and Bavelier's chapters in this volume for further discussion of this theory). Without a token representation, the occurrence of an item is unreportable. The loss of reportable information about the occurrence of the second of two identical items (RB) is due to a bias in the visual system against the immediate retokenizing of the same type: instead, the second occurrence, which does activate the type representation, is taken to be part of the first occurrence, which has already been tokenized.

One can ask whether CSTM consists of type activation or new tokens or both. CSTM is a form of representation in which old (recognizable) items are activated to form new structures, so it is clear that existing types (and their associations) must be activated in CSTM. Insofar as structuring occurs in CSTM processing, the new structures must be represented by establishing tokens of the relevant types and their relationships. For example, to process even a simple novel sentence successfully requires the activation of one's knowledge of the word types, of associations among the concepts constrained by parsing mechanisms, and a token representation of the resulting meaningful structure. The finding that syntactic and pragmatic constraints have little or no effect on repetition blindness for the second occurrence of a word in a sentence (Kanwisher 1987; Kanwisher & Potter 1990) suggests that failure to create a token for the second occurrence of a word prevents it from entering into the structuring process, so that the sentence "Nancy spilled the ink and there was ink all over" is processed and recalled as the ungrammatical string "Nancy spilled the ink and there was all over." For sentence processing, a failure to include a token of the second "ink" apparently makes it invisible to the parser.

Thus, although structuring in CSTM makes use of types and their connections as represented in LTM, it seems likely that copies or tokens of these activated types are what enter into the structuring process in CSTM, at least in the case of syntactic processing. Repetition blindness would prevent an item from participating in CSTM. On the other hand, Bavelier (in the present volume; Bavelier 1994; Bavelier & Potter 1992) has argued that some forms of repetition blindness, particularly those between nonidentical visual stimuli that share only an identical phonological representation (e.g., a picture of the sun and the written word *son*), arise only after an initial token has been opened for the second item; as more information (e.g., phonological information) becomes activated, the opened token will become subject to RB if the added information leads to sufficiently similar representations of C1 and C2.

That is, Bavelier proposes that tokenization is not an all-or-nothing process, but occurs over a period of tens or hundreds of milliseconds as more information about a type is accrued, either stabilizing the token or, in RB, making it similar enough to an earlier token to cause the two to merge. This view implies that such items are represented at least partially in CSTM, albeit briefly. Such a fleeting representation may account for the preservation of semantic priming from a repeated homophone in lexical decision (e.g., none . . . nun PRIEST) despite evidence for RB for *nun* in recall (Coltheart, this volume). Bavelier notes that RB effects tend to be considerably weaker between visually dissimilar items than between highly similar or identical visual items, suggesting that much of the time both items are at least briefly available in CSTM.

In understanding the basis for RB it is important to note that visual similarity and phonological similarity of the names of visual stimuli can both produce RB, but there is little or no evidence for conceptually based repetition blindness. Synonyms such as "couch" and "sofa" do not produce RB (Altarriba & Soltano 1996; Kanwisher & Potter 1990; but see MacKay & Miller 1994; and MacKay, Abrams, Pedroza, & Miller 1996). This suggests that the tokenizing process is concerned with the representation of visual entities, not their meanings. A further question is whether an analog of RB is found with auditory stimuli: repetition deafness (RD). While Miller and MacKay (1994, 1996) did report evidence for RD in lists of words (but not sentences), Downing, Kanwisher, and Potter (1998) failed to find either RD or a cross-modal repetition deficit; if anything, they obtained a repetition benefit (positive priming) in the auditory case. As Potter, Chun, et al. (1998) speculated with respect to the absence of an auditory or cross-modal attentional blink, it seems likely that the auditory system has a robust mechanism for representing rapid sequences of sounds, a mechanism that would buffer rapidly changing information more effectively than in the visual system.

Summary: RB   The loss of a stimulus when it is identical or similar to a stimulus seen within the last 0.5 sec points to the vulnerability of rapidly presented stimuli to forgetting. The very structuring process that stabilizes associated items in CSTM appears to collapse two events into one when they arrive in quick succession and are categorized visually, orthographically, or phonologically under the same heading—even when they are in fact distinct not only temporally but also in terms of their visual properties (uppercase versus lowercase letters, homophones, pictures and words, etc.).

Understanding RSVP Sentences
Given the marked problems in encoding just two stimuli in the target-search tasks used to investigate the attentional blink, it is striking that one can read an RSVP sentence at the same rate (10 words/sec), and both understand and recall it (Potter 1983, 1984a; Potter et al. 1986). Although part of the difference between search tasks and sentences is due to the special processing demands when selecting a target from among distractors, another major factor appears to be the difficulty of retaining unrelated items even briefly. In this section I review some of the evidence for this claim, which is central to the CSTM hypothesis.

Differences Between Lists and Sentences   The memory span for words is 5 or 6, when the presentation rate is consistently 1/sec. But when lists of 2, 3, 4, 5, or 6 nouns were presented at higher rates using RSVP, I found that immediate recall declined to a mean of 2.6 words for 5-word lists (2.4 for six-word lists) at the rate of 12 words/sec, as shown in figure 2.3 (Potter 1982, 1993). This was evidently not because participants could not recognize the words at that rate, because a list of just 2 words (followed by a mask) was recalled almost perfectly at 12/sec: instead, some additional process was necessary to stabilize the words in short-term memory. At the rate of 10/sec, about 3 words were remembered (for lists of 3 to 6 words), at 3/sec, about 4 words (for lists of 4 to 6 words). In another study I found that the presentation of two related words on a 5-word RSVP list (separated by another word) resulted in improved recall for both words, suggesting that both words were activated to a level at which an association could be

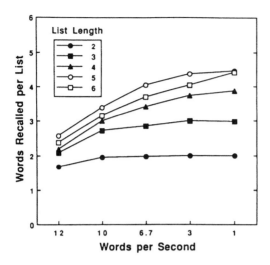

Figure 2.3
Immediate recall of RSVP lists of 2, 3, 4, 5, and 6 nouns presented at rates between 1 and 12 words/sec (Potter 1982). A mask followed each list. (Adapted from Potter 1993, figure 2.)

retrieved. This hinted at the sort of process that might stabilize or structure information in CSTM.

In contrast to lists, 14-word sentences presented at rates up to at least 12 words/sec can be recalled quite accurately (see Potter 1984a; Potter et al 1986), at least if they are not syntactically complex and if they convey straightforward ideas. The findings with lists versus sentences strongly support the CSTM assumption that each word can be identified and understood with an 83–100 msec exposure, even when it is part of a continuing series of words. The results also support the second assumption that representations of the words remain activated long enough to allow them to be bound into whatever syntactic and conceptual structures are being built on the fly. When, as with a list of unrelated words, there is no ready structure to hand, all but 2 or 3 of the words are lost.

How Are RSVP Sentences Remembered? The Regeneration Hypothesis Before addressing the question of how rapidly presented sentences are retained, one should address the prior question of why sentences heard or read at *normal* rates are easy to repeat immediately, even when they are two or three times as long as the list that can be repeated accurately. The difference in capacity between lists and sentences is thought to be due to some form of chunking, although it has also been assumed that sentences can be stored in some verbatim form temporarily (see the review by Von Eckardt & Potter 1985). Potter and Lombardi (1990) proposed a different hypothesis: immediate recall of a sentence (like longer-term recall) is based on a conceptual or propositional representation of the sentence. The recaller regenerates the sentence, using normal speech production processes to express the propositional structure. We proposed that recently activated words were likely to be selected to express the structure. In consequence, the recalled sentence is normally verbatim, but not because there is a sequential verbatim representation of the words (e.g., a phonological representation) that is simply parroted.

To test this hypothesis, Potter and Lombardi (1990) presented distractor words in a secondary task immediately before or after the to-be-recalled sentence, and on some trials one of the words was a good substitute for a word in the sentence (such as "castle" for "palace"). As we predicted, that word was frequently intruded in recall, as long as the rest of the sentence was consistent with the substitution. Thus, recall was guided by a conceptual representation, not by a special verbatim representation.

Further studies (Lombardi & Potter 1992; Potter & Lombardi 1998) indicated that syntactic priming from having processed the sentence plays a role in the syntactic accuracy of immediate recall of sentences. Syntactic priming (e.g., Bock 1986) is a temporary facilitation in the production of a recently processed syntactic structure, as distinguished from direct memory for the syntactic structure of the prime sentence. Among the reasons that sentences are no longer recalled verbatim after one intervening sentence (e.g., Sachs 1967, 1974) are that the conceptual structure is now more complex (if the sentences are related), the relevant words are no longer as activated, and syntactic priming may have decayed or been interfered with by the intervening sentence.

The Potter-Lombardi hypothesis that sentences are regenerated rather than "recalled verbatim" is consistent with the CSTM claim that propositional structures are built rapidly, as a sentence is read or heard. More directly relevant is one of the Potter–Lombardi (1990) experiments in which the sentences were presented at a rate of 10 words/ sec, rather than the moderate 5 words/sec of their other experiments: the intrusion results were essentially the same, showing that the relevant conceptual processing had also occurred at the higher rate.

Reading RSVP Paragraphs: More Evidence for Immediate Use of Structure   A single RSVP sentence apparently is easy to comprehend and recall when presented as fast at 12 words/sec, so that recall is close to ceiling. Does that mean that longer-term retention of the sentence will be as good as if it had been presented more slowly? To answer that

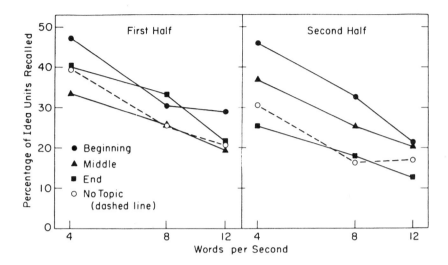

Figure 2.4
RSVP paragraphs presented at 3 rates; percentage of idea units recalled in each half of
the paragraph, as a function of the position of the topic sentence in the paragraph.
(Adapted from Potter et al. 1980, figure 20.2.)

question, we (Potter et al. 1980) presented RSVP paragraphs of about
100 words at three rates: 4, 8, and 12 words/sec, with the equivalent
of a two-word pause between sentences (the net rates averaged 3.3,
6.7, and 10 words/sec). Immediately after presentation, participants
wrote down the paragraph as accurately as possible. To allow us to
evaluate both single-word perception and use of discourse-level information, we used paragraphs that appeared to be ambiguous and poorly
integrated unless the reader knew the topic (see Bransford & Johnson
1972; Dooling & Lachman 1971). We included a sentence that mentioned
a one-word topic (e.g., "pizza") at the beginning, the middle, or the
end of the paragraph, or we omitted the topic. Our predictions were
that the topic word would be recalled, that any part of the paragraph
that followed the topic would be recalled more accurately than any
part that preceded it (so that having the topic at the end of the paragraph
would be no better than omitting it entirely), and that both predictions
would be true at all rates of presentation. We also expected that the
higher the rate, the less the recall.

Whether we scored only verbatim recall or used a more liberal score
of idea units recalled, recall was improved after the topic was presented
(but not before), at all three rates of presentation: therefore, even at
the highest rate the discourse topic could be used to structure the
paragraph (figure 2.4). This suggests that the discourse topic, once it

became evident, remained active as a source of structure as the rest of the paragraph was read. (The topic word was perceived and recalled by more than 80% of the subjects regardless of rate or condition). At the same time, there was a marked main effect of rate: recall declined as rate of presentation increased, from 37% of the idea units at 4 words/sec to 26% at 8 words/sec to 20% at 12 words/sec, averaging over all topic conditions. Clearly, even though there was internal evidence that discourse-level structuring was occurring at all rates of presentation, some process of consolidation was beginning to fail as rate increased.

Putting the paragraph results together with those for lists and single sentences, we see that structuring can occur rapidly, and more structure results in better memory (comparing lists with sentences, or comparing a string of seemingly unrelated sentences with sentences structured by having a topic). Nonetheless, rapid conceptual processing is not sufficient for accurate retention if there is no additional time for consolidation: the gist may survive, but details will be lost in immediate recall, just as they are in longer-term memory.

Mechanisms of Structuring in RSVP Sentence Processing   Although I have repeatedly invoked the idea that there is rapid structuring of information represented in CSTM, I have had little to say about just how this structuring occurs. In the case of sentences, it is evident that parsing and conceptual interpretation must occur virtually word by word, because any substantial delay would outrun the persistence of unstructured material in CSTM (as one sees in the case of the attentional blink). Here I will briefly describe three studies that have investigated the process of selecting an appropriate interpretation of a given word in an RSVP sentence, a key process in comprehension, given the extent of lexical ambiguity in English and in most other languages.

THE INFLUENCE OF SENTENCE CONTEXT ON WORD AND NONWORD PERCEP-TION   In one study (Potter, Moryadas, Abrams, & Noel 1993) we took advantage of the propensity of RSVP readers to convert a nonword into an orthographically similar word. We presented nonwords such as *dack* that are one letter away from two other words (*deck, duck*), in sentences biased toward one or the other of these words or neutral between them, as in the following examples. Note that when we presented a real word in the biased sentences, it was always the mismatching word. Subjects recalled the sentence; they were told to report misspelled words or nonwords if they saw them.

Neutral: "The visitors noticed the *deck/duck/dack* by the house."
Biased: "The child fed the *deck/dack* at the pond."
"The sailor washed the *duck/dack* of that vessel."

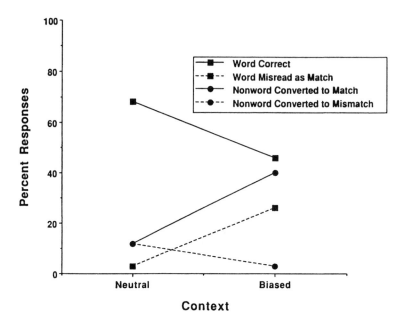

Figure 2.5
Percent report of the critical word (always the mismatch word) or nonword (similar to both the match and mismatch words) as the match or mismatch word. In the neutral condition the match and mismatch words were equally plausible; in the biased context only the match word was plausible. Subjects were instructed to report incongruous or misspelled words, if any. (Adapted from Potter et al. 1993, experiment 2.)

As figure 2.5 shows, we found that readers were much more likely to convert the nonword in the biased direction (40% of trials) than in the other direction (3% of trials). Similarly, when the inappropriate word was put in the biased sentence, misreadings increased dramatically and accurate reports dropped, although the incongruous word was still reported correctly on almost half the trials. Thus, context can bias word and nonword perception even when reading at 10 words/ sec. More surprisingly, we found that even selective context that does not appear until as much as three words (300 msec) after the critical word or nonword can influence perception, suggesting that multiple word candidates (and their meanings) are activated as the nonword or word is perceived, and may remain active for at least 300 msec after the word or nonword has been masked by succeeding words. This supposition that multiple possible words and their meanings are briefly activated during word perception accords with the Swinney hypothesis (1979) that multiple meanings of ambiguous words are

Table 2.1
Percentages of double words (matching and nonmatching) recalled in each context condition (before and after) as part of the sentence.

Double Word	Context Condition	
	Before	After
Matching	75	65
Nonmatching	10	15

Before: Maggie carried the kitten in a $\overset{\text{basket}}{\underset{\text{pencil}}{******}}$ to her house.

After: Maggie used a $\overset{\text{basket}}{\underset{\text{pencil}}{******}}$ to carry the kitten.

Adapted from Potter et al. 1998, experiment 1.

briefly activated: both results are consistent with the CSTM view. In the present study and in the case of ambiguous words, the process of activation and selection appears to occur unconsciously for the most part, an issue considered in a later section.

DOUBLE-WORD SELECTION   In another study (Potter, Stiefbold, & Moryadas 1998) we presented two orthographically distinct words simultaneously (one above and one below the line) in the course of an RSVP sentence, instructing the participant to select the one that fit into the sentence and include it when immediately recalling the sentence. We regarded this as an overt analog of lexical ambiguity resolution. The sentence was presented at about 7.5 words/sec; the two-word ("double word") display, for 83 msec. As table 2.1 shows, sentence context had a massive influence on selection, both when the relevant context arrived before the double words and when it arrived later (up to 1 sec later, in one experiment), showing that readers could activate and maintain two distinct lexical possibilities. Subjects were asked to report the "other" word (the mismatching word) after they recalled the sentence, but most of the time they were unable to do so, showing that the unselected word was usually forgotten rapidly. Again, this illustrates the existence of fast and powerful processors that can build syntactically and pragmatically appropriate structures from briefly activated material, leaving unselected material to be rapidly forgotten.

LEXICAL DISAMBIGUATION   Miyake, Just, and Carpenter (1994) carried out two experiments on self-paced reading of sentences with ambiguous words that were not disambiguated until 2–7 words after the ambiguous word. They found that readers with low or middling reading spans were slowed down when the disambiguation was toward the subordinate meaning, especially with a delay of 7 words. (High-span readers had no problems in any of the conditions.) In an unpublished experiment we presented subjects with a similar set of sentences that included an ambiguous word, using RSVP at 10 words/sec; the task was to decide whether or not the sentence was plausible, after which we gave a recognition test of a subset of the words, including the ambiguous word. Our hypothesis was that sentences that eventually turned out to require the subordinate meaning of an ambiguous word would sometimes be judged to be implausible, implying that only the dominant reading had been retrieved. Unambiguously implausible and plausible sentences were intermixed with the ambiguous sentences.

Subjects were more likely to judge a plausible sentence to have been implausible when a subordinate meaning of the ambiguous word was required (27% versus 11% errors), when the disambiguating information appeared after a greater delay (23% versus 16% errors), and especially when there were both a subordinate meaning and late disambiguation (32% errors, versus 9% for the dominant/early condition). A mistaken judgment that the sentence was implausible suggests that on those trials only one meaning, the wrong one, was still available at the point of disambiguation. Interestingly, the ambiguous word itself was almost always correctly spotted on a recognition test of a subset of words from the sentence, even when the sentence had mistakenly been judged implausible. The results suggest that although multiple meanings of a word are indeed briefly activated (in CSTM), the less frequent meaning will sometimes fall below threshold within a second, when sentences are presented rapidly.

Understanding Pictures and Scenes

In the previous sections I have focused on CSTM as it is revealed in studies in which letters, digits, words, and sentences were presented in RSVP. In this section I review evidence that comprehension of pictures or scenes also involves rapid understanding followed by rapid forgetting.

In an early study (Potter & Levy 1969) 128 color photographs of a wide variety of scenes—close-ups of objects and people, indoor and outdoor scenes—were presented sequentially at rates between about 1 every 2 sec and 9/sec, followed by a recognition test of the presented pictures mixed with an equal number of new pictures. No picture was ever shown more than once. The rationale for presenting sequences of still pictures was that that is the way we normally take in visual information: by successive fixations (separated by brief saccades). With normal viewing, the stimulus onset asynchrony (SOA) between one fixation and the next ranges from about 100 to 500 msec, averaging about 300 msec; longer fixations occur when the viewer focuses on a fine detail or a difficult-to-see stimulus.

In our studies we bracketed the normal range of fixation durations, concentrating on rates between 125 and 333 msec.[2] The main finding of our initial study (Potter & Levy 1969) was that the 16 pictures in a sequence were easily recognized in the test that followed the sequence if they had been presented for 1 or 2 sec each, but with shorter presentations, recognition memory declined, reaching almost chance at an exposure duration of 125 msec. These same pictures were easy to remember if they were presented singly for 90 or 120 msec, followed by a visual mask (Potter 1976): the problem seemed not to be that an exposure of 125 msec is too short to comprehend the picture, but rather that the presentation of the following to-be-attended picture cut off further processing in a way that the visual mask did not. I concluded that visual masking occurs with short SOAs (under 100 msec), whereas conceptual masking occurs with SOAs up to 500 msec or more (Potter 1976; see also Intraub this volume, 1980, 1981; Loftus & Ginn 1984; Loftus, Hanna, & Lester 1988).

In the next set of experiments (Potter 1975, 1976) I asked viewers of the picture sequences to detect a picture described by a brief title that was not explicit about pictorial details (e.g, "a boat," "a picnic on the beach," "two people drinking"). As shown in figure 2.6, the detection results were very different from recognition memory results with the same set of pictures: detection was above 60% at 125 msec per picture and above 80% at 250 msec per picture, when recognition memory (corrected for false yeses) was about 12% and 30%, respectively. Thus there was a strong indication that a viewer can comprehend a scene in 100–200 msec but cannot retain it without additional time (a median time of about 400 msec) for processing or consolidation, during which time it is vulnerable to conceptual masking from the next picture. This result is a prime example of CSTM, in a case in which there is no opportunity for linking the unrelated pictures into some kind of structure, so that most of the pictures in a sequence are simply forgotten at the higher rates.

Further studies by Intraub (1980, 1981, 1984; and see her chapter in the current volume) have provided more controlled tests of the disparity between visual search and later memory, and have examined the important role of attention. Intraub (1984) found that deliberately attending to the briefer of alternating brief and longer-duration pictures increased the probability of remembering the briefer pictures while decreasing the probability of remembering the longer pictures. This attentional trade-off is reminiscent of the attentional blink effect.

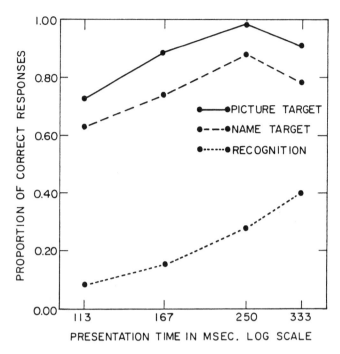

Figure 2.6
Proportion of correct detection responses to a target picture in a rapid sequence of pictures, when the target was shown in advance or was described by a brief title; the proportion of correct recognition responses (corrected for false yeses) is also shown. (From Potter 1976, experiment 1.)

Another approach to the question of picture comprehension versus picture memory is that of McConkie and Currie (1996) and Rensink, O'Regan, and Clark (1997), as well as the work of Wolfe (see his chapter in the present volume). McConkie and Currie, Rensink et al. have shown that our ability to recognize changes in a picture from one glimpse to the next (such as a change in size of the picture, or the addition or subtraction of one person from a group, a change in the color of a piece of clothing, a shift in the position of an item) is surprisingly poor; it is mainly a change in the object we are currently attending to (or planning a saccade to) that we notice. In these studies the change is made following a brief interruption to the scene, such as a blank interval of 80 msec or a saccade by the viewer, because a change made without such an interruption produces visual transients that attract attention. Some investigators (see O'Regan 1992) have concluded that we actually perceive much less in a scene than we subjectively suppose.

But another possibility, consistent with the CSTM hypothesis, is that we do perceive a great deal while we are actually viewing the scene, but only a subset of that information is still available once the next scene is presented: the new scene replaces the previous one, and little survives from the previous glimpse that can be compared with the present scene, other than the gist plus focally attended specifics.

Summary: Rapid Conceptual Processing Followed by Rapid Forgetting
In each of the experimental domains discussed—the attentional blink in selective search; repetition blindness; comprehension and retention of RSVP word lists, sentences, and paragraphs; studies of word perception and selection; and the experiments on picture perception and memory just reviewed—there is evidence for comprehension of the meaning or meanings of a stimulus early in processing (possibly before conscious awareness), followed by rapid forgetting unless conditions are favorable for retention. The two kinds of favorable conditions examined in these studies were selection for attention (e.g., T1 in the attentional blink procedure, and selection of a target picture from among rapidly presented pictures) and the availability of associations or meaningful relations between momentarily active items (as in sentence and paragraph comprehension and in word perception, selection, or disambiguation as a sentence is processed). The power of these two factors_selective attention that is defined by conceptual properties of the target, and the presence of potential conceptual structure_is felt early in processing, before conventional STM for the stimuli has been established, thereby justifying the claim that CSTM is separate from STM and working memory, as they are usually defined.

Further Questions About CSTM

As presented here and in Potter (1993), conceptual short-term memory is a functional construct that brings together diverse phenomena, all of which embody rapid conceptual activation of material that will be deactivated or forgotten almost immediately, but that remains active long enough for structure-building processes of perception, language, and thought to transform relevant material into a stable conceptual representation. CSTM is underspecified in many respects, and indeed no such construct could be fully specified until we know much more about the phenomena in question and about cognition more generally; the present volume moves us closer to that goal. In this section I raise some questions about CSTM and speculate about possible answers.

What Factors Determine Activation of Information in CSTM?
A distinction is often made between primary recognition or categorization of a stimulus and subsequent associations to that stimulus, but recognition and categorization themselves may involve associations, as was evident in misperception of a nonword like *dack* in the presence of a context word like *pond* versus *sailor* (Potter et al. 1993). A stimulus produces activation at many levels in the visual system and higher levels of processing, as incorporated in models such as those of McClelland and Rumelhart (1981) and Norris (1986) for word perception. This activation provides multiple possible interpretations of the stimulus at each level, requiring mechanisms for selecting the best fit among competing interpretations. Such mechanisms use semantic or pragmatic context associated with one or another interpretation to bias the outcome of the competition.

Psychologists have focused on word associations as an important source of memory activation and have used norms from the word association task as a measure of associative strength between words. Greater semantic priming between items with high than with low normative associations shows that word association norms capture something about the associative structure of the mind. However, the malleability of the word association task (which depends on the mental set of the subject, age, and the like) and the uncertainty about whether the norms measure association between lexical items, between concepts, or some combination of the two makes word association norms a questionable basis for a model of associative structure. Efforts to characterize and model human knowledge have had limited success: semantic networks, expert systems, schemata, prototypes, scripts, frames, and lexicographic approaches (to mention only a few examples) have each provided insights, but collectively they do not provide explicit constraints on what kinds of associations would be expected to result in activation of concepts in CSTM. All we can be sure of is that activation must be rapid, and hence only relatively direct associations are likely to be involved, at least in the first few hundred msec after presentation of a word (but see the discussion of LSA, below, for a different possibility).

What Are the Structuring Processes Within CSTM, and How Do They "Consolidate" Memory?
I assume that structuring in CSTM is not different in principle from the slower processes of comprehension that happen as we gradually understand a difficult text or an initially confusing picture, or solve a chess problem over a period of seconds and minutes. By definition, a difference between CSTM structuring and these slower processes is

the speed with which "solutions" are reached, and thus the relative absence of awareness that alternatives have been weighed and that many possibilities have been considered and rejected, at least implicitly. As in slower and more conscious problem-solving, a viewer's task or goal makes a major difference in what happens in CSTM, because one's intentions activate processing routines such as sentence-parsing, target specifications in search tasks, and the like. Thus the goal partially determines what enters CSTM and how structuring takes place.

The presence of many activated items at any moment, in CSTM, allows for compound cuing (e.g., McKoon & Ratcliff 1992)—the convergence of two or more weak associations on an item. The power of converging cues, familiar to any crossword puzzle fan, is likely to be central to structure-building in CSTM. A recent and radical proposal for the acquisition of knowledge (Landauer & Dumais 1997), latent semantic analysis (LSA), provides a suggestive model for how structure may be extracted from haphazard material. LSA's focus is on the slow buildup of "knowledge" of word meanings through massive exposure to texts, simply by analyzing the co-occurrence of words in paragraphs or other small units of text. The word co-occurrence matrix is subjected to an analysis similar to principal components analysis or factor analysis, which extracts N dimensions (factors or components) that capture the greatest variance in the matrix—300 dimensions were optimal in Landauer and Dumais's tests of LSA. A new text sample is interpreted by projecting it onto this 300-D space, a process that is fast. Although LSA is concerned with acquisition and only secondarily with comprehension, some such procedure may be involved in the rapid comprehension characteristic of CSTM (see also McKoon & Ratcliff 1998). However, there is no syntactic parser in LSA, and it is clear from RSVP research that we do parse rapidly presented sentences (see Potter, Stiefbold, & Moryadas 1998, experiment 4, for a recent example); thus, the LSA approach is at best a partial explanation of processing in CSTM.

Memory consolidation requires time, so that if the to-be-remembered material is presented sufficiently slowly, even arbitrary lists of items can be retained. But when information is presented more rapidly (as in RSVP), the more interconnected or structured or "chunked" the information to be remembered, the more time will be available to consolidate each chunk or unified structure—assuming that a unified structure can be consolidated in about the same time that an unconnected item can be. This is a version of Miller's original chunking hypothesis for short-term memory (1956), although in the original theory, chunking depended on preexisting units in memory such as letter groups that form words or acronyms. In CSTM, existing knowledge is used to build structures that include new elements. Few sentences that we read or hear are recognized as a whole since most have never been encountered before, and yet a normal RSVP sentence is easily structured and retained long enough to be recalled immediately afterward. (I say "normal," because it would be easy enough to write a sentence with so many new elements and relations that it could not be successfully processed and retained in a single pass.) Similarly, with extensive practice a subject studied by Chase and Ericsson (1982) was able to develop coding schemes for structuring random sequences of digits, eventually expanding his digit span to over 80 digits. Clearly, the new structures were stored in long-term memory (except for the most recent digits that had not as yet been structured). Note that in this study the digits were presented at 1/sec; it is doubtful that the skill was sufficiently developed to have permitted structuring at a rate such as 10/sec.

If the structuring that occurs in conjunction with CSTM is in the same form or forms as the structuring characteristic of information in long-term memory, should one say that the resulting structure is "in" LTM? In terms of block diagrams of information flow, my answer is yes, but with the caveat that information in LTM can vary markedly in durability. Freshly structured information in CSTM must undergo a process of consolidation if it is to endure long enough to be recalled, and consolidation itself is a continuous variable. The details of our daily experience enter LTM for a time, but forgetting begins immediately and only the main incidents of the day are likely to be recallable the next day, and even less a week later. Information structured in CSTM is the leading edge of this negatively accelerated forgetting curve. In this view, conceptually structured experience is represented in a single memory system with a single consolidation process and a single forgetting function. (Adjunct memory systems such as phonologically based STM or imagery representations, with their own dynamics, may subserve the cuing or construction of conceptual memory.) However, the hypothesis that there is a single conceptual memory system may be oversimplified, given evidence from amnesics such as H.M. who seem to have intact CSTM (Potter, unpublished data) and yet totally forget new information within minutes (Milner, Corkin, & Teuber 1968).

How Does CSTM Interact with STM?
If conventional STM is largely irrelevant to most cognitive processing, which is carried out in conjunction with CSTM, then what is the role of STM and how does it interact with CSTM? By STM I mean conventional short-term memory as embodied in studies ranging from Miller's classic paper (1956) to Baddeley's (1986) working memory, in particular the articulatory loop system. (The visuospatial sketchpad and the central

executive, the other components of Baddeley's model, I do not discuss here: whether visualization is rapid enough to play a role in CSTM is doubtful, and the central executive is a residual memory device whose characteristics have only begun to be specified; see Baddeley 1996.)

This question about the relation between CSTM and STM is closely related to the assumption in the preceding section that more effortful and slower reasoning and thinking are carried out by essentially the same processes as in CSTM. The processes leading from one inference to the next may be the same, but more deliberate reasoning may require chains of inferences. The reasoner may need to pass over the material again and again before the needed conjunctions of ideas are made, and STM may be used to maintain relevant information in a retrievable form, reentering it into CSTM as such successive passes are made. The actual processes leading to a solution may be carried out stepwise in CSTM, with a longer latency between steps or with a longer chain of steps. On the other hand, it seems clear that one can use verbal STM or the visuospatial sketchpad to manipulate representations in the interest of solving a problem. (However, a surprising contrary result was recently reported by Butterworth, Cipolotti, and Warrington [1996], who studied an individual with a markedly impaired digit span who appeared to have normal ability to perform mental arithmetic.) There is evidence that patients with reduced memory spans may have trouble processing sentences with complex structures or temporary "garden paths," suggesting that sentence-processing does rely to some extent on the articulatory loop system—contrary to what Potter and Lombardi (1990) hypothesized (see above). But it is striking that many such patients adequately understand sentences, even though they para-phrase rather than report them verbatim (see Saffran and Martin's chapter in the present volume).

The performance of experts represents almost the opposite case: the prolonged training and practice required to become an expert in chess or medical diagnosis, or the playing of a musical instrument (Ericsson & Lehmann 1996), results in rapid recognition and action that is like "normal" CSTM, coupled with excellent memory. Ericsson and Kintsch (1995) have proposed that expert performance provides evidence for a long-term working memory (LT-WM) that keeps track of the status of a task in a particular domain, such as a chess game, permitting experts to play several games at the same time. In our terms, experts have developed the ability to structure and consolidate information in their special domain much more rapidly than nonexperts, as a result of their long training and current level of practice.

It is possible (as Ericsson & Kintsch 1995 suggest) that ordinary people (nonexperts) are in fact experts in the cognitive processing of everyday life: perception and action in the (normal) environment, inferences about causal relations, language comprehension and production, reading, and so on. Independent of the question of innate endowment for performing these feats, it is evident that extensive practice in childhood is necessary for optimal performance in all these domains. Long practice can lead to a shift from slow, STM-bound processing to rapid CSTM processing (see the shift from a declarative to a procedural mode of processing, Anderson 1983).

Why Are the Most Convincing Demonstrations of CSTM All Visual (and Mostly Sequential)?
To examine the workings of the hypothesized CSTM, it is necessary to minimize the availability of other forms of memory, particularly conventional STM. Since the articulatory–phonological system that supports STM is derived from speech, auditory input virtually guarantees representation in this system. The phonological store provides an effective temporal buffer for short sequences of speech or other auditory input, so processing can be spread out over time. The buffer has some limitations, however. Using compressed speech (speech that is sped up without raising its pitch), Yntema, Wozencraft, and Klem (1964) showed that listeners became overloaded when more than 3 or 4 compressed digits were presented at a rate of 10/sec, forgetting many of them—just as viewers in our experiments with RSVP lists of words forgot most of them at that rate. But, unlike a visual presentation at 10/sec, compressed speech at that rate is markedly degraded; although it is possible to train a subject to recognize a finite set of one-syllable words such as digit names, it is difficult or impossible to comprehend sentences that use an unconstrained vocabulary at such high rates.

Sequential presentation is used to control the rate of processing and to examine continuous processing rather than processing of a single tachistoscopic stimulus. Because the viewer is obliged to attend to a succession of stimuli, performance reflects the capacity to process items and integrate them at a given rate. Normal reading rate is limited by the rate of eye movements and by ingrained reading habits, but RSVP reading demonstrates that people can process single sentences when reading more than twice as fast as they normally would. It is then possible (as in the paragraphs study, for example) to discover what processes begin to fail as reading is speeded up. In the present context, the advantage of using RSVP is that one is able to reveal phenomena that cannot be explained in the standard framework that includes only sensory memories, STM (including the visuospatial sketchpad), and LTM.

But does rapid visual presentation of sentences or other stimuli actually prevent material from entering standard STM? That is not yet clear. On the one hand, there is strong evidence that RSVP readers do retrieve some phonological representation of the words they are reading (Bavelier & Potter 1992; Petrick 1981; Petrick & Potter 1979; and see Coltheart's chapter in this volume). On the other hand, concurrent articulation during RSVP reading does not appear to interfere with processing and immediate memory for the sentence (Potter 1984b), nor does it interfere with phonologically based repetition blindness between homophones such as ate/eight in RSVP sentences (Bavelier & Potter 1992). Besner and Davelaar (1982) have proposed that there are two phonological codes, the first of which is generated immediately, perhaps directly from the orthography, and contributes to lexical access. The second code is postaccess and constitutes the rehearsable phonological component of the articulatory loop model of STM. Only the second code is interfered with by articulatory suppression. If this hypothesis is correct, then it is likely that the early phonological code is the one activated during RSVP reading, whereas the late code, associated with STM, is not—but see Coltheart's chapter in the present volume for a different view.

Is CSTM Conscious?
At this point the question probably cannot be answered, because we have no clear independent criterion for consciousness other than availability for report. And, by hypothesis, report requires some form of consolidation, and therefore only what persists in a structured form will be reportable. Thus, while the evidence we have reviewed demonstrates that there is conceptual processing of material that was subsequently forgotten, it does not tell us whether we were briefly conscious of that material, or whether the activation and selection occurred unconsciously.

It seems unlikely, however, that multiple competing concepts (such as the multiple meanings of a word) that become active simultaneously could all be conscious in the ordinary sense, although preliminary structures or interpretations that are quickly discarded might be conscious. People do sometimes become aware of having momentarily considered an interpretation of a spoken word that turns out to be false, for example. And in viewing rapidly presented pictures, people have a sense of recognizing all the pictures but forgetting them. But such experiences seem to be the exception rather than the rule. Thus, I adopt the working hypothesis that much of CSTM activation and selection and structuring happens before one becomes aware: it is the structured result, typically, of which one is aware, which is why perception and cognition seem so effortless and accurate.

Conclusions

Evidence for conceptual short-term memory has appeared in a wide variety of tasks. The purpose of this chapter has been to review and discuss some of this evidence for early accessing of cognitive information and rapid selective structuring of that information. Rapid structuring can occur only if the material permits it and if the skills for discovering latent structure are highly practiced: for example, object and word recognition, lexical retrieval, sentence parsing, causal inference, search for a target, and the like. These are just the cognitive skills, each highly complex, that make comprehension seem trivially easy most of the time.

CSTM is the working memory that supports these processes, lasting just long enough to allow multiple options to be entertained before one is selected and the unused fragments evaporate, in most cases without entering awareness. The labored thoughts and decisions we are aware of pondering are a tiny fraction of those we make effortlessly. Even these worked-over thoughts may advance stepwise, by recirculating the data through CSTM until the next step occurs to us. We are aware of slowly shaping an idea or solving a problem, but not of precisely how each step occurs. More work will be needed to gain a full understanding of just what takes place in this largely preconscious stage of cognitive processing.

Notes

1. In most AB studies "lag 1" is defined as the item immediately following T1, whereas in many RB studies the immediately following item is considered to be at lag 0, and the next item is at lag 1. In this chapter I use "lag 1" to refer to the item immediately following T1 or C1.
2. The pictures were presented sequentially, and the viewer did not have to move his or her eyes to scan the picture; in one check on eye movements, we found that the viewers' eyes rarely moved in this task when the pictures were presented for 250 msec or less (Potter & Levy 1969).

References

Allport, D. A., Styles, E. A., & Hsieh, S. (1994). Shifting intentional set: Exploring the dynamic control of tasks. In C. Umilta & M. Moscovitch (eds.), *Attention and performance XV* (pp. 421–452). Hillsdale, NJ: Lawrence Erlbaum Associates.

Altarriba, J., & Soltano, E. G. (1996). Repetition blindness and bilingual memory: Token individuation for translation equivalents. *Memory & Cognition, 24,* 700–711.

Anderson, J. R. (1983). *The architecture of cognition.* Cambridge, MA: Harvard University Press.

Anderson, J. R. (1993). *Rules of the mind.* Hillsdale, NJ: Lawrence Erlbaum Associates.

Arnell, K., & Jolicoeur, P. (1995). Allocating attention across stimulus modalities: Evidence from the attentional blink phenomenon. Poster session presented at the 36th annual meeting of the Psychonomic Society, Los Angeles, November.

Arnell, K., & Jolicoeur, P. (1997). The attentional blink across stimulus modalities: Evidence for central processing limitations. Manuscript submitted for publication.

Baddeley, A. (1986). *Working memory.* Oxford: Clarendon Press.

Baddeley, A. (1996). Exploring the central executive. *Quarterly Journal of Experimental Psychology, 49A,* 5–28.

Bavelier, D. (1994). Repetition blindness between visually different items: The case of pictures and words. *Cognition, 51,* 199–236.

Bavelier, D., & Potter, M. C. (1992). Visual and phonological codes in repetition blindness. *Journal of Experimental Psychology: Human Perception and Performance, 18,* 134–147.

Besner, D., & Davelaar, E. (1982). Basic processes in reading: Two phonological codes. *Canadian Journal of Psychology, 36,* 701–711.

Bock, J. K. (1986). Syntactic persistence in language production. *Cognitive Pychology, 18,* 355–387.

Bransford, J. D., & Johnson, M. K. (1972). Contextual prerequisites for understanding: Some investigations of comprehension and recall. *Journal of Verbal Learning and Verbal Behavior, 11,* 717–726.

Butterworth, B., Cipolotti, L., & Warrington, E. K. (1996). Short-term memory impairment and arithmetical ability. *Quarterly Journal of Experimental Psychology, 49A,* 251–262.

Chase, W. G., & Ericsson, K. A. (1982). Skill and working memory. In G. H. Bower (ed.), *The psychology of learning and motivation* (vol. 16, pp. 1–58). New York: Academic Press.

Chun, M. M. (1997a). Types and tokens in visual processing: A double dissociation between the attentional blink and repetition blindness. *Journal of Experimental Psychology: Human Perception and Performance, 23,* 738–755.

Chun, M. M. (1997b). Temporal binding errors are redistributed by the attentional blink. *Perception & Psychophysics, 59,* 1191–1199.

Chun, M. M., Bromberg, H. S., & Potter, M. C. (1994). Conceptual similarity between targets and distractors in the attentional blink. Poster session presented at the 35th annual meeting of the Psychonomic Society, St. Louis, November.

Chun, M. M., & Potter, M. C. (1995). A two-stage model for multiple target detection in rapid serial visual presentation. *Journal of Experimental Psychology: Human Perception and Performance, 21,* 109–127.

Coltheart, M. (1983). Iconic memory. *Philosophical Transactions of the Royal Society of London, B302,* 283–294.

Dooling, D. J., & Lachman, R. (1971). Effects of comprehension on retention of prose. *Journal of Experimental Psychology, 88,* 216–222.

Downing, P., Kanwisher, N. C., & Potter, M. C. (1998). A crossmodal repetition deficit for RSVP and compressed-speech sequences. Manuscript under revision.

Ericsson K. A., & Kintsch, W. (1995). Long-term working memory. *Psychological Review, 102,* 211–245.

Ericsson, K. A., & Lehmann, A. C. (1996). Expert and exceptional performance: Evidence of maximal adaptation to task constraints. *Annual Review of Psychology, 47,* 273–305.

Forster, K. I. (1970). Visual perception of rapidly presented word sequences of varying complexity. *Perception & Psychophysics, 8,* 215–221.

Intraub, H. (1980). Presentation rate and the representation of briefly glimpsed pictures in memory. *Journal of Experimental Psychology: Human Learning and Memory, 6,* 1–12.

Intraub, H. (1981). Rapid conceptual identification of sequentially presented pictures. *Journal of Experimental Psychology: Human Perception and Performance, 7,* 604–610.

Intraub, H. (1984). Conceptual masking: The effects of subsequent visual events on memory for pictures. *Journal of Experimental Psychology: Learning, Memory and Cognition, 10,* 115–125.

Just, M. A., & Carpenter, P. A. (1992). A capacity theory of comprehension: Individual differences in working memory. *Psychological Review, 99,* 122–149.

Kahneman, D., & Treisman, A. M. (1984). Changing views of attention and automaticity. In R. Parasuraman & D. R. Davies (eds.), *Varieties of attention* (pp. 29–61). New York: Academic Press.

Kanwisher, N. G. (1987). Repetition blindness: Type recognition without token individuation. *Cognition, 27,* 117–143.

Kanwisher, N. G., & Potter, M. C. (1990). Repetition blindness: Levels of processing. *Journal of Experimental Psychology: Human Perception and Performance, 16,* 30–47.

Kintsch, W. (1988). The role of knowledge in discourse comprehension: A construction–integration model. *Psychological Review, 95,* 163–183.

Kutas, M., & Hillyard, S. A. (1980). Reading senseless sentences: Brain potentials reflect semantic incongruity. *Science, 207,* 203–205.

Landauer, T. K., & Dumais, S. T. (1997). A solution to Plato's problem: The latent semantic analysis theory of acquisition, induction and representation of knowledge. *Psychological Review, 104,* 211–240.

Lawrence, D. H. (1971a). Temporal numerosity estimates for word lists. *Perception & Psychophysics, 10,* 75–78.

Lawrence, D. H. (1971b). Two studies of visual search for word targets with controlled rates of presentation. *Perception & Psychophysics, 10,* 85–89.

Loftus, G. R. (1983). Eye fixations on text and scenes. In K. Rayner (ed.), *Eye movements in reading: Perceptual and language processes* (pp. 359–376). New York: Academic Press.

Loftus, G. R., & Ginn, M. (1984). Perceptual and conceptual masking of pictures. *Journal of Experimental Psychology: Learning, Memory and Cognition, 10,* 435–441.

Loftus, G. R., Hanna, A. M., & Lester, L. (1988). Conceptual masking: How one picture captures attention from another picture. *Cognitive Psychology, 20,* 237–282.

Lombardi, L., & Potter, M. C. (1992). The regeneration of syntax in short-term memory. *Journal of Memory and Language, 31,* 713–733.

Luck, S. J., Vogel, E. K., & Shapiro, K. L. (1996). Word meanings can be accessed but not reported during the attentional blink. *Nature, 382,* 616–618.

MacKay, D. G., Abrams, L., Pedroza, M. J., & Miller, M. D. (1996). Cross-language facilitation, semantic blindness, and the relation between language and memory: A reply to Altarriba and Soltano. *Memory & Cognition, 24,* 712–718.

MacKay, D. G., & Miller, M. D. (1994). Semantic blindness: Repeated concepts are difficult to encode and recall under time pressure. *Psychological Science, 5,* 52–55.

Maki, W. S., Couture, T., Frigen, K., & Lien, D. (1997). Sources of the attentional blink during rapid serial visual presentation: Perceptual interference and retrieval competition. *Journal of Experimental Psychology: Human Perception and Performance, 23,* 1393–1411.

Maki, W. S., Frigen, K., & Paulson, K. (1997). Associative priming by targets and distractors during rapid serial visual presentation: Does word meaning survive the attentional blink? *Journal of Experimental Psychology: Human Perception and Performance, 23,* 1014–1034.

McClelland, J. L., & Rumelhart, D. E. (1981). An interactive model of context effects in letter perception: Part 1. An account of basic findings. *Psychological Review, 88,* 375–407.

McConkie, G. W., & Currie, C. B. (1996). Visual stability across saccades while viewing complex pictures. *Journal of Experimental Psychology: Human Perception and Performance, 22,* 563–581.

McKoon, G., & Ratcliff, R. (1992). Spreading activation versus compound cue accounts of priming: Mediated priming revisited. *Journal of Experimental Psychology: Learning, Memory, and Cognition, 18,* 1155–1172.

McKoon, G., & Ratcliff, R. (1998). Memory-based language processing: Psycholinguistic research in the 1990s. *Annual Review of Psychology, 49,* 25–42.

Meiran, N. (1996). Reconfiguration of processing mode prior to task performance. *Journal of Experimental Psychology: Learning, Memory, and Cognition, 22,* 1423–1442.

Miller, G. A. (1956). The magical number seven, plus or minus two: Some limits on our capacity for processing information. *Psychological Review, 63,* 81–97.

Miller, M. D., & MacKay, D. G. (1994). Repetition deafness: Repeated words in computer-compressed speech are difficult to encode and recall. *Psychological Science, 5,* 47–51.

Miller, M. D., & MacKay, D. G. (1996). Relations between language and memory: The case of repetition deafness. *Psychological Science, 7,* 347–351.

Milner, B., Corkin, S., & Teuber, H. L. (1968). Further analysis of the hippocampal amnesic syndrome: 14-year follow up study of H. M. *Neuropsychologia, 6,* 215–234.

Miyake, A., Just, M. A., & Carpenter, P. A. (1994). Working memory constraints on the resolution of lexical ambiguity: Maintaining multiple interpretations in neutral contexts. *Journal of Memory and Language, 33,* 175–202.

Monsell, S. (1996). Control of mental processes. In V. Bruce (ed.), *Unsolved mysteries of the mind: Tutorial essays in cognition* (pp. 93–148). Hove, E. Sussex: Erlbaum (UK) Taylor & Francis.

Neely, J. H. (1991). Semantic priming effects in visual word recognition: A selective review of current findings and theories. In D. Besner & G. W. Humphreys (eds.), *Basic processes in reading: Visual word recognition* (pp. 264–336). Hillsdale, NJ: Lawrence Erlbaum Associates.

Norris, D. (1986). Word recognition: Context effects without priming. *Cognition, 22,* 93–136.

O'Regan, J. K. (1992). Solving the "real" mysteries of visual perception: The world as an outside memory. *Canadian Journal of Psychology, 46,* 461–488.

Petrick, S. (1981). Acoustic and semantic encoding during rapid reading. Ph.D. dissertation, Massachusetts Institute of Technology.

Petrick, S., & Potter, M. C. (1979). RSVP sentences and word lists: Representation of meaning and sound. Paper presented at the 20th annual meeting of the Psychonomic Society, Phoenix, November.

Potter, M. C. (1975). Meaning in visual search. *Science, 187,* 965–966.

Potter, M. C. (1976). Short-term conceptual memory for pictures. *Journal of Experimental Psychology: Human Learning and Memory, 2,* 509–522.

Potter, M. C. (1982). Very short-term memory: In one eye and out the other. Paper presented at the 23rd annual meeting of the Psychonomic Society, Minneapolis, November.

Potter, M. C. (1983). Representational buffers: The eye–mind hypothesis in picture perception, reading, and visual search. In K. Rayner (ed.), *Eye movements in reading: Perceptual and language processes* (pp. 413–437). New York: Academic Press.

Potter, M. C. (1984a). Rapid serial visual presentation (RSVP): A method for studying language processing. In D. Kieras & M. A. Just (eds.), *New methods in reading comprehension research* (pp. 91–118). Hillsdale, NJ: Lawrence Erlbaum Associates.

Potter, M. C. (1984b). Articulatory suppression and very-short-term memory for sentences. Paper presented at the 25th annual meeting of the Psychonomic Society, San Antonio, TX, November.

Potter, M. C. (1993). Very short-term conceptual memory. *Memory & Cognition, 21,* 156–161.

Potter, M. C., Chun, M. M., Banks, B. S., & Muckenhoupt, M. (1998). Two attentional deficits in serial target search: The visual attentional blink and an amodal task-switch deficit. *Journal of Experimental Psychology: Learning, Memory, and Cognition, 24,* 979–992.

Potter, M. C., Chun, M. M., & Muckenhoupt, M. (1995). Auditory attention does not blink. Paper presented at the 36th annual meeting of the Psychonomic Society, Los Angeles, November.

Potter, M. C., Kroll, J. F., & Harris, C. (1980). Comprehension and memory in rapid sequential reading. In R. Nickerson (ed.), *Attention and performance VIII* (pp. 395–418). Hillsdale, NJ: Lawrence Erlbaum Associates.

Potter, M. C., Kroll, J. F., Yachzel, B., Carpenter, E., & Sherman, J. (1986). Pictures in sentences: Understanding without words. *Journal of Experimental Psychology: General, 115,* 281–294.

Potter, M. C., and Levy, E. I. (1969). Recognition memory for a rapid sequence of pictures. *Journal of Experimental Psychology, 81,* 10–15.

Potter, M. C., & Lombardi, L. (1990). Regeneration in the short-term recall of sentences. *Journal of Memory and Language, 29,* 633–654.

Potter, M. C., & Lombardi, L. (1998). Syntactic priming in immediate recall of sentences. *Journal of Memory and Language, 38,* 265–282.

Potter, M. C., Moryadas, A., Abrams, I., & Noel, A. (1993). Word perception and misperception in context. *Journal of Experimental Psychology: Learning, Memory and Cognition, 19,* 3–22.

Potter, M. C., Stiefbold, D. R., & Moryadas, A. (1998). Word selection in reading sentences: Preceding versus following contexts. *Journal of Experimental Psychology: Learning, Memory and Cognition, 24,* 68–100.

Raymond, J. E., Shapiro, K. L., & Arnell, K. M. (1992). Temporary suppression of visual processing in an RSVP task: An attentional blink? *Journal of Experimental Psychology: Human Perception and Performance, 18,* 849–860.

Rayner, K. (ed.). (1983). *Eye movements in reading: Perceptual and language processes.* New York: Academic Press.

Rensink, R. A., O'Regan, J. K., & Clark, J. J. (1997). To see or not to see: The need for attention to perceive changes in scenes. *Psychological Science, 8,* 368–373.

Rogers, R. D., & Monsell, S. (1995). Costs of a predictable switch between simple cognitive tasks. *Journal of Experimental Psychology: General, 124,* 207–231.

Sachs, J. S. (1967). Recognition memory for syntactic and semantic aspects of connected discourse. *Perception & Psychophysics, 2,* 437–442.

Sachs, J. S. (1974). Memory in reading and listening to discourse. *Memory & Cognition, 2,* 95–100.

Sereno, S. C., & Rayner, K. (1992). Fast priming during eye fixations in reading. *Journal of Experimental Psychology: Human Perception and Performance, 18,* 173–184.

Shapiro, K., Driver, J., Ward, R., & Sorenson, R. E. (1997). Priming from the attentional blink: A failure to extract visual tokens but not visual types. *Psychological Science, 8,* 95–100.

Shulman, H. G. (1971). Similarity effects in short-term memory. *Psychological Bulletin, 75,* 399–415.

Sperling, G., Budiansky, J., Spivak, J. G., & Johnson, M. C. (1971). Extremely rapid visual search: The maximum rate of scanning letters for the presence of a numeral. *Science, 174,* 307–311.

Swinney, D. A. (1979). Lexical access during sentence comprehension: (Re)consideration of context effects. *Journal of Verbal Learning and Verbal Behavior, 18,* 645–659.

Von Eckardt, B., & Potter, M. C. (1985). Clauses and the semantic representation of words. *Memory & Cognition, 13,* 371–376.

Yntema, D. B., Wozencraft, F. T., & Klem, L. (1964). Immediate serial recall of digits presented at very high rates. Paper presented at the 5th annual meeting of the Psychonomic Society, November.

Chapter 3

Understanding and Remembering Briefly Glimpsed Pictures: Implications for Visual Scanning and Memory

Helene Intraub

The world we perceive is made up of complex, interrelated collections of objects and backgrounds. Yet, at no moment in time does an observer perceive a scene in its entirety. During visual scanning, each eye fixation delivers only a partial view of a continuous environment, and each partial view can be quite brief. For example, when studying a picture of a scene, the viewer's average fixation frequency can be as high as 3 per sec (Yarbus 1967). A classic issue in perception has been how to account for our ability to perceive and remember the meaningful spatial relations that comprise real-world scenes, given the brief and piecemeal character of the visual input.

Research on picture perception and memory provides one avenue for addressing this question. Hochberg (1978, 1986), for example, proposed a theory of visual integration of partial views based primarily upon an analysis of the viewer's ability to understand dynamic pictorial displays. In one experiment he demonstrated that when viewers looked at a moving display through an aperture, although they never saw the whole display at once, they rapidly integrated their partial views into an understandable whole. He proposed that the perception of the whole is achieved through the use of a mental schema—an abstract representation that serves to guide interpretation and integration of successive views of the visual world. The schema can be thought of as an abstract representation of the layout and major landmarks that characterize a scene without preserving sensory detail. Hochberg (1986) argued that, contrary to our subjective experience, "there is much in the world that simply goes unnoticed and unrepresented in the structure that we use to store and to assimilate new views" (22:58).

Consistent with this characterization of scene perception, recent research has shown that observers are surprisingly poor at detecting a change in a scene when the change is preceded by a transient such as a brief mask (Rensink, O'Regan, & Clark 1997) or a shift in viewpoint (Simons & Levin 1997). For example, in one experiment, a videotape was made of two actors at a table, talking. When the camera panned away from the table to focus on one actor for 4 sec, a central item on the table (a large soda bottle that had been conspicuously used) was replaced with a cardboard box. When the camera returned to the original view, remaining for 30 sec, none of the viewers noticed that the bottle had "become" a box (Simons 1996).

Similarly, it has been demonstrated that various types of changes made to a scene during a saccade (when the eye rapidly travels from one region of a scene to another) have been surprising resistant to detection (Grimes, 1996; McConkie & Currie, 1996; also see O'Regan, 1992). There has been a growing number of studies supporting the idea that transsaccadic memory is abstract rather than sensory in nature (e.g., Irwin, Brown, & Sun 1988; Irwin 1991; McConkie & Zola 1979; Rayner & Pollatstek 1992; see also Intraub 1997).

If a schematic representation of spatial layout underlies the integration of successive views during visual scanning, then each briefly viewed glimpse of the world would have to be very rapidly analyzed and understood, readily activating expectations about the surrounding area. This possibility has been explored in various ways. In this chapter, I will describe three lines of research from my own lab that are relevant to this possibility. These are (a) recognition memory for briefly glimpsed pictures, (b) target detection during rapid continuous presentation of pictures, and (c) memory for a scene's boundaries, that is, its spatial expanse.

Memory for Briefly Glimpsed Pictures

When photographs are presented in rapid succession, at rates that mimic or surpass the average fixation frequency of the eye, the viewer's ability to recognize them moments later is very poor. At a rate of 3 pictures per sec (similar to the scanning rate reported by Yarbus 1967), recognition memory performance on tests using dissimilar distractors has shown that subjects remember fewer than 50% of the stimuli (e.g., Potter 1976; Potter & Levy 1969). Why is recognition memory so poor following a presentation rate that mimics the rate at which scenes are normally fixated?

One possibility is that under these artificial conditions of presentation, most of the unrelated scenes that flash by are not understood by the viewer and are therefore not remembered. After all, although the rapid sequences used in these experiments mimic the rate at which viewers can shift their fixation during visual scanning, they do not mimic the redundancy and continuity of the information gleaned from successive fixations on a stable environment. The continuity among successive views during normal scanning may result in the develop-

Figure 3.1
Examples of the pictures of objects that were used in the brief presentation and RSVP experiments The actual stimuli were presented in color. (Intraub 1979, 1980, 1984, 1985, 1989.)

ment of expectations that serve to guide and facilitate perception. Therefore, although the scanning rate is quite rapid, the viewer has a good idea of what each fixation will bring into view (Neisser 1976). On the other hand, poor memory following rapid continuous presentation of unrelated pictures might be caused by the viewer's inability to identify rapidly changing, unpredictable visual events. However, research on scene perception has suggested that the meaning and layout of a scene are acquired so rapidly that they can affect identification of objects within the scene, at durations as brief as 50–150 msec (Biederman 1972, 1981; Biederman, Mezzanotte, & Rabinowitz 1982). Thus, poor memory following rapid presentation may actually reflect limitations on memory rather than on perception.

To explore the viewers' ability to remember briefly presented unrelated pictures, I conducted a series of experiments that tested recognition memory under a variety of time constraints. This research showed that recognition memory for briefly glimpsed pictures could be quite good, as long as viewers were allowed some time between pictorial presentations. This strongly suggested that the poor performance following rapid continuous presentation was not attributable to the viewer's inability to extract information from a very brief glimpse of an isolated pictorial event. Figure 3.1 provides a sample of photographs of objects used in these experiments.

In one series of experiments, Intraub (1979) presented 12 color photographs of common objects for 110 msec each at 6 different stimulus onset asynchronies (SOAs). These ranged from 110 msec to 1.5 sec. At the shortest SOA (110 msec) there was no interstimulus interval (ISI); each briefly presented picture was immediately followed by the next. At the slower SOAs, each 110-msec picture was followed by a gray field that remained on the screen for the full ISI. To test the effects of "nameability" on picture memory, photographs of objects were selected that were "equally easy to see," based upon visual duration thresholds, but that were not equally easy to name, based on each picture's mean naming latency. Subjects' memory was tested using either free recall or a serial recognition test in which 12 nonconfusable objects served as distractors.

Recognition memory for the briefly glimpsed pictures improved markedly from 19% to 92% (corrected for guessing) as the time between stimuli was increased. Free recall of the pictures yielded the same pattern of results, with percent recalled ranging from 13% in the fastest presentation condition to 52% in the slowest. The possibility that this improvement was due to verbal mediation at slower rates (see Paivio 1971; Paivio & Csapo 1969) was not supported because there was no relationship between a picture's nameability (in terms of its naming latency) and whether or not it was remembered. This was true both for recognition and for recall. It seemed likely that something other than a simple name was being encoded during the brief ISIs that were tested—perhaps information related to pictorial detail. This possibility was supported when it was shown that the ability to remember left–right orientation of objects presented for 110 msec increased with increases in ISI (Intraub 1980).

Recall, recognition, and memory for mirror reversal all improved when the time between briefly presented pictures was increased. Apparently encoding continued following offset of a complex visual event. These early experiments, however, could not determine the degree to which this poststimulus encoding may have relied on the presence of an iconic representation of each picture. The gray field shown during the ISI would not be expected to act as a visual mask.

If during continuous presentation (no ISI) visual masking of each picture by the next was the primary reason for poor recognition performance, then in a sequence with ISIs, presentation of a visual mask rather than a blank field during the ISI should cause a dramatic decrease in recognition memory. To test this prediction, Intraub (1980) compared recognition memory for photographs of objects under conditions in which the ISI did or did not contain a mask (see figure 3.2).

One hundred and fifty color photographs were presented for 110 msec each, at a rate of 1 picture every 6 sec (see diagram at the top of figure 3.2). In one condition a blank field was presented during the ISI. In another condition, to present a display during the ISI that would have the same masking potential as pictures in a rapid sequence, two pictures from the same stimulus pool were selected. Each picture was used for half of the subjects in this condition. The subjects were familiarized with their designated picture prior to presentation, and then that picture was presented during each ISI in the sequence. Therefore, although subjects in the two ISI conditions were allowed the same amount of time between stimuli, in the blank-field ISI condition no masking stimulus was presented, whereas in the repeating-picture ISI condition each stimulus was followed by a potential visual mask. Finally, a third group of subjects viewed the same 150 pictures for the same 110 msec duration each, but with no ISI (this is depicted in the lower diagram in figure 3.2). In all three conditions, subjects were instructed to pay attention to and to try to remember the briefly presented pictures. If the poor performance typically obtained following rapid continuous presentation is caused by visual masking of each picture's iconic representation, then memory in the repeating-picture ISI condition should drop to this same low level.

After viewing 150 unrelated pictures, subjects in the blank-ISI and repeating-ISI conditions recognized 77% and 73% of the test items, respectively. The 4% difference in performance did not approach significance. Other experiments showed that presentation of a picture during the ISI did not diminish recognition memory for left-right orientation (Intraub 1980; experiment 3), nor did it diminish the viewer's ability to report pictorial details (Intraub 1980, experiment 4). However, when the same briefly presented pictures were shown with no ISI, recognition accuracy plummeted to 21% correct.

It is important to point out that across experiments, the small decrement in recognition memory between the blank-ISI condition and the repeating-ISI condition sometimes reached significance and sometimes did not (Intraub 1980, 1984). This small difference may have been due to the disruptive effects of visual masking on the iconic representation of each picture (see Loftus, Hanna, & Lester 1988; Loftus, Johnson, &

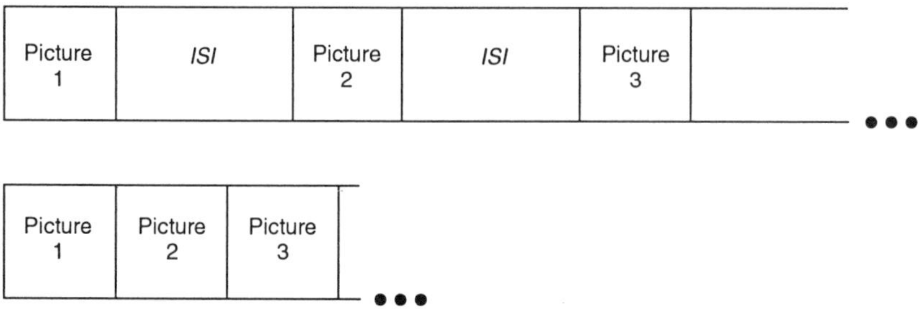

Picture 1	ISI	Picture 2	ISI	Picture 3	

• • •

Picture 1	Picture 2	Picture 3

• • •

Figure 3.2
Schematic representation of the sequences when there was an ISI (top) and when there was no ISI (bottom). Stimulus pictures were presented for 110 msec each in all conditions. Depending on condition, either a blank field or a familiar picture was presented during the 5890 msec ISI. (Intraub 1980, experiment 1.)

Shimamura 1985; Loftus & Ginn 1984). However, this relatively small decrement in performance does not approach the level of poor performance obtained in the continuous presentation condition. This suggested that something in addition to visual masking was contributing to the viewers' inability to remember pictures that they had just viewed.

Visual Search, Memory, and the Conceptual Short-Term Store

Some years earlier, Potter (1976; also see Potter 1993) had proposed that during rapid continuous presentation, unrelated pictures are momentarily understood and then immediately forgotten. She argued that although each picture is momentarily grasped, conceptual processing initiated by the next *new* picture in the sequence disrupts consolidation in memory.

Potter argued that a picture is identified within about 100 msec. Until the item is identified, it is vulnerable to visual masking by a new visual event. Once identification is complete, however, the pictorial representation is maintained in a conceptual short-term store for a few hundred milliseconds. It is during this time that the information is consolidated in memory. Although the representation is no longer subject to visual masking, its consolidation into memory can be disrupted by "conceptual masking." Conceptual masking can occur if a new, *meaningful* visual event is presented to the observer before consolidation of the previous event is complete. The new, meaningful visual event elicits conceptual processing and replaces the previous item in the conceptual short-term store. Potter argued that the store can maintain only one item at a time. If a picture is consolidated in memory before onset of a new picture, it is likely to be remembered.

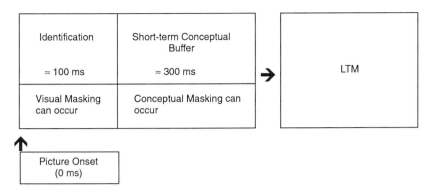

Figure 3.3
Schematic representation of Potter's (1976) model.

If not, although the viewer will have momentarily understood the picture, it will be forgotten by the time he or she has understood the next picture in the sequence. A schematic diagram of Potter's model is presented in figure 3.3.

The relatively good recognition memory for briefly glimpsed pictures that is obtained when a second or more is allowed between presentations (even when a repeating picture is presented during those ISIs) is consistent with this proposal, because the timing would eliminate the interfering effects of a conceptual mask.

To test if subjects could indeed momentarily grasp more than they could remember during continuous presentation, Potter (1976) contrasted subjects' ability to detect cued pictures with other subjects' ability to remember pictures at the end of each sequence. She reasoned that if viewers understand more than they can remember, on-line detection will be superior to immediate recognition memory. Conversely, if memory is poor following rapid presentation because observers can identify only a few unrelated visual events and remember only those that were identified, then detection accuracy should be no better than recognition memory.

She presented 16 unrelated color photographs of scenes in a continuous stream (no ISIs) at SOAs ranging from 113 to 333 msec per picture. One picture in each sequence was cued either by being presented in advance or by being described in advance, using a brief verbal title (e.g., "a road with cars"). The rationale was that whereas a correct detection based on the pictorial cue could be made on the basis of physical characteristics alone, correct detection based on the verbal cue could occur only if the viewer conceptually identified the target picture's meaning as it flashed by. Comparison of the two conditions was intended to provide insight into the extent to which target detection relies on specific visual detail as opposed to conceptual analysis. The proportion of targets detected based on the verbal cue was interpreted as reflecting the minimum proportion of pictures identified during presentation of the sequence. In the recognition memory condition, subjects were instructed to remember as many pictures as possible, and immediately following each sequence they participated in a recognition test in which all 16 presentation pictures were mixed with 16 distractor pictures.

In the detection conditions, subjects pressed a key as soon as they detected the cued picture. Responses falling between 250 and 900 msec following target onset were counted as correct. Results showed that subjects could identify unrelated scenes remarkably well at presentation rates that were equivalent to the average eye fixation frequency of 3 per sec, and those that were considerably more rapid. On the basis of the verbal cue, detection accuracy for rates of 113, 167, 250, and 333 msec/picture was 64%, 74%, 89%, and 78%, respectively (the apparent decrease at the slowest rate was due to an increased number of anticipation responses). Performance with the verbal cue was almost as good as seeing the picture itself in advance. Furthermore, in all cases, detection accuracy far surpassed recognition memory, with recognition accuracy ranging from 11% correct at the fastest rate to 42% correct at the slowest rate.

These results showed that completely unrelated scenes presented at rates equal to or faster than the average fixation frequency could be conceptually analyzed and matched to a verbal cue, although memory for the pictures immediately following presentation was relatively poor. The results were replicated and extended by Intraub (1981), using a number of design modifications that provided perhaps even more compelling support for Potter's (1976) model.

Although Potter (1976) had used general titles as cues to avoid facilitating perception of the target picture, one could argue that "a road with cars" narrows the visual expectations of the viewer enough to enhance perception of the target picture (see, e.g., Carr & Bacharach 1976; Neisser 1976). This would artificially inflate the detection rate. Intraub (1981) attempted to reduce expectancy by using not only descriptive titles as cues in a search task, but also cues that provide no specific visual details about the target. These latter cues were "category cues" and "negative cues." This was accomplished by presenting subjects with 12-item sequences that contained 11 items from a single general category (e.g., animals) and 1 from a different category. The odd item was cued by its basic-level name (e.g., chair), its superordinate category (e.g., "house furnishings or decorations"), or a negative cue (e.g., the item that is not an animal). The pictures used in this experiment were color photographs of objects similar to those shown in figure 3.1.

Sequences were presented at rates of 114, 172, and 258 msec/picture with no ISIs. Photographs were selected that were as visually dissimilar as possible. For example, the category "animals" contained creatures as diverse as a frog, a dog, a giraffe, and a butterfly. The target picture did not differ noticeably in size or general coloration from the other pictures in the sequence. The subject's task was to press a key upon detection, and then to describe the target picture. This meant that unlike Potter's experiment, rather than inferring correct detection from the key press alone, correct detection was based on the subject's ability to describe the target. Finally, to provide subjects in the recognition condition with a better chance to demonstrate good recognition memory, Intraub (1981) used a less taxing recognition test than Potter had (4 items instead of 32). The test always included two pictures that had been shown during presentation (one was the "odd" picture) and two distractors (one from the general category presented in the sequence, and one from a new category that differed from all the pictures, including the "odd" picture).

The results were consistent with those obtained by Potter (1976). As can be seen in table 3.1, subjects were able to detect and describe target pictures whether they had been cued by name, by superordinate category, or by negative cue. Furthermore, in all conditions, detection accuracy surpassed immediate recognition memory. The viewers' success in detecting and describing these target pictures on the basis of cues that provided no direct information about their visual characteristics, strongly supports the argument that a large proportion of the rapidly presented pictures were at least momentarily understood although they were rapidly forgotten. It is interesting to note that when subjects in the recognition condition were asked to describe the sequences they had just seen, all reported that the pictures were grouped by category and 83% specifically reported that there was a category-plus-odd-picture arrangement. In spite of having noticed this, they were very poor at recognizing the odd picture immediately following presentation.

The detection experiments showed that viewers can very rapidly identify a picture's meaning, but that identification alone is not sufficient to ensure later recognition. What is it that prevents consolidation during rapid presentation? To test Potter's (1976) argument that it is the presentation of a new, meaningful visual event (i.e., a conceptual mask), Intraub (1984) presented 16 pictures for 112 msec each with a 1.5 sec ISI. The ISI contained a blank field, a repeating to-be-ignored picture, or a new picture each time (see upper diagram in figure 3.2). Subjects were instructed to memorize the briefly presented stimulus

Table 3.1
Proportion of pictures detected by name, category, and negative category, and the proportion of target pictures recognized at each rate of presentation.

Rate (msec/picture)	Detection			Recognition Memory*
	Name	Cat.	Neg.	Target
258	.89	.69	.79	.58
172	.86	.71	.58	.49
114	.71	.46	.35	.19

Cat., category; neg., negative category.
*Recognition scores were corrected for guessing.
Based on Intraub 1981, table 1.

pictures. Once again, there was not a large difference in performance between the blank-ISI and the repeating-ISI conditions: recognition accuracy was 89% and 80% (which did not differ significantly). However, when a new, to-be-ignored picture was presented in the ISI each time (changing-ISI condition), recognition accuracy for the briefly presented pictures dropped to 63% correct.[1]

What is it about a new, to-be-ignored picture that disrupts processing more than a familiar repeating picture? According to Potter's view it is the conceptual processing that is elicited by each new, meaningful picture. However, another possibility is that it is not the "meaningfulness" of the new ISI pictures per se, but the novelty of each new ISI picture, that draws the subject's attention. To tease apart these two possible forms of interference, Intraub (1984) presented one of the following during each ISI: (a) a familiar, repeating picture, (b) a new picture, or (c) a new, colorful nonsense picture. The nonsense pictures were created by tracing the outline of each changing-ISI picture and filling it with splotches of color that did not follow any of the original contours within the picture. A new, nonsense picture was no more disruptive to memory than was a familiar, repeating picture: subjects recognized 87% of the pictures in the changing-nonsense-picture condition, and 90% in the repeating condition. Presentation of a new picture during each ISI, however, resulted in a significant reduction in recognition accuracy to 73% correct. During rapid presentation, apparently it is not simply the presentation of a new visual event that disrupts consolidation of individual pictures, but presentation a new *meaningful* event—a conceptual mask.

Loftus and Ginn (1984) provided converging evidence for conceptual masking and demonstrated a clear distinction between visual masking and conceptual masking. Pictures were presented for 50 msec, followed by either a visual noise mask or a conceptual mask (a new meaningful picture). The mask occurred either immediately or after a 300 msec delay. In addition, the mask was presented at one of two illumination levels. As predicted, in the immediate condition, luminance (a variable known to affect visual masking) affected the subjects' ability to report details of the picture, but type of mask did not. At the 300 msec delay (which allowed enough time for identification to be complete), luminance did not affect report, but type of mask did. A display with new conceptual information (i.e., a picture mask) resulted in fewer correct details being reported than did the visual noise mask.

In Intraub (1984), although presentation of a new picture in the ISI disrupted encoding more than had a familiar, repeating picture, memory did not drop to the low level obtained following rapid continuous presentation (19–21% correct),[1] a condition in which numerous new pictures follow a given picture. This argues against Potter's (1976) claim that the conceptual short-term store can hold only one picture at a time and that the information is "bumped" from the buffer when conceptual processes are elicited by the *next new picture in the sequence*. Subjects apparently could continue some processing of the briefly glimpsed pictures during the changing-ISI sequence. Given this result, Intraub (1984) sought to determine if the ability to continue processing was to some degree under the observer's control.

Subjects viewed the changing-ISI condition but were now provided with one of three attention instructions: attend to the brief pictures (112 msec), attend to the long-duration pictures (1.5 sec), or attend to both types of pictures equally (see upper diagram of figure 3.2). If conceptual masking by the new ISI picture automatically "bumps" the previous briefly presented picture from the store, then attention instructions should have no effect on memory. Subjects' recognition accuracy for the long and brief pictures as a function of attention instruction is shown in figure 3.4. Results showed a pronounced effect of attention instructions on memory for both the 112 msec and the 1.5 sec pictures. This demonstrated that the viewer has more control over these early stages of processing than was originally thought.

Intraub (1984) argued that the conceptual buffer must be able to hold more than one picture at a time. Consistent with this view, Intraub and Nicklos (1981; Intraub 1985a) presented 24 pictures in a sequence in which a blank interval was presented after each picture or after each group of 2, 3, or 4 pictures. The effect of grouping these pictures indicated that the buffer could hold up to three complex pictures. Subjects could encode successively presented pictures as long as the series was not too long.

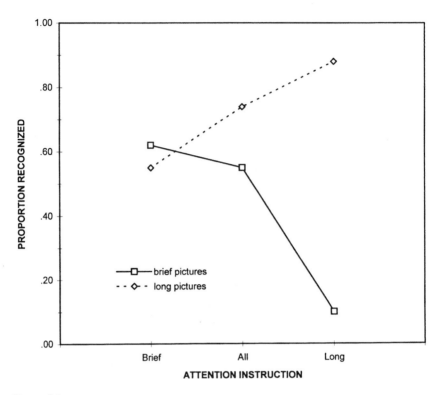

Figure 3.4
Proportion of long-duration and brief-duration pictures recognized (corrected for guessing) following each attention instruction. (From Intraub 1984.)

Visual Dissociation

The conceptual short-term buffer can hold more than one picture at a
time. A phenomenon referred to as "visual dissociation" of pictures
suggests that identification and integration of components of pictures
can be ongoing for more than one picture at a time (Bishop & Intraub
1996; Intraub 1985b, 1989). Visual dissociation occurs during rapid
presentation, when a searched-for feature migrates to a temporally
adjacent picture in the sequence and the subject perceives an illusory
conjunction of the picture and the feature.

In one experiment, Intraub (1985b) presented subjects with color
photographs of objects at a rate of 9 pictures/sec. They were instructed
to report which object in each 12-picture sequence was surrounded by
a black outline frame. Although subjects were often confident and
correct, they were frequently confident and wrong (30–50% of the
time). Subjects, when wrong, almost always reported the immediately

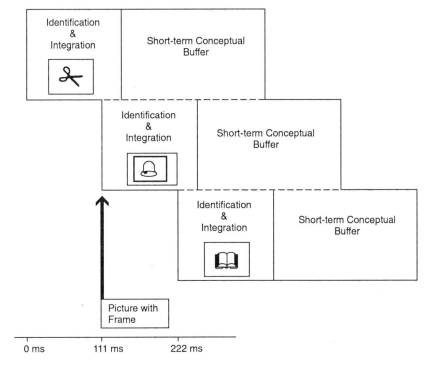

Figure 3.5

In this example, 3 successive items from an RSVP sequence are depicted (actual stimuli were color photographs). The picture of the bell is presented with the black frame. When the frame is detected early, it is likely to become integrated with the previous picture in the sequence (the scissors). When frame detection is relatively late (e.g., an additional 26 msec), it is likely to become integrated with the following picture in the sequence (the book). Dotted lines indicate places of potential overlap, where 2 pictures may undergo similar processing at the same time.

preceding or immediately following object in the sequence as the one with the frame. When subjects made an error, they often described the target object (the one actually in the black frame) as a "frameless" picture. This type of report shows that the subjects had perceived and remembered both the target picture and the temporally adjacent picture. Apparently, both were identified and understood, but under time pressure the frame had become integrated with the wrong stimulus, while both were being simultaneously processed.

In another experiment in which the procedure was the same except that in addition to the verbal response, subjects pressed a key as soon as they detected the frame, reaction time was clearly associated with the "direction" of the frame's migration (i.e., to the preceding or following picture in the sequence). Frame detection times were 26 msec faster on those trials associated with frame migration to the preceding picture than those associated with frame migration to the following picture. In other words, when the frame was rapidly detected, it was more likely to become integrated with the "tail-end" of processing associated with the previous picture, but when frame detection was relatively slow, it was more likely to become integrated with processes that were just initiated on a new picture (Intraub 1989, experiment 2). A schematic representation of a modified version of the original Potter (1976) model that characterizes these results is presented in figure 3.5.

The same type of temporal migration was obtained when subjects were required to search for a specified object (e.g., an outline drawing of a chair) in a sequence of outline scenes (e.g., a living room, a bedroom, and a study; Intraub 1989). In this case subjects would frequently, and confidently, report the object as occurring in the preceding or following scene in the sequence. Yet if these stimuli are presented at a rate of 3–4 pictures per sec, the searched-for element (frame or object) does not become integrated with temporally adjacent pictures. At rates such as these, the successive views have apparently reached a stable state in which they are immune to integration errors.

This can also be seen in Hochberg's (1986) aperture viewing experiment. In this case, subjects were informed that the ambiguous display they would see was actually an outline cross moving behind a circular aperture. They could perceive the display as such when the presentation rate was 2–3 views per sec. At more rapid rates of presentation (e.g., 10 views per sec), the views became visually integrated and could not each be evaluated in terms of the mental schema.

The discussion of timing is an important one. Potter (1976) raised the question of why, if the visual system is capable of identifying a picture within 100 msec, visual scanning would have an upper limit of about 3–4 fixations per sec. She speculated that the average fixation frequency of 3 per sec may be a compromise between the need for rapid identification of each fixated part of the visual world (which can occur within 100 msec) and the need to retain some portion of what has been seen (by allowing consolidation of information in the conceptual short-term store). The visual dissociation experiments and the research on the effects of presentation rate on aperture viewing suggest that this limitation on the scan rate also serves the important purpose of minimizing the likelihood of visual integration errors during visual scanning.

To summarize, research on detection and memory of briefly presented views shows that a picture's conceptual content can be very rapidly accessed, but that consolidation in memory takes a somewhat longer amount of time. Although the characteristics of a display can affect consolidation of the previously glimpsed picture, the viewer possesses considerable control over the allocation of attention to previous and current visual events. These capabilities would be instrumental to a system that interprets the visual world by integrating successive views within a larger schematic context. The next question to be considered is whether there is any evidence to suggest that a mental schema is in fact activated by a single glimpse of a scene.

Boundary Extension

If activation of a mental schema occurs in response to the detection of a partial view of a scene, might there be a detectable "residue" of this activation when the scene is later remembered? A possible affirmative answer is provided by research on "boundary extension," a memory distortion reported by Intraub and Richardson (1989). What they observed was that viewers tended to remember having seen a greater expanse of a scene than had been shown in a photograph (see figure 3.6). Subjects' drawings of remembered photographs, and their responses in a recognition/rating test, revealed that they remembered having seen information that did not exist in the photograph, but that would be expected to exist just outside the camera's field of view.

Boundary extension has been observed under a wide variety of conditions in which pictures are presented for relatively long periods of time (e.g., 15 sec). It occurs regardless of whether objects are cropped by the edges of the picture (Intraub, Bender, & Mangels 1992; Intraub & Bodamer 1993); thus ruling out an explanation based on the Gestalt principle of object completion (see Ellis 1955). It occurs following presentation of as few as 3 pictures (Intraub & Bodamer 1993, see demonstration condition) or presentation of as many as 20 pictures for 15 sec each (Intraub & Richardson 1989). It also has been obtained using a variety of memory tests including recall (subjects draw remembered pictures), boundary recognition tests, and even a test in which subjects physically moved markers to indicate the remembered boundaries of a photograph (Intraub 1992; Intraub & Bodamer 1993; Intraub & Richardson 1989; Legault & Standing 1992; Nyström 1993).

A possible explanation of boundary extension is that when viewers detect a partial view of a scene, this activates a mental schema that represents the general layout of what would be seen if the viewer actually could make an eye fixation just beyond the picture's boundaries. In terms of this formulation, comprehension of a partial view involves mentally locating the view with respect to the larger scene. For example, when viewing a portrait-style photograph of a smiling

Figure 3.6
Panel A shows a close-up version of a scene with main objects cropped. Panel B shows a slightly more wide-angle version of the scene with no objects cropped. The subjects' drawings in panels C and D are representative drawings of the photographs in panels A and B, respectively. In comparing drawings with the photographs, be sure to pay attention to four picture boundaries. (Intraub & Richardson 1989.)

friend, we do not perceive the picture as depicting a disembodied head. The rest of the friend and the rest of the background are understood to "exist" just outside the picture's boundaries. Interpretation of the partial view includes these spatial assumptions about the layout of the continuous scene from which the partial view was culled.

We have proposed that the viewer remembers seeing not only what was actually presented but also what was understood to exist just beyond the picture's boundaries, thus causing the viewer to recall having seen a greater expanse of the scene than was shown (Intraub 1992; Intraub, Bender, & Mangels 1992). An interesting point to consider is that although this results in a nonveridical representation of the picture, it will often result in a veridical representation of the real-world scene that extends beyond the picture's boundaries. This can be seen in figure 3.6. A comparison of the close-up photograph and the subject's drawing of that photograph shows that boundary extension occurred. If one then compares that same drawing with the wide-angle photograph of the scene, it is clear that although the subject did not correctly remember the close-up, the subject's error included information that actually did exist outside the close-up's boundaries! The "error" shows that the observer had successfully extrapolated information regarding the scene's layout.

Several studies following the initial report of boundary extension have supported the hypothesis that the phenomenon reflects activation of a scene schema during perception. This has been referred to as the "perceptual schema hypothesis." In one test of the hypothesis, Intraub and Bodamer (1993) sought to eliminate the phenomenon by drawing the viewer's attention to the pictures' boundaries. Their rationale was that if boundary extension reflects a fundamental aspect of picture perception (i.e., understanding the partial view within its larger expected context), then it should be difficult to prevent even when the viewer attempts to do so.

Subjects viewed 12 photographs of scenes for 15 sec each and were told to remember them in as much detail as possible, including the background and the layout of the objects in the picture space. In the control condition, that is all they were told. In the test-informed condition, they were told about the boundary memory test in advance—so they knew that memory for the pictures' boundaries would be especially important. In the demo condition, prior to the experimental sequence, they were given a demonstration of boundary extension using 3 pictures. All subjects drew pictures with extended boundaries. This was pointed out to them, and the phenomenon was described. Prior to presentation of the experimental sequence, they were specifically told to try to prevent the distortion from occurring.

Both a drawing task and a recognition memory test (in which distractors showed both boundary extension and boundary restriction) revealed that subjects in the test-informed and demo conditions experienced boundary extension. The effect was attenuated in comparison with the control condition, but was not eliminated. Even when subjects were forewarned, they were unsuccessful in their attempts to prevent its occurrence.

In other research, Intraub, Gottesman, and Bills (1998) directly tested the perceptual schema hypothesis by comparing memory for spatial expanse in a condition in which the pictures depicted a partial view of a scene (which should activate the schema), and a condition in which the pictures did not (and therefore should not active the schema). They presented subjects with 16 photographs of scenes, 16 outline drawings of the scenes (traced from the photographs), or 16 outline objects (traced from the photographs without including any indication of a background). Both a boundary recognition test and a drawing task showed that boundary extension occurred for both types of scenes, but not for the pictures of objects that had been presented without scene structure. Converging results were reported by Legault and Standing (1992), who found that photographs of objects in scenes yielded boundary extension, whereas pictures showing an outline drawing of the main object from each scene did not.

The type of schematic expectations that yield boundary extension are apparently limited to cases in which the viewer understands the stimulus to be a partial view of a continuous scene. To determine if the perceptual schema could be activated via a top-down route, Intraub et al. (1998) presented the outline objects, described the photographs from which the objects had been traced, and instructed the subjects to attempt to imagine the photograph and "mentally project" it onto the outline object. Subjects were instructed to remember the size and placement of each object in as much detail as possible. They were told that the purpose of the exercise was to determine if imagining the scene from which the object was drawn would aid memory.

While subjects viewed each of the 16 outline objects for 15 sec each, the experimenter read a description of the photograph that the subject was to try to imagine. For example, while studying the outline drawing of a man in a cross-legged sitting position, the subjects heard the following, "The man is sitting on a concrete pebbled ground. Directly behind him is a red brick wall which fills the picture space." In the control condition, subjects were also instructed to remember the size and placement of each object in as much detail as possible, but no mention of scenes was made.

Although subjects in both conditions saw the same stimuli (outline drawings of objects), subjects remembered the size of the objects differently in the two conditions. In the control group, there was no overall directional distortion. Some objects were remembered as being larger and some as being smaller[2]. In the imagination group, however, results yielded the typical pattern associated with boundary extension. Consistent with remembering a more wide-angle view, subjects tended to remember the main object as having taken up less of the picture space. Furthermore, as has been found repeatedly with photographs of scenes, objects traced from close-up versions of the pictures showed a greater degree of distortion than did objects traced from the wide-angle views.

Finally, to determine if it was the imagination task per se that resulted in boundary extension, they again presented the outline objects along with an imagination task. However, this time, the subjects were provided with a description of each object's colors and were asked to mentally project those colors onto the outline objects (with no mention of scenes or partial views). In this case, boundary extension was not obtained and the pattern of results was the same as in the control condition. Apparently, the schema is only activated in response to the understanding of a partial view of a potentially continuous environment (i.e., a scene).

This research suggests that activation of the perceptual schema can be initiated by either bottom-up or top-down indications of a continuous scene. Perception and imagination of scenes apparently share a common underlying structure, a notion that has been applied to other types of stimuli (e.g., Farah 1988; Finke 1985; Reisberg 1996). For the purposes of the present discussion, however, the most important point is that when the observer encounters a partial view of a continuous scene (regardless of whether it is physically presented or imagined), expectations about the continuation of the scene's layout are automatically activated. If the same schema also underlies the integration of eye fixations, then we should be able to find evidence for it under conditions that mimic the temporal characteristics of visual scanning.

Intraub, Gottesman, Willey, and Zuk (1996) conducted two experiments using brief presentations of pictures to address this question. In experiment 1, they sought to determine if boundary extension would occur following a brief exposure to a scene. Prior to their experiments, multisecond stimulus durations had been used in boundary extension experiments, with durations usually as long as 15 sec. If boundary extension reflects the activation of a schema that serves to guide and integrate successive views, then a brief glimpse should be sufficient to cause boundary extension. On the other hand, if a single glimpse allows only for the extraction of the "gist" of a scene (in terms of its semantic meaning alone), then boundary extension should not occur. In the latter case, although subjects would not be expected to have an accurate memory for the boundaries (i.e., they might sometimes expand them and sometimes contract them), without schema activation there would be no reason to expect a unidirectional error.

To test these hypotheses, Intraub et. al (1996) used a design that was similar in many ways to the recognition memory experiments described earlier (e.g., Intraub 1979, 1980), except that memory for boundaries was tested. Seven scenes were presented with an SOA of 5 sec. The pictures were presented for either 250 msec each or 4 sec each, with a black-and-white visual noise mask during the ISI. Subjects saw either close-up or wide-angle views of the same 7 scenes. Presentation was followed by a drawing task and a boundary recognition task. Subjects' performance on both types of tests showed that they remembered the pictures with extended boundaries. If anything, the unidirectional distortion was slightly more pronounced in the 250 msec condition than the 4 sec condition. Memory for pictures presented at both stimulus durations replicated the pattern of results reported in numerous boundary extension experiments (e.g., Intraub et al. 1992; Intraub & Berkowits 1996): close-ups yielded a strong degree of boundary extension and wide-angle views yielded little or no directional distortion.

This experiment clearly demonstrated that boundary extension is not limited to stimuli with long durations. To explore the early time course of the phenomenon further, in another experiment Intraub et al. (1996) sought to determine if the same memory distortion would occur with an SOA that is brief enough to mimic a fixation frequency of 3 views per sec. Subjects were presented with 72 sequences. Each contained 3 unrelated photographs of scenes presented for 333 msec each with no ISI. The third picture was followed by a visual noise mask for 1 sec, followed by the test picture. The test picture was always identical to one of the pictures the subject had just seen. Subjects rated the view depicted in the test picture using a 5-point boundary scale (ranging from a score of -2 to +2) as "much too close," "slightly too close," "same," "slightly too far," or "much too far," and then provided a confidence rating of "sure," "pretty sure," or "not sure."

What happened was that test pictures tended to be rated as being "too close" to be the original, which indicates that the original was remembered with extended boundaries. The mean boundary scores and .95 confidence limits as a function of the serial position of the picture that was tested, are presented in table 3.2. As can be seen in the table, the directional bias was significant regardless of the serial position of the stimulus, and the removal of "not sure" responses, if anything, resulted in a stronger unidirectional distortion of the pictures' boundaries. Given only 3 pictures presented in rapid succession, and a 1 sec retention interval, boundary extension occurred. In addition to grasping the conceptual meaning of each unrelated, briefly glimpsed picture, viewers had apparently extrapolated each scene's layout. Merely a glimpse of a scene was sufficient to activate schematic expectations beyond the picture's physical boundaries.

Summary and Conclusions

We possess a fleeting memory for unrelated objects and scenes that are presented in rapid succession at rates that mimic or surpass the average fixation frequency of the eye. At presentation rates ranging from about 110 msec to 333 msec per picture, the subjective experience is a very interesting one of grasping and losing large amounts of information within moments. The research reviewed in this chapter supports the contention that under conditions in which scenes change far more rapidly than they ever do in normal visual scanning, and with far less predictability, our capacity to understand each brief glimpse at least

Table 3.2
Mean boundary score and the upper limit and lower limit of the .95 confidence interval in each serial position

Position	Boundary Score		Confidence Interval	
	M	SD	UL	LL
	All Responses			
1	−.37	.21	−.32	−.42
2	−.41	.26	−.34	−.47
3	−.38	.21	−.32	−.43
	High Confidence Responses			
1	−.44	.24	−.38	−.50
2	−.50	.29	−.43	−.57
3	−.43	.27	−.36	−.50

Boundary score range is −2 to +2.
UL, upper limit; LL, lower limit.
High confidence responses are "Sure" and "Pretty sure."
Taken from Intraub et al. 1966.

momentarily is remarkably good, although our ability to remember those glimpses suffers. Not only can viewers extract the gist of a picture under these extreme conditions, they can extrapolate the scene's layout and understand the view within the context of the larger, real-world scene from which it was culled.

The visual system rapidly activates schematic expectations of spatial layout, given only a single glimpse of a complex scene. It also has considerable flexibility in terms of the allocation of attention, allowing viewers to minimize the effects of conceptual masking if they adopt the appropriate strategy. If these remarkable capabilities exist (a) for sequences of completely unrelated photographs (e.g., asparagus, moose, stove, man, easy chair, soldier, etc.) and, (b) under the unyielding time constraints of rapid continuous visual presentation, then it is difficult to believe that they do not take place with even greater facility during normal visual scanning. Under normal viewing conditions, a mental schema elicited by a single view could be extended and embellished as additional fixations on the scene are made. The continuity and redundancy of the successive views gleaned during visual scanning limit the likelihood of conceptual masking. The fact that both the placement and the duration of individual eye fixations can be controlled during visual scanning (something that is not possible under the artificial constraints of rapid continuous presentation) makes it seem quite feasible that a schematic representation of the spatial layout of a scene plays an important role in our comprehension of the visual environment and in the integration of briefly fixated views.

Notes

1. In the changing-ISI condition, subjects saw twice as many pictures prior to the recognition test than subjects in the repeating-ISI condition. Perhaps this, rather than online cognitive masking, resulted in greater confusion on the recognition test. This hypothesis was rejected when the ISI pictures from the changing-ISI condition were shown to subjects prior to presentation of a repeating-ISI sequence and the same results were obtained (Intraub 1984, experiment 3).

   A note about the type of equipment used in the different experiments being described here is in order. In Intraub (1984), all conditions were presented using 16 mm cine film. This differs from Intraub (1980), in which the continuous sequence was presented using cine film, and the ISI sequences were presented using a tachistoscope. The same results were obtained regardless of whether the same mode (cine film) or different modes (film and tachistoscope) were used.

2. This pattern (normalization toward the average view in the set) was predicted on the basis of the Extension-Normalization Model (Intraub 1992; Intraub et al. 1992; Intraub et al. 1996). This model provides an account of the changes in boundary memory for scenes that occur over relatively long retention intervals (e.g., 2 days).

References

Biederman, I. (1972). Perceiving real-world scenes. *Science, 177*, 77–80.

Biederman, I. (1981). On the semantics of a glance at a scene. In M. Kubovy & J. R. Pomerantz (eds.), *Perceptual organization* (pp 213–253). Hillsdale, NJ: Lawrence Erlbaum Associates.

Biederman, I., Mezzanotte, R. J., & Rabinowitz, J. C. (1982). Scene perception: Detecting and judging objects undergoing relational violations. *Cognitive Psychology, 14*, 143–177.

Bishop, P. J., & Intraub, H. (1996). Visual dissociation of digitized photographs. *Behavior Research Methods, Instruments and Computers, 28*, 365–371.

Carr, T. H., & Bacharach, V. R. (1976). Perceptual tuning and conscious attention: Systems of input regulation in visual information processing. *Cognition, 4*, 281–302.

Ellis, W. D. (ed. and trans). (1955). *A source book of Gestalt psychology.* London: Routledge & Kegan Paul.

Farah, M. J. (1988). Is visual imagery really visual? Overlooked evidence from neuropsychology. *Psychological Review, 95*, 307–317.

Finke, R. A. (1985). Theories relating mental imagery to perception. *Psychological Bulletin, 98*, 236–259.

Hochberg, J. (1978). *Perception* (2nd ed.). Englewood Cliffs, NJ: Prentice-Hall.

Hochberg, J. (1986). Representation of motion and space in video and cinematic displays. In K. J. Boff, L. Kaufman, & J.P. Thomas (eds.), *Handbook of perception and human performance* (vol. 1, pp. 22:1–22:64). New York: John Wiley & Sons.

Intraub, H. (1979). The role of implicit naming in pictorial encoding. *Journal of Experimental Psychology: Human Learning and Memory, 5*, 78–87.

Intraub, H. (1980). Presentation rate and the representation of briefly glimpsed pictures in memory. *Journal of Experimental Psychology: Human Learning and Memory, 6*, 1–12.

Intraub, H. (1981a). Identification and processing of briefly glimpsed visual scenes. In D. F. Fisher, R. A. Monty, & J. W. Senders (eds.), *Eye movements: Cognition and visual perception*. Hillsdale, NJ: Lawrence Erlbaum Associates.

Intraub, H. (1981b). Rapid conceptual identification of sequentially presented pictures. *Journal of Experimental Psychology: Human Perception and Performance, 7*, 604–610.

Intraub, H. (1984). Conceptual masking: The effects of subsequent visual events on memory for pictures. *Journal of Experimental Psychology: Learning, Memory and Cognition, 10*, 115–125.

Intraub, H. (1985a). Conceptual masking of briefly glimpsed photographs. In R. Groner, G. W. McConkie, & C. Menz (eds.), *Eye movements and psychological processes*. North-Holland.

Intraub, H. (1985b). Visual dissociation: An illusory conjunction of pictures and forms. *Journal of Experimental Psychology: Human Perception and Performance, 11*, 431–442.

Intraub, H. (1989). Illusory conjunctions of forms, objects and scenes during rapid serial visual search. *Journal of Experimental Psychology: Learning, Memory and Cognition, 15*, 98–109.

Intraub, H. (1992). Contextual factors in scene perception. In E. Chekaluk, & K. R. Llewellyn (eds.), *The role of eye movements in perceptual processes* (pp. 45–72). Amsterdam: Elsevier Science Publishers.

Intraub, H. (1977). The representation of visual scenes, *Trends in Cognitive Sciences, 1*, 217–222.

Intraub, H., Bender, R. S., & Mangers, J. A. (1992). Looking at pictures but remembering scenes. *Journal of Experimental Psychology: Learning, Memory and Cognition, 18*, 180–191.

Intraub, H., & Berkowits, D. (1996). Beyond the edges of a picture. *American Journal of Psychology, 109*, 581–598.

Intraub H., & Bodamer, J. A. (1993). Boundary extension: Fundamental aspect of pictorial representation or encoding artifact? *Journal of Experimental Psychology: Learning, Memory and Cognition, 19*, 1387–1397.

Intraub, H., Gottesman, C. V., & Bills, A. J. (1998). Effects of perceiving and imagining scenes on memory for pictures. *Journal of Experimental Psychology: Learning, Memory and Cognition, 24*, 186–201.

Intraub, H., Gottesman, C. V., Willey, E. V., & Zuk, I. J. (1996). Boundary extension for briefly glimpsed pictures: Do common perceptual processes result in unexpected memory distortions? *Journal of Memory and Language, 35*, 118–134.

Intraub, H., & Nicklos, S. (1985). Levels of processing and picture memory: The physical superiority effect. *Journal of Experimental Psychology: Learning, Memory, and Cognition, 11*, 284–298.

Intraub, H., and Richardson, M. (1989). Wide-angle memories of close-up scenes. *Journal of Experimental Psychology: Learning, Memory and Cognition, 15*, 179–187.

Irwin, D. E.(1991). Information integration across saccadic eye movements. *Cognitive Psychology, 23*, 420–456.

Irwin, D. E., Brown, J. S., & Sun, J. (1988). Visual masking and visual integration across saccadic eye movements. *Journal of Experimental Psychology: General, 117*, 276–287.

Legault, E., & Standing, L. (1992). Memory for size of drawings and of photographs. *Perceptual and Motor Skills, 75*, 121.

Loftus, G. R. (1985). Picture perception: Effects of luminance on available information and information extraction rate. *Journal of Experimental Psychology: General, 114*, 342–356.

Loftus, G. R., & Ginn, M. (1984). Perceptual and conceptual masking of pictures. *Journal of Experimental Psychology: Learning, Memory and Cognition, 10*, 435–441.

Loftus, G. R., Hanna, A. M., and Lester, L. (1988). Conceptual masking: How one picture captures attention from another picture. *Cognitive Psychology, 20*, 237–282.

Loftus, G. R., Johnson, C. A. and Shimamura, A. P. (1985). How much is an icon worth? *Journal f of Experimental Psychology: Human Perception and Performance, 11*, 1–13.

McConkie, G. W., & Currie, C. B. (1996). Visual stability across saccades while viewing complex pictures. *Journal of Experimental Psychology: Human Perception and Performance, 22*, 563–581.

McConkie, G., & Zola, D. (1979). Is visual information integrated across successive fixations in reading? *Perception and Psychophysics, 25*, 221–224.

Neisser, U. (1976). *Cognition and reality*. San Francisco: Freeman.

Nystrom, L., & McClelland, J. (1992). Trace synthesis in cued recall. *Journal of Memory and Language, 31*, 591–614.

Nyström, M. (1993). Is picture memory wide-angle? *Psychological Research Bulletin, 33*, 1–16.

Paivio, A. (1971) *Imagery and Verbal Processes*. New York: Holt, Rinehart, and Winston.

Paivio, A., & Csapo, K. (1969). Concrete image and verbal memory codes. *Journal of Experimental Psychology, 80*, 279–285.

Potter, M. C. (1976). Short-term conceptual memory for pictures. *Journal of Experimental Psychology: Human Learning and Memory, 2*, 509–522.

Potter, M. C. (1993). Very short-term conceptual memory. *Memory Cognition, 21*, 156–161.

Potter, M. C., & Levy, E. I. (1969). Recognition memory for pictures. *Journal of Experimental Psychology, 81*, 10–15.

Rayner, K., & Pollatsek, A. (1992). Eye movements and perception. *Canadian Journal of Psychology, 46*, 342–376.

Reisberg, D. (1996). The nonambiguity of mental images. In C. Cornoldi, R.H. Logie, M. A. Brandimonte, G. Kaufmann, & D. Reisberg *Stretching the imagination* (pp. 119–171). New York: Oxford University Press.

Resink, R. A., O'Regan, J. K., & Clark, J. J. (1997). To see or not to see: The need for attention to perceive changes in scenes. *Psychological Science, 8*, 368–373.

Simons, D. J. (1996). In sight, out of mind: When object representations fail. *Psychological Science, 7*, 301_305.

Simons, D. J. & Levin, D. T. (1997). Change blindness. *Trends in Cognitive Sciences, 1*, 261–267.

Yarbus, A. (1967). *Eye movements and vision*. New York: Plenum Press.

Chapter 4

Inattentional Amnesia

Jeremy M. Wolfe

Imagine that you are on the street and someone pulls you aside to ask for directions. You begin to engage this person in conversation. For mysterious reasons, in the middle of this conversation, workers, carrying a door, walk between you and the other person. When the door is gone, the original person has been replaced by a different person. Would you notice if Stranger 1 was replaced by Stranger 2? The intuitive answer is "Of course, I would." How could you fail to realize that you were no longer talking to the same person? The empirical answer, from a clever experiment by Dan Simons and Dan Levin (1997), is that people fail to notice this change about 50% of the time. Surprising as this finding might be, it is not an isolated phenomenon. In recent years, a growing number of reports have seemed to show that we see much less than we think we see. Simons and Levin have produced a number of variations on this basic theme. In one series of experiments, subjects watch a videotape of a conversation. The camera cuts from one speaker to the other. Speaker 1 is sitting at a table. She pours herself a cup of Diet Pepsi. The camera cuts to Speaker 2. When the camera returns to Speaker 1, the Pepsi bottle has been replaced with a cardboard box. Subjects may remember that Speaker 1 poured herself a drink, but they frequently fail to notice that the bottle has vanished (Simons 1996).

Grimes (1996) obtained a similar effect when he changed the contents of images during eye movements. He found that observers were strikingly insensitive to substantial alterations in the content of scenes. These were unsubtle changes, such as trees disappearing from front yards. Blackmore et al. (1995) did a different version of this experiment. In their study, subjects viewed one image. The image was then moved to a new location. Subjects had to move their eyes to refoveate it. They then needed to decide if the second image was the same as or different from the first. Performance was quite poor. Again, subjects missed substantial changes from one image to the next. Irwin and his colleagues have asked, in various ways, what information about a scene is preserved when observers make an eye movement (Irwin 1996; Irwin &

Carlson-Radvansky 1996; Irwin, Yantis, & Jonides 1983). For instance, they have asked how well subjects perform tasks that require the combination of information from successive fixations. They find that subjects perform such tasks quite poorly, and they conclude that very little visual information is preserved across saccades. Henderson (1997) reaches a similar conclusion. Information about the goal of the eye movement is retained, but there is little evidence for the idea that a rich visual percept is built up over a series of fixations (Breitmeyer 1984; McConkie & Rayner 1976).

Rensink, O'Reagan, and their collaborators have shown that observers can fail to report changes in an image even if those changes are not made during an eye movement or a camera movement (O'Regan, Rensink, & Clark 1996; Rensink, O'Regan & Clark 1995; 1996). In one version of their experiment, observers look at a natural scene. At regular intervals, the scene is very briefly replaced by a white field. When the scene reappears, *something* has changed. The observer's task is to find the change, which oscillates back and forth from frame to frame. Observers are surprisingly bad at this task (see exp. 2 of Blackmore et al. 1995). Even though they may be looking at the images for several seconds, subjects fail to notice that jet engines appear on and disappear from an airplane. They fail to notice that a bridge crosses a pond on the even-numbered frames and stops in the middle of the pond on the odd-numbered frames. Observers notice the change only if they happen to be attending to the changing object or location from frame to frame. It is not necessary to blank the entire screen. A distracting "mud splash" will produce the same effect (O'Regan et al. 1996). As in the other examples, the implication would seem to be that we actually see far less than we think we see when we look at a scene (Dennett 1991).

Mack and Rock (1997) propose a way of understanding such phenomena that they call "inattentional blindness." The hypothesis is that we do not consciously perceive objects to which we have not attended. Their own evidence for this hypothesis comes from a line of heroic experiments—heroic because each experimental session yields just one trial per observer. Observers are asked to view a briefly presented "cross" and to judge if the vertical or horizontal component line is longer. After a few trials of this sort comes the critical trial. On this trial, some irrelevant stimulus is flashed in one of the quadrants formed by the cross. After the trial, observers are asked if they saw anything out of the ordinary. Observers fail to report stimuli that are easily seen if they are aware that such stimuli might appear (hence, one critical trial per observer) (Mack, Tang, Tuma, & Kahn 1992). Mack and Rock argue that in the absence of attention, the irrelevant stimuli never rose to the level of conscious perception.

An experiment by Joseph et al. (1997) seems to support this view. In their experiment, using a rapid serial visual presentation (RSVP) task at fixation, they produced an "attentional blink" (see Chun & Potter 1995; Raymond, Shapiro, & Arnell 1992; and see the chapter by Shapiro and Luck in this volume). If a visual search stimulus is presented during the "blink," subjects are unable to detect a target of one orientation among homogenous distractors of another orientation. It could be argued that the attentional blink task entirely consumes attention during the blink and, as a result, the search stimulus is simply not seen—"inattentional blindness."[1]

We can apply the inattentional blindness argument to the first examples discussed in this chapter. Why don't observers notice changes in unattended objects when those changes are made during eye movements or under cover of a distracting event like a screen flash or mud splash? Inattentional blindness argues that the changes are not seen because the stimuli that changed were not attended and, thus, not consciously perceived. On the other hand, inattentional blindness is not an entirely convincing explanation of the Simons and Levin or Rensink et al. experiments. The stimuli are present for a relatively long time in these tasks. Surely, observers in the Simons and Levin experiment were attending to the person who was asking for directions. Surely that person was perceived. Why, then, was a change in his identity not noted? Moreover, inattentional blindness seems at odds with introspection. When we look at a scene, we seem to consciously perceive *something* throughout the visual field. Even at stimulus onset, conscious perception does not seem to be restricted to the object of attention. This sort of introspective argument is unsatisfying, because it is extremely difficult to test experimentally. Indeed, there are serious problems with any experimental effort to directly ask subjects if something is consciously perceived without attention. The direct approach would be to ask subjects to attend to visual stimulus A and report about the perception of stimulus B. However, this proves to be impossible because the demand to report on B directs attention to B. If you do not attend to a stimulus, then you cannot report on that stimulus, regardless of whether or not you saw the stimulus. Thus, the problem of perception without attention is a difficult experimental nut to crack, if one is willing to accept that it is possible to see stimuli that cannot, for one reason or another, be reported.

The widely employed solution to this methodological problem involves presenting a stimulus, arranging for the subject not to attend to that stimulus, removing that stimulus, and then, after the unattended stimulus is gone, asking the subject to report on its properties. The usual finding, as seen in the examples given above, is that subjects are very poor at after-the-fact reporting on the properties of unattended stimuli. Note, however, that an inability to report is not the same as an inability to see. Sperling (1960) made this point almost forty years ago. A subject, asked to report all the letters in a briefly flashed, 12-letter display, could report only about 25–30% of the letters. However, the subject would do much better if cued, after the display was gone, to report on the letter at a specific location.

Sperling's subjects responded after the stimulus had been removed but could still attend to the icon, if not to the physical stimulus. All of the experimental examples given thus far involve reporting after the removal of the stimulus and after the destruction or dissipation of any icon representation. In the Mack and Rock experiment, observers were asked if they saw anything unusual on the previous trial. In the Simons and Levin experiment, subjects had to compare the current speaker with a speaker who was present before the door moved past, and so forth. Even when the subject knew the question, report was made after the stimulus was gone (e.g., Joseph et al. 1997). The common thread in these experiments is that unattended stimuli cannot be accurately reported after they are gone. Unfortunately, there are at least two plausible explanations for this failure. First, as suggested by the inattentional blindness hypothesis, the stimuli may not be *seen* if they are not attended. Second, the stimuli may have been seen but not *remembered*. I wish to argue that the explanation of these apparent failures of perception is not inattentional blindness but *inattentional amnesia*.

The Inattentional Amnesia Hypothesis

The inattentional amnesia hypothesis has four parts:

> 1. Under normal circumstances we consciously perceive visual *stuff* at all locations in the visual field. (Visual "stuff" will be more precisely defined below.)
> 2. At the current locus of attention, visual information can make enhanced contact with other mental processes. This permits, for instance, object recognition and transfer into memory. Attention may change the visual representation so that things look different while attended. Overt responses, from eye movements to key presses, demand attention.
> 3. The present conscious visual representation is composed of the visual stuff of 1 and the effects of attention as sketched in 2.
> 4. This visual representation has no memory. It exists solely in the present tense. When a visual stimulus is removed, its contents are lost to the visual system. Similarly, when attention is deployed

away from some previously attended object or locus, no trace of the effects of attention remain in the visual representation.

If vision has no memory and if attention is the gateway to other mental representations, it follows that unattended visual stimuli may be seen, but will be instantly forgotten; hence, *inattentional amnesia.*

In the bulk of this chapter, I will describe experiments that motivate the various pieces of the inattentional amnesia hypothesis. At the end, we will return to the phenomena described above and show how they can be understood in this context.

Preattentive Vision and Visual "Stuff"
The greater part of research on visual perception deals with what can be called "attentive vision." A stimulus is placed before an observer and the observer is asked to respond to that stimulus. The situation requires and expects that observers will focus attention on the stimulus. It is somewhat more difficult to assess visual function away from the present locus of attention. For more than 20 years, visual search experiments have been among the most effective tools for examining the nature of "preattentive vision," vision prior to the arrival of attention. In standard visual search experiments, observers look for one item, the "target" among a variable number of "distractor" items. The search display can be briefly flashed, in which case the dependent measure is accuracy. Alternatively, the display can remain visible until a response is made, in which case the dependent measure is reaction time (RT). Our experiments use RT methods.

As shown in figure 4.1, search tasks differ in their efficiency. "Feature" searches are searches where the target is distinguished from the distractors by a unique basic feature. In figure 4.1, the feature is orientation and the target is uniquely horizontal ("shallow" may be a more accurate description (Wolfe, Friedman-Hill, Stewart, & O'Connell 1992). Many feature searches are very efficient, with RT essentially independent of set size. This independence suggests that all items can be processed at the same time ("in parallel") (Treisman & Gelade 1980). There are perhaps a dozen basic features that support efficient search (reviewed in Wolfe 1997b). These include color, orientation, size, and various cues to depth.

Parallel processing of basic features across the entire stimulus is thought to occur before any attentional bottleneck in processing. Thus feature processing is said to be "preattentive" (Neisser 1967). Attention seems to limit processing to one or perhaps a few objects at a time (Baylis & Driver 1995a, 1995b; Tipper & Weaver 1996), possibly by constricting receptive fields in some cortical areas to cover only the attended item(s) (Moran & Desimone 1985).

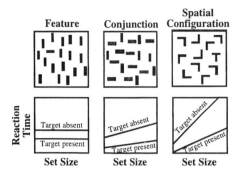

Figure 4.1
Typical searches and patterns of RT data.

This is not the place for a full discussion of the properties of preattentive vision. However, it is worth noting that there is more to preattentive visual processing than parallel extraction of a dozen basic features. For our purposes, the most important of these properties is that preattentive processing includes some division of the image into candidate objects (Wolfe & Bennett 1997). Attention is probably deployed from preattentive object to object rather than from location to location (Baylis 1994; Baylis & Driver 1993; Duncan 1984; Gibson 1994; Vecera & Farah 1994), though it is possible to direct attention to a location, too (Gibson & Egeth 1994). Moreover, there is some evidence that preattentive processing is sensitive to the structure of objects and can assign one attribute to the whole object and another attribute to a part. As an example, while it is difficult to search for a target defined by two colors (e.g., the item that is red and green; Wolfe, Yu, Stewart, Shorter, Friedman-Hill, & Cave 1990), preattentive processing makes it relatively easy to find a whole item of one color with a part of another color (e.g., the red item with a green part; Bilsky & Wolfe 1995; Wolfe, Friedman-Hill, & Bilsky 1994).

Returning to figure 4.1, most searches in the real world are conjunction searches. In these searches, no single feature defines the target, but basic feature information is part of the definition of the target. In the middle panel of figure 4.1, the target is black and horizontal. We probably do not have preattentive "black horizontal" processors (for a theoretical account, see Tsotsos 1990). However, if a color processor *guided* attention toward black items and an orientation processor guided attention toward vertical items, the intersection of those two sources of guidance would tend to direct attention toward black vertical items. The result is relatively efficient search for conjunctions of basic features. This idea that preattentive processes can guide attention in a useful manner is the heart of the Guided Search model (Wolfe 1994; Wolfe, Cave, & Franzel 1989; Wolfe & Gancarz 1996; see also Egeth, Virzi, & Garbart 1984; Hoffman 1979; Tsotsos 1995; Tsotsos et al., 1995). For present purposes, the important point is that the target is not identified until attention is deployed to the target object. Only with attention can the relationships between basic features be used as a basis for an overt response.

The role of attention is more marked in tasks where basic feature information is of no use, as in the *spatial configuration* search in the third panel of figure 4.1. Here the target is a T and the distractors are L's. Target and distractors have the same basic features—a vertical line and a horizontal line. Preattentive processes cannot guide attention in this case, and search proceeds in what appears to be a serial manner from item to item until attention stumbles upon the target (Kwak, Dagenbach, & Egeth 1991).

Whether search is efficient or inefficient, the items in a search display are present in the conscious visual representation prior to the arrival of attention. A glance at the T vs. L search in figure 4.1 makes it clear that there are several vertical and horizontal items present. You see them but do not know if a specific item is a T or an L until attention visits that item. This illustrates the first three parts of the inattentional amnesia hypothesis: (1) We see something everywhere. That "something" is preattentive vision; (2) Attention can take the preattentive feature information and create a different perception; and (3) The current contents of the visual representation are preattentive vision augmented by the current work of attention.[2]

Postattentive Vision
From the vantage point of a book on fleeting memories, the interesting questions begin to arise not in preattentive or attentive vision but in what can be called "postattentive vision" (Wolfe, 1997a). When the eyes first open on a new scene, preattentive processes extract features and assign them, loosely, to preattentive objects. Typically, attention will be deployed to one object. That act of attention allows the features of the object to be organized and processed in a way that permits object recognition. The attended object is perceived differently than the not-yet-attended objects in the scene. Assuming this to be the case, what happens when attention is deployed to the next object? Does the visual representation have a *memory* of the work of attention? The possibilities can be illustrated by analogy. Consider a model airplane. In its "preattentive" state, it is a collection of pieces in a box. When a child directs "attention" to those pieces, they can be formed into a recognizable object. When the child's attention is directed elsewhere, the model

remains glued together. This postattentive representation has a memory for the effects of attention. Alternatively, consider a set of juggling balls. When our talented child directs attention to the balls, they can be juggled into a recognizable figure. However, when the child's attention is directed elsewhere, the balls no longer describe an oval in the air. They return to their unjuggled, preattentive state This postattentive representation has no memory.

Measuring Postattentive Vision: The Repeated Search Task   In a series of experiments, we have asked if the visual representation has any memory for the perceptual effects of attention. We find that the answer is "no." When attention is deployed elsewhere, the visual representation of an object appears to revert to its preattentive state. The first series of experiments used a *repeated search* method. The basic stimulus and experimental design are illustrated in figure 4.2.

In repeated search, the search stimulus remains the same over several trials. In the version shown in the top part of figure 4.2, five letters form the search display. These are presented in a circle around fixation. At the center of the display, a probe letter is presented. The observer's task is to determine if the probe letter can be found in the search array. Thus, in the first trial shown in figure 4.2, the probe is an "r" and the answer is "no"; it is not present. The second probe is "a," which is present. And so forth. The postattentive logic of this experiment is shown in the second part of figure 4.2. When the display first appears, the letters are represented preattentively. The blobs in the figure denote preattentive object files, shapeless bundles of basic features (Wolfe & Bennett 1997). As time progresses from left to right in the figure, attention is deployed to first one and then another object. Attention allows the letter to be read and the observer to determine that no "r" is present in the display. After the subject responds to the probe letter, "r," it is replaced with an "a" probe.[3] There is an A in the display. Presumably, it must have been identified in order to determine that it was not an R in the previous trial. Does this act of attending and identifying the A on one trial have any impact on the course of the search for the A in the next? Put another way, does the visual stimulus A retain some postattentive quality that makes it easier to find on the next trial, or does the display revert to its preattentive state?

Note that, for the logic of this experiment, it does not really matter if one holds that attention is deployed in series from item to item (as proposed here) or if one believes that attention is deployed in parallel across all items. In either case, for the "r" to be rejected, all letters in the search display must be identified. Does that speed subsequent searches through the same display?

Repeated Search: Five repetitions

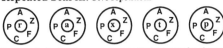

The search display does not change. Only the probe changes.

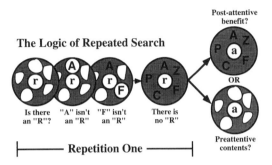

Figure 4.2
The repeated search paradigm. The top panel shows a sequence of 5 repeated searches through a single display. The bottom panel shows the presumed action of attention during the first search.

In the actual experiment, observers searched through the same display 5 times. The search display could contain either 3 or 6 items. The center of each item lay on an invisible circle of radius 2.6 deg. The probe, identifying the target on each trial, was presented in the circle at the center of the display. On 50% of the trials, the probe item was present in the search display. Subjects responded by pressing one key if the target was present and another if the target was absent. Reaction time and accuracy were recorded. Accuracy feedback was given by coloring the central circle after each repetition—blue for correct responses, red for incorrect. Subjects were tested for 20 practices and 100 trials (or $5 \times 20 = 100$ and $5 \times 100 = 500$ total searches). For the version presented here, the first test probe appeared 300 msec prior to the onset of the search display and subsequent probes appeared 50 msec after the previous response was recorded. We have repeated the experiment with the first probe appearing at the same time as the search display and with longer intervals between response and the next probe. These manipulations do not alter the basic results described below. The search display remained continuously visible with no change during the 5 search repetitions. Experiments were run on Macintosh computers using MacProbe software (Hunt 1994, #3325).

We have performed this experiment with letters, meaningless closed curves, meaningful pictures, and conjunctions of color, orientation, and size. In all versions, the results were similar to the results for conjunction stimuli shown in figure 4.3. The conjunction stimuli could be red, green, yellow, or blue rectangles that could be oriented vertically, horizontally, or obliquely. The rectangles also could be large or small.

Looking first at the reaction time data, it is clear that the RTs do not change markedly as a function of repetition. More important than the absolute RTs, however, are the slopes of the RT × set size function, since these slopes are the measure of the efficiency of visual search. The slope is derived from the difference between RTs for set sizes 3 and 6. The RT graph shows that this separation is not decreasing. The slopes themselves are plotted in the lower portion of figure 4.3. On the first appearance of the stimuli, search is quite inefficient. Though many conjunction searches are very efficient (Cohen & Ivry 1991; Driver 1992; Nakayama & Silverman 1986; Quinlan & Humphreys 1987; Theeuwes & Kooi 1994; Treisman & Sato 1990; Wolfe et al. 1989), this search would not be expected to be efficient because of high distractor inhomogeneity (Duncan & Humphreys 1989) and, more important, because the target changes on each trial (inconsistent mapping) (Schneider & Shiffrin 1977; Shiffrin & Schneider 1977). Here, search is inefficient on repetition 1 and repeated search does not improve efficiency.

This seems surprising, because observers must have been learning something about the display. Why weren't they using this knowledge to improve search efficiency? Perhaps the observers did not have enough exposure to the search display. To test this hypothesis, we had observers search 400 times through the same set of 3 or 5 letters. As in the previous experiment, the search display remained unchanged—this time through all of the 400 trials. By the end of the 400 trials, observers were *very* familiar with the stimuli. If asked, they could easily recite the 3 or 5 letters they had been examining. Nevertheless, while search efficiency improved a little, slopes were still in the decidedly inefficient range of > 50 msec/item after 400 trials.

Knowing the letters in the search display did not improve search efficiency, because knowing is not seeing. If an observer knew that the letters in the display were C, V, and N, she could search through that remembered set rather than searching through the visual display. However, that memory search would proceed at a rate equivalent to 30–40 msec/item (McElree & Dosher 1989; Sternberg 1969)—a rate not notably different from an inefficient visual search. In fact, our repeated search paradigm reveals the unexpectedly impoverished state of postattentive vision precisely because memory can be of so little help. In more realistic search tasks, memory is useful. If I want to find a book

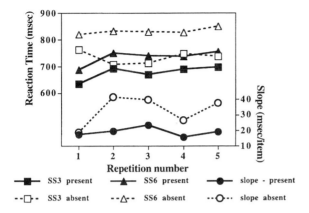

Figure 4.3
Repeated search—results for conjunction stimuli. (Data from Wolfe 1997a.)

on a colleague's shelf, I must engage in a fairly inefficient visual search. If I want to find a book on my shelf, my search is speeded by my knowledge of the layout of my library. I don't *see* my shelves differently from the way I see my colleagues' shelves. I *know* more about them. The repeated search tasks employed here do not benefit from memorization of the display because memory access is no more efficient than visual access for these tasks. For the present purposes, the important point is that repeated application of attention to a search display does nothing to the visual representation that makes search more efficient.

Once the search display has been committed to memory, the visual stimulus may actually serve to interfere with search. For example, after 400 trials of search through the same set of letters, we removed the search display and asked observers to continue to respond to the probes based on their memory of the contents of the display. The resulting RTs were about 100 msec *faster* in these memory searches than in the visual searches. The slopes of the memory search functions were 30 msec/item for items in the memory set and 50 msec/item for items that were not in the set. These are comparable with the results of Sternberg (1969). A series of experiments comparing memory search and visual search suggests that the visual search display acts to mask the probe at the center of the display (Wolfe 1997a).

A Second Repeated Search Task   We replicated the repeated search result with a modified version of the task. The goal of the new task was to unconfound trial number and the pre/postattentive status of an item. That is, in the original version, all of the items are represented preattentively at the onset of trial 1. No new items could appear after that.

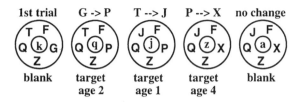

Figure 4.4
A second repeated search paradigm. Note: Repeated letters moved a little from trial to trial (see text). This is not shown in the figure.

The visual representation of the display can only become increasingly postattentive. Figure 4.4 illustrates a method that allows new items to appear during a session.

The observer's task is the same as in the previous version of repeated search. Is the probe letter present in the search display? In this version, however, one item in the search array could change on each trial. In figure 4.4, the changes are described above each display. On each trial after the first, each letter in the search display was moved by a small amount. On half of the trials, one of these letters changed to a new letter. The movement of all letters masked the transients that would otherwise have alerted subjects to the change in one letter (Yantis & Johnson 1990). Thus, from trial 1 to trial 2, the G becomes a P. On some trials (e.g., trial 5) nothing changed. In the figure, the "age" of the target, shown below the display, is the number of trials that the target has been present in the display. With this method, age of the target is uncoupled from trial number. It becomes possible to have targets of age 1 appearing throughout a series of trials (e.g., trial 3).

In this experiment, no feedback was given between repetitions and a 500 msec interval was placed between the response to trial N and the presentation of the target probe for trial N+1. Targets were presented on 60% of trials. After 30 practice searches, each subject was tested for 2 blocks of 800 trials—one with set size 3, the other with set size 5. Other details can be found in Wolfe (1997a).

Since we are interested in the age of the target, it is only the target-present trials that are of use here. Figure 4.5 shows the results, averaged over 10 observers. It makes very little difference if the target item is new to the display or if it has been present for several trials. The time required to find a letter is about the same whether that letter is represented preattentively or postattentively.

The results of the repeated search experiments suggest that attention to an item does nothing persistent to the visual representation of that item; at least, nothing that can be used to make visual search more efficient. Couched in terms of fleeting memories, this means that the

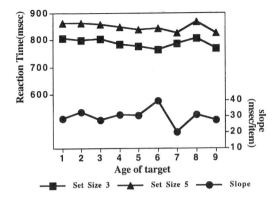

Figure 4.5
Repeated search—results for conjunction stimuli. (Data redrawn from Wolfe 1997a.)

visual representation's memory for the effects of attention is fleeting indeed. Attention does something to the representation of items. In many cases (e.g. letters), items are not recognized until attention is applied to them. Once attention is deployed elsewhere, however, any trace of that attentional effect on the visual representation vanishes very rapidly.

Curve Tracing: A Different Postattentive Paradigm

While the results of the repeated search experiments seem very clear, it is unwise to base conclusions on a single line of research. Accordingly, we have performed another series of postattentive experiments using an entirely different task. Here we use a curve-tracing task introduced by Jolicoeur et al. (1986). The basic idea is illustrated in figure 4.6.

Jolicoeur's subjects were asked to determine if two dots were on the same curve or on different curves (as at the left in figure 4.6). The basic finding was that reaction times depended on the distance along the curves and not the linear distance between the dots. Jolicoeur et al. proposed that the task was performed by having an attentional operator, a "visual routine," move along the curve from one dot to the other. We reasoned that this could be a useful task in an investigation of postattentive vision. If attention changed the visual representation of the curve, then the dependence of RT on distance might be reduced with extended exposure to the same curves. The basic task is shown in figure 4.7.

In the upper row, we have an example of the repeated-curve tracing task. In the actual experiment, the curves remained fixed on the screen. The dots changed position from trial to trial. Subjects made a forced-

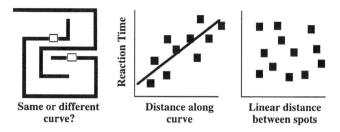

Figure 4.6
The Jolicoeur et al. (1986) curve-tracing paradigm. RT to determine if the spots are on the same curve depends on the distance along the curve between the 2 dots and not on the physical separation of the dots.

choice response that the dots were either on the same curve or on different curves.

What might we expect if postattentive vision showed the persistent effects of attention? Perhaps attention serves to individuate one curve from the other. If a subject knew that one dot was on curve A and the other was on curve B, we can presume that it would not be necessary to trace the curves. This would be akin to asking if two people reside in the same town. If you say that one person is in California and the other is in Massachusetts, you do not need to scan the town. You simply know that the people are not in the same town. In the context of curve tracing, we can examine the consequences of individuating the curves by using curves of different colors, as shown schematically in the lower portion of figure 4.7. With different-color curves, tracing is not necessary. If one dot is on a yellow curve and the other is on a blue curve, it is safe to say that they are on different curves. Can attention "paint" the curves so that tracing becomes unnecessary following extended exposure to one set of curves?

The methods were similar to those used for the repeated search task. Subjects performed 5 trials with each pair of curves. The curves were unchanging during those 5 trials. Only the position of the dots changed. Ten subjects ran a total of 500 trials with curves of the same color and 500 trials with each curve having a different color.

Our experiment replicated the basic findings of the original Jolicoeur et al. (1986) study. RTs over 5000 msec were discarded. The average correlation of RT with distance along the curve ($R^2 = 0.14$) was significantly greater than the correlation with the linear distance between points ($R^2 = 0.025$; paired $t(9) = 6.75$, $p < 0.001$). Our particular interest is in the efficiency of the task as reflected in the slope of the function relating RT to distance along the curve. The average slopes are shown in figure 4.8.

Are the dots on the same or different curves?

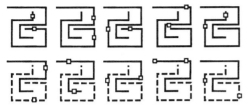

Figure 4.7
The repeated curve-tracing task.

There is no improvement in the efficiency of the curve-tracing task as a function of repetition. The Different Color condition produces faster tracing (shallower slopes) than the Same Color condition. This means that there was room for improvement in the Same Color condition, but no improvement is seen. One might wonder why there is any evidence for tracing in the Different Color condition. It is hard to see why subjects should bother tracing at all. However, Pringle and Egeth (1988) have shown that slopes are greater than 0 even for very simple stimuli. Perhaps some tracing is automatic and mandatory.

As in the repeated search case, we were concerned that we had not given postattentive vision enough of a chance to show the enduring benefits of attention. Accordingly, we had 9 subjects do the curve-tracing task 100 times for each of 10 curves. If we compare the first 25 trials with the last 25, we see that there is little change (figure 4.9). The slowest subjects show some improvement. However, performance in the Same Color condition never approaches the efficiency of performance in the Different Color condition.

To determine if two dots lie on the same line, it may be necessary to use an attentional operator to trace the curve from one dot to the next. The results of these experiments suggest that any such attentional tracing leaves not a trace behind. The tracing done on one trial must be done again on the next. There is no evidence for a postattentive benefit in curve tracing.

Discussion

What Does Vision Remember?
Evidence, converging from many experiments in many labs, argues that vision does not remember very much, if anything. Is there a spatiotopic visual representation that remembers the contents of one fixation and fuses them with the contents of the next fixation? We get a negative answer from almost all of the recent experiments on transsaccadic mem-

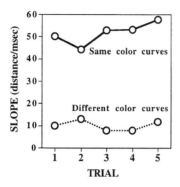

Figure 4.8
Repeated curve-tracing. Subjects trace no faster on the fifth repetition than they do on the first.

ory. Subjects are poor at noticing changes in a scene when they move their eyes over the scene (Grimes 1996) or when the scene moves and the eyes follow (Blackmore et al. 1995). Subjects are poor at noticing changes in the contours of an object across fixations (Henderson 1997). They do not integrate patterns over fixations (Irwin et al. 1983). If the visual stimulus does not move, subjects still fail to notice large changes to items that are not the present subject of attention (Rensink et al. 1995b). These changes can include alterations in basic, preattentive features like color. In one of Rensink's demonstrations, for example, a boat's change from blue to yellow is not immediately noticed. This argues that even the preattentive contents of the image are not remembered from one moment to the next. In one frame you may see a blue boat. In the next frame you may see a yellow boat. However, unless you were attending to the color of the boat, no memory of the boat's previous color is available to compare with the boat's present color.

If you attend to the boat over the course of the change from one image to the other, you can encode the fact that the boat *was* blue and *is* yellow, and, therefore, must have changed color. That attention, however, is not changing the visual representation. The postattentive experiments described in this chapter find no persistent visual effects that can be used to speed visual search or curve tracing. Memory for the color of the boat or, indeed, for anything else seems to be quite separate from the actual experience of seeing. Vision exists in the present tense. It remembers nothing.

Note that it is rather hard to explain something like the failure to notice a change in boat color by saying that the color was not seen. If you ask subjects about the gist of the scene, they will tell you that the picture included a boat pulled up on the shore. How could the boat

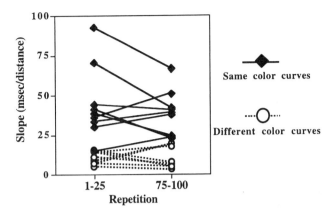

Figure 4.9
Even 100 trials do not eliminate the need to trace a curve. Each line connects 1 subject's slope value for the first 25 trials with that subject's slope for the last 25 trials.

be seen without seeing a color? What was seen at the location of the yellow (or blue) pixels that made up the side of the attended and perceived boat?

How Long Is the Present Tense?
It is not entirely fair to say that vision has no memory. If a visual stimulus is extinguished, its effects remain for some period of time; 100 msec might be a good estimate for the duration of this fleeting visual memory (the "sensible present" in James's terms (1890, p. 608). For example, Phillips (1974) had subjects compare 2 random dot patterns. If these patterns were briefly presented and separated by less than 100 msec, subjects could detect small changes between the patterns, suggesting that they could compare all of the past stimulus with all of the present stimulus. As the ISI increased, performance dropped markedly and subjects behaved as though only a small subset of information on the first frame was available to be compared with the second frame. As a quite different example, consider that for durations of less than 100 msec, light intensity and duration trade off so that 10 units of light for 100 msec looks like 100 units presented for 10 msec (Bloch's law; Hood & Finkelstein 1986). For the present argument, nothing very important rests on the duration of the present tense. The visual representation probably persists for some short period of time beyond the extinction of the physical stimulus. However, by the time the subject can be asked about the contents of that representation, it is gone.

But What About Cases Where Perception Takes Time to Develop?
There are a number of famous cases of visual stimuli that do change with continued inspection. Examples would include the Dalmation dog picture that looks like black and white blobs until you "get it," and complex stereograms like Julesz's (1971) spiral or the "Magic Eye" autostereograms (Tyler & Clarke 1990). These cases seem to show exactly what the postattentive experiments do not show. With sustained attention, the visual representation seems to build up over time. Moreover, after it is built, it stays built in the sense that the dog and the spiral are more rapidly seen on subsequent presentation (Frisby & Clatworthy 1974; Kumar & Glaser 1993; Ramachandran 1976).

In the case of complex stereograms, the slow development of the percept probably reflects the slow time course of preattentive processing. If the visual representation is the result of preattentive processing plus the current work of attention, then the percept will evolve if the preattentive processes require a significant amount of time to complete their work. There is good evidence for the preattentive processing of disparity information (He & Nakayama 1992; Nakayama & Silverman 1986).

It is interesting that complex stereograms are learned and seen more rapidly on subsequent trials, but this is not directly germane to the claims of inattentional amnesia. Whatever is being learned is somehow stored in a memory that persists for a long time and exists in the absence of the visual stimulus. The learning is not an example of change in the visual representation.

The stereoscopic spiral slowly develops as you look at it. The blob dog example is somewhat different. Subjects either see the dog or they don't see the dog. This does not seem to be an example of a slow preattentive process. Rather, it is a failure of attentive object recognition. This example illustrates the second tenet of the inattentional amnesia hypothesis. At the locus of attention, contact with other cognitive processes can alter the visual representation. On initial exposure, the blob dog fails to make contact with any stored material. Once the subject learns to see the blob dog as a dog, it is seen as a dog. The claim of the inattentional amnesia hypothesis would be that the blobs are seen as a dog only when attended and that the postattentive representation of the blob dog, like the preattentive representation (Wolfe & Bennett 1997), is a collection of blobs. Of course, the hypothesis makes the same claim about all objects. They are seen as recognizable objects only when attended.

Attention as the Bridge to Memory
Attention is the pathway around what would otherwise be the crippling effects of inattentional amnesia. The objects of attention reach into

memory. The temporal details of the paths from vision to cognition are the subject of a number of chapters in this book. Potter's chapter proposes a "conceptual short-term memory" (CSTM) that is "conceptually structured and tightly linked to long-term memory." It is a bridge between the contents of the visual representation and the stored information that can give meaning to those contents. The chapters on the attentional blink (Shapiro and Luck) and repetition blindness (Kanwisher) describe some of the limits on this first conceptual stage of processing. When this bridge is blocked or overloaded, stimuli are not remembered. For example, the Joseph et al. (1997) experiment shows that simple feature search cannot be done during the attentional blink. Inattentional amnesia holds that the search stimuli were seen. However, the search task could not be performed until the blink had passed. By that time, it was too late. The stimulus had disappeared into James's "bottomless abyss of oblivion" (James 1890, p. 643).

It is interesting to ask how much processing can be done without leaving a usable trace in explicit memory. For example, Luck et al. (1996) performed an experiment that is similar in spirit to the Joseph et al. experiment. They presented words during the attentional blink. Like the blinked search task of Joseph et al., the blinked words could not be recalled, but the meanings of those words had an impact on the N400 wave of the ERP. Apparently, the words were read and understood at some level in the system but left no mark in explicit memory.

Blindness or Amnesia?
The Luck et al. result returns us to the difficult task of choosing between inattentional blindness and inattentional amnesia. There are two choices. One can argue that the words in the Luck et al. experiment were not seen but were, nevertheless, processed to a level of word meaning sufficient to produce semantic effects on the ERP (evoked response potential).[4] Alternatively, one could argue that the word was seen. It reached something like the conceptual short-term memory described by Potter (1993). This would account for its ability to influence the ERP. However, because of the temporal dynamics of CSTM, the word failed to create a more lasting explicit memory. In this account, the word was seen, fleetingly remembered, and then forgotten before it could be reported.

To some extent, this argument rides on the definition of what it means to consciously perceive something. Can one be said to consciously see something if one cannot remember seeing it an instant later? I see no reason why not.[5] If I showed a subject a picture and then gave him electroconvulsive shock, he would have no conscious memory of having seen the picture, but it seems wrong to me to assert that he did not have a conscious experience of the picture. Dreams may provide a more benign analogy. We have all had the experience of waking out of a dream and feeling its contents evaporate. Indeed, within moments we may recall nothing more than the feeling that we had a dream. Consider that vision is like a dream. While you are dreaming, attending, or seeing, the products of those processes are all very real and very present to you.[6] However, the moment you are not dreaming, attending, or seeing, "These, our actors, . . . are melted into air, into thin air . . . the baseless fabric of this vision, . . . this insubstantial pageant faded, leave(s) not a rack behind."[7]

Notes

1. Braun and Sagi (1990, 1991), using a somewhat different method, concluded that subjects could do feature search tasks while attention was diverted elsewhere, but one could always argue that they did not divert attention as fully as Joseph et al. (1997).
2. One could argue that a diffuse attention to the whole display is required to see the items, and that focused attention is required to identify the items (Nakayama 1990). We will discuss this issue later, but for the time being, what matters is that you see *something* before you find the target and, after you find the target, you see something different at the target location.
3. In the figure the probes are shown in lowercase Times and the search stimuli in uppercase **HELVETICA BOLD**, so that there is not a perfect visual match between probe and target. We have done these experiments with matching and nonmatching probes and targets; it does not seem to matter.
4. This points to a connection between inattentional blindness and late selection theories (Deutsch & Deutsch 1963; Lavie 1995). Similar late selection thoughts can be provoked by the finding by Mack and her colleagues (1992) that complex stimuli like one's own name may be reported in her inattentional blindness paradigm while simple stimuli like gratings are not reported.
5. Others disagree (e.g., Kihlstrom 1997).
6. Having discussed these matters a bit with my philosophical friends (Ned Block, Daniel Dennett; personal communications), I will leave it to them to say exactly what it is that is real or present in either seeing or dreaming.
7. Shakespeare, *The Tempest,* act 4, scene 1.

References

Baylis, G. C. (1994). Visual attention and objects: Two object cost with equal convexity. *Journal of Experimental Psychology: Human Perception and Performance, 20*(1), 208–212.

Baylis, G. C., & Driver, J. (1993). Visual attention and objects: Evidence for hierarchical coding of location. *Journal of Experimental Psychology: Human Perception and Performance, 19*(3), 451–470.

Baylis, G. C., & Driver, J. (1995a). One-sided edge assignment in vision: 1. Figure-ground segmentation and attention to objects. *Current Directions in Psychological Science, 4*(5), 140–146.

Baylis, G. C., & Driver, J. (1995b). One-sided edge assignment in vision: 2. Part decomposition, shape discrimination, and attention to objects. *Current Directions in Psychological Science, 4*(6), 201–206.

Bilsky, A. A., & Wolfe, J. M. (1995). Part-whole information is useful in size x size but not in orientation x orientation conjunction searches. *Perception & Psychophysics, 57*(6), 749–760.

Blackmore, G. B. (S. J.), Nelson, K., & Trosciansko, T. (1995). Is the richness of our visual world an illusion? Transsaccadic memory for complex scenes. *Perception, 24.* 1075–1081.

Braun, J., & Sagi, D. (1990). Vision outside the focus of attention. *Perception & Psychophysics, 48*(1), 45–58.

Braun, J., & Sagi, D. (1991). Texture-based tasks are little affected by second tasks requiring peripheral or central attentive fixation. *Perception, 20,* 483–500.

Breitmeyer, B. G. (1984). *Visual masking: An integrative approach.* Oxford: Oxford University Press.

Chun, M. M., & Potter, M. C. (1995). A two-stage model for multiple target detection in rapid serial visual presentation. *Journal of Experimental Psychology: Human Perception and Performance, 21*(1), 109–127.

Cohen, A., & Ivry, R. B. (1991). Density effects in conjunction search: Evidence for coarse location mechanism of feature integration. *Journal of Experimental Psychology: Human Perception and Performance, 17*(4), 891–901.

Dennett, D. C. (1991). *Conscious explained.* Boston: Little, Brown.

Deutsch, J. A., & Deutsch, D. (1963). Attention: Some theoretical considerations. *Psychological Review, 70,* 80–90.

Driver, J. (1992). Motion coherence and conjunction search: Implications for guided search theory. *Perception & Psychophysics, 51*(1), 79–85.

Duncan, J. (1984). Selective attention and the organization of visual information. *Journal of Experimental Psychology: General, 113,* 501–517.

Duncan, J., & Humphreys, G. W. (1989). Visual search and stimulus similarity. *Psychological Review, 96,* 433–458.

Egeth, H. E., Virzi, R. A., & Garbart, H. (1984). Searching for conjunctively defined targets. *Journal of Experimental Psychology: Human Perception and Performance, 10,* 32–39.

Frisby, J. P., & Clatworthy, J. L. (1974). Learning to see complex random-dot stereograms. *Perception, 4,* 173–178.

Gibson, B. S. (1994). Visual attention and objects: One vs two or convex vs concave? *Journal of Experimental Psychology: Human Perception and Performance, 20*(1), 203–207.

Gibson, B. S., & Egeth, H. (1994). Inhibition of return to object-based and environment-based locations. *Perception & Psychophysics, 55*(3), 323–339.

Grimes, J. (1996). On the failure to detect changes in scenes across saccades. In K. Akins (ed.), *Perception* (pp. 89–110). New York: Oxford University Press.

He, Z. J., & Nakayama, K. (1992). Surfaces versus features in visual search. *Nature, 359,* 231–233.

Henderson, J. M. (1997). Transsaccadic memory and integration during real-world object perception. *Psychological Science, 8*(1), 51–55.

Hoffman, J. E. (1979). A two-stage model of visual search. *Perception & Psychophysics, 25,* 319–327.

Hood, D. C., & Finkelstein, M. A. (1986). Sensitivity to light. In K. R. Boff, L. Kaufmann, & J. P. Thomas (eds.), *Handbook of perception and human performance* (vol. 1, chap. 5). New York: John Wiley and Sons.

Hunt, S. (1994). MacProbe: A Macintosh-based experimenter's workstation for the Cognitive Sciences. *Behavior Research Methods, Instruments & Computers, 26,* 345–351.

Irwin, D. E. (1996). Integrating information across saccadic eye movements. *Current Directions in Psychological Science, 5*(3), 94–100.

Irwin, D. E., & Carlson-Radvansky, L. A. (1996). Cognitive suppression during saccadic eye movements. *Psychological Science, 7*(2), 83–88.

Irwin, D. E., Yantis, S., & Jonides, J. (1983). Evidence against visual integration across saccadic eye movements. *Perception & Psychophysics, 34*(1), 49–57.

James, W. (1890). *The principles of psychology*. New York: Henry Holt.

Jolicoeur, P., Ullman, S., & MacKay, M. (1986). Curve tracing: A possible basic operation in the perception of spatial relations. *Memory & Cognition, 14*(2), 129–140.

Joseph, J. S., Chun, M. M., & Nakayama, K. (1997). Attentional requirements in a "preattentive" feature search task. *Nature, 387*, 805–807.

Julesz, B. (1971). *Foundations of cyclopean perception*. Chicago: University of Chicago Press.

Kihlstrom, J. F. (1997). Conscious vs unconscious cognition. In R. Sternberg (ed.), *The nature of cognition*. Cambridge, MA: MIT Press.

Kumar, T., & Glaser, D. A. (1993). Initial performance, learning, and observer variability for hyperacuity tasks. *Vision Research, 33*(16), 2287–2300.

Kwak, H., Dagenbach, D., & Egeth, H. (1991). Further evidence for a time-independent shift of the focus of attention. *Perception & Psychophysics, 49*(5), 473–480.

Lavie, N. (1995). Perceptual load as a necessary condition for selective attention. *Journal of Experimental Psychology: Human Perception and Performance, 21*(3), 451–468.

Luck, S. J., Vogel, E. K., & Shapiro, K. L. (1996). Word meanings can be accessed but not reported during the attentional blink. *Nature, 382*, 616–618.

Mack, A., & Rock, I. (1998). *Inattentional Blindness*. Cambridge, MA: MIT Press.

Mack, A., Tang, B., Tuma, R., & Kahn, S. (1992). Perceptual organization and attention. *Cognitive Psychology, 24*, 475–501.

McConkie, G. W., & Rayner, K. (1976). Identifying the span of the effective stimulus in reading: Literature review and theories of reading. In H. Singer & R. B. Ruddell (eds.), *Theoretical models and processes of reading* (pp. 137–162). Newark, DE: International Reading Association.

McElree, B., & Dosher, B. A. (1989). Serial position and set size in short-term memory: The time course of recognition. *Journal of Experimental Psychology: General, 118*(4), 346–373.

Moran, J., & Desimone, R. (1985). Selective attention gates visual processing in the extrastriate cortex. *Science, 229*, 782–784.

Nakayama, K. I. (1990). Vision: Coding and efficiency. The iconic bottleneck and the tenuous link between early visual processing and perception. In C. Blakemore (ed.), *Vision: Coding and efficiency* (pp. 411–422). Cambridge: Cambridge University Press.

Nakayama, K., & Silverman, G. H. (1986). Serial and parallel processing of visual feature conjunctions. *Nature, 320*, 264–265.

Neisser, U. (1967). *Cognitive psychology*. New York: Appleton-Century-Crofts.

O'Regan, J. K., Rensink, R., & Clark, J. J. (1996). "Mud splashes" render picture changes invisible. *Investigative Ophthalmology & Visual Science, 37*(3), S213.

Phillips, W. A. (1974). On the distinction between sensory storage and short-term visual memory. *Perception & Psychophysics, 16*(2), 283–290.

Potter, M. C. (1993). Very short-term conceptual memory. *Memory & Cognition, 21*(2), 156–161.

Pringle, R., & Egeth, H. (1988). Mental curve tracing with elementary stimuli. *Journal of Experimental Psychology: Human Perception and Performance, 14*(4), 716–728.

Quinlan, P. T., & Humphreys, G. W. (1987). Visual search for targets defined by combinations of color, shape, and size: An examination of the task constraints on feature and conjunction searches. *Perception and Psychophysics, 41*, 455–472.

Ramachandran, V. S. (1976). Learning-like phenomena in stereopsis. *Nature, 262*, 382–384.

Raymond, J. E., Shapiro, K. L., & Arnell, K. M. (1992). Temporary suppression of visual processing in an RSVP task: An attentional blink? *Journal of Experimental Psychology: Human Perception and Performance, 18*(3), 849–860.

Rensink, R., O'Regan, J. K., & Clark, J. J. (1995). Image flicker is as good as saccades in making large scene changes invisible. *Perception, 24 (suppl.)*, 26–27.

Rensink, R., O'Regan, J. K., & Clark, J. J. (1997). To see or not to see: The need for attention to perceive changes in scenes. *Psychological Science, 8,* 368–373.

Schneider, W., & Shiffrin, R. M. (1977). Controlled and automatic human information processing: I. Detection, search, and attention. *Psychological Review, 84,* 1–66.

Shiffrin, M. R., & Schneider, W. (1977). Controlled and automatic human information processing: II. Perceptual learning, automatic attending, and a general theory. *Psychological Review, 84,* 127–190.

Simons, D. J. (1996). In sight, out of mind: When object representations fail. *Psychological Science, 7*(5), 301–305.

Simons, D. J., & Levin, D. T. (1997). Failure to detect changes to attended objects. *Investigative Ophthalmology and Visual Science, 38*(4), S707.

Sperling, G. (1960). The information available in brief visual presentations. *Psychological Monographs, 74,* 1–29.

Sternberg, S. (1969). High-speed scanning in human memory. *Science, 153,* 652–654.

Theeuwes, J., & Kooi, J. L. (1994). Parallel search for a conjunction of shape and contrast polarity. *Vision Research, 34*(22), 3013–3016.

Tipper, S. P., & Weaver, B. (1996). The medium of attention: Location-based, object-based, or scene-based? In R. Wright (ed.), *Visual attention.* Oxford: Oxford University Press.

Treisman, A., & Gelade, G. (1980). A feature-integration theory of attention. *Cognitive Psychology, 12,* 97–136.

Treisman, A., & Sato, S. (1990). Conjunction search revisited. *Journal of Experimental Psychology: Human Perception and Performance, 16*(3), 459–478.

Tsotsos, J. K. (1990). Analyzing vision at the complexity level. *Brain and Behavioral Sciences, 13*(3), 423–469.

Tsotsos, J. K. (1995). Toward a computational model of visual attention. In T. Papathomas, C. Chubb, A. Gorea, & E. Kowler (eds.), *Early vision and beyond* (pp. 207–218). Cambridge, MA: MIT Press.

Tsotsos, J. K., Culhane, S. N., Wai, W. Y. K., Lai, Y., Davis, N., & Nuflo, F. (1995). Modeling visual attention via selective tuning. *Artificial Intelligence, 78,* 507–545.

Tyler, C. W., & Clarke, M. B. (1990). The autostereogram. *Proceedings of the Society of Photographic and Illuminating Engineers (SPIE), 1256,* 182–197.

Vecera, S. P., & Farah, M. J. (1994). Does visual attention select objects or locations? *Journal of Experimental Psychology: General, 123*(2), 146–160.

Wolfe, J. M. (1994). Guided Search 2.0: A revised model of visual search. *Psychonomic Bulletin and Review, 1*(2), 202–238.

Wolfe, J. M. (1997a). Post-attentive vision. *Investigative Ophthalmology and Visual Science, 37*(3), S214.

Wolfe, J. M. (1997b). Visual search. In H. Pashler (ed.), *Attention.* London: University College Press.

Wolfe, J. M., & Bennett, S. C. (1997). Preattentive object files: Shapeless bundles of basic features. *Vision Research, 37*(1), 25–44.

Wolfe, J. M., Cave, K. R., & Franzel, S. L. (1989). Guided search: An alternative to the Feature Integration model for visual search. *Journal of Experimental Psychology: Human Perception and Performance, 15,* 419–433.

Wolfe, J. M., Friedman-Hill, S. R., & Bilsky, A. B. (1994). Parallel processing of part/whole information in visual search tasks. *Perception & Psychophysics, 55*(5), 537–550.

Wolfe, J. M., Friedman-Hill, S. R. Stewart, M. I., & O'Connell, K. M. (1992). The role of categorization in visual search for orientation. *Journal of Experimental Psychology: Human Perception and Performance, 18*(1), 34–49.

Wolfe, J. M., & Gancarz, G. (1996). Guided Search 3.0: A model of visual search catches up with Jay Enoch 40 years later. In V. Lakshminarayanan (ed.), *Basic and clinical applications of vision science* (pp. 189–192). Dordrecht, Netherlands: Kluwer Academic.

Wolfe, J. M., Yu, K. P., Stewart, M. I., Shorter, A. D., Friedman-Hill, S. R., & Cave, K. R. (1990). Limitations on the parallel guidance of visual search: Color x color and orientation x orientation conjunctions. *Journal of Experimental Psychology: Human Perception and Performance, 16*(4), 879–892.

Yantis, S., & Johnson, D. N. (1990). Mechanisms of attentional priority. *Journal of Experimental Psychology: Human Perception and Performance, 16*(4), 812–825.

Chapter 5

The Attentional Blink: A Front-End Mechanism for Fleeting Memories

Kimron L. Shapiro and Steven J. Luck

In the past few years, there has been an increasing interest in the study of attention over time, as opposed to attention over space. Since the latter area of study is often referred to as *spatial* attention, the former may conveniently be referred to as *temporal* attention. The popularity, though not the origin, of this temporal approach lies with Broadbent (Broadbent & Broadbent 1987), as do many phenomena in the field of attention. In studies of temporal attention, there is a reliable finding that attention is not available to identify or even to detect a second target for approximately 500 msec after successful report of a first target. Most studies have examined this phenomenon with visual stimuli, but recently reports have emerged that point to similar outcomes with auditory targets and even cross-modal (visual and auditory) stimuli. Since 1994, this topic has come under close scrutiny by a number of laboratories, particularly those of Raymond and Shapiro and their colleagues. In a research report in that year, Shapiro, Raymond, and Arnell (1994; see also Raymond, Shapiro, & Arnell 1992) refined the paradigm for studying temporal attention and referred to the above failure to sustain attention as the attentional blink (AB), in an effort to note the similarity between limitations of attentional processing and visual information processing, the latter occurring during an eye blink.

The purpose of this chapter is twofold. First, we seek to provide an empirical and theoretical update to those interested in temporal attentional phenomena, particularly as regards the AB paradigm, and second, to relate such phenomena to the topic of this volume, *fleeting memories*. It is beyond the scope of this chapter to present the full history of research on the AB, and we refer the reader to two previous reviews (Shapiro & Raymond 1994; Shapiro & Terry 1998) for further development of issues that will be mentioned here in passing. To accomplish our purpose, we will begin by discussing the basic methods and typical outcome of the AB and then move on to discuss the latest models, including their successes and shortcomings. Next, we will discuss the recent experiments on the role of masking in the attentional blink phenomenon. Third, we will present new data collected from patients with neuropsychological damage that may provide a key to understanding basic deficits in visual neglect and related disorders. In the final section, we will examine very recent data from Luck's laboratory, where modern neurophysiological techniques have been successful in assessing the degree of information-processing occurring during the AB.

Attentional Blink Method and Typical Outcome

The basic method for examining the AB and the typical outcome that results are described in this section. The reader is advised to note that the terminology used here is different in a few key respects from that used in previous descriptions of this phenomenon. Reference to previously used terminology, along with the changes, is made to provide a transition between this and previous work by Shapiro and his colleagues. The change in terminology is in pursuit of the goal of achieving a common set of terms, which seems to be emerging in the literature. A schematic of a typical RSVP experiment is shown in figure 5.1. The top panel of this figure is an example of the critical items in a given trial, as well as the temporal parameters. The bottom panel of this figure schematizes the total sequence of events in a given RSVP trial.

In a typical AB experiment, participants are required to observe a stream (previously referred to as *distractor set*) of black letters and, in the dual-target condition (previously referred to as the *experimental* condition), to identify the white letter (T1; previously referred to as the *target*). Participants in the single-target condition (previously referred to as the *control* condition) are instructed to ignore T1. A further stream of 8 black letters follows T1, and participants in both single- and dual-target conditions are required to report whether or not the letter X (T2; previously referred to as *probe*) occurred. T2 can occur in any one of the 8 post-T1 positions, randomly chosen from trial to trial. On a random half of trials, T2 does not occur, enabling a false alarm rate for T2 to be calculated. The dual-target condition enables us to assess the effect (or dwell time[1]) of the T1 task on a participant's ability to reallocate attention to T2 subsequent to processing T1. The single-target condition allows us to assess the "baseline" ability of participants to deal with the identical perceptual information encountered by participants in the dual-target condition but unaffected by any prior constraint to process T1.

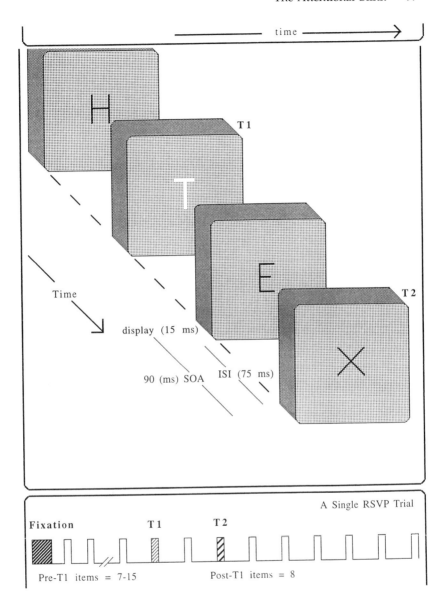

Figure 5.1
An illustration of the RSVP stimuli presentation used in the experiment described. The target (T1), embedded in the stimulus stream, was a white letter that subjects were required to identify. The probe (T2) was always a black ''X' presented at a variable serial position after the target. Below is a diagram of the temporal arrangement used in stimulus presentation. (Adapted from Shapiro & Raymond 1994.)

A representative outcome (see figure 5.2) shows the typical AB effect. Percent correct report of T2 is plotted on the Y-axis only for those trials when T1 was identified correctly (dual-target condition). As can be seen, whereas individuals in the single-target condition are able to report T2 correctly on approximately 90% of trials, regardless of the relative position of T2, participants in the dual-target condition experience a marked deficit in correct T2 report between 100 and 400 msec post target. This deficit is the attentional blink.

It is useful here to note that not all of the stream of items presented are critical for production of the AB. Duncan, Ward, and Shapiro (1994; see also Ward, Duncan, & Shapiro 1996) have demonstrated that only T1, T2, and the respective stream items following each are necessary. The items just following T1 and T2 can be thought of, and likely are acting, as masks for their respective targets (see Seiffert & Di Lollo 1997; Ward & Treisman 1998). These items, which were referred to in earlier reports as the T+1 and P+1 items, will be referred to as T1 and T2 masks, respectively. T1 and T2 in this modification of the basic method are separated by a varying stimulus onset asynchrony (SOA) and do not have to appear in the same spatial location.

A wide variety of other conditions involving various combinations of detection and identification of T1 and T2 and various types of stimuli have been conducted. The reader is referred to Shapiro and Terry (1998) for a compendium of such conditions and their associated outcomes. Is the attentional blink a fleeting memory that is lost once acquired, was it never acquired in the first place, or was it acquired in a way that does not enable report but does entail some other type of processing? We turn our efforts now to answering these questions.

The Interference Model

The interference model was specified by Shapiro, Raymond, and Arnell (1994) as a late-selection account of the AB. This account was predated by an "inhibitory model" (Raymond, Shapiro, & Arnell 1992) that was found to be inadequate to explain certain outcomes reported by Shapiro et al. (1994).[2] As distinct from the account offered by Raymond et al., the interference model suggests that stimuli after T1 (specifically T2) are processed but are unavailable for report. The inability to process these stimuli effectively arises from interference occurring between the two targets and their respective masks, which enter a short-term visual store from which they are then selected for report. Evidence in support of the contention that T2 is processed comes from two experiments that will be described here briefly and from an additional one that will be described in the final section on neurophysiological bases of the

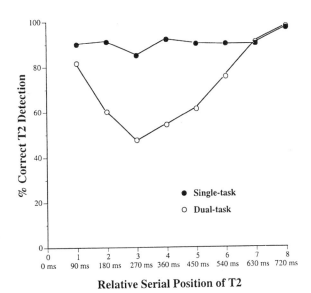

Figure 5.2
The group mean percentage of trials in which the probe was correctly detected, plotted as a function of the relative serial position of the probe in experiment 2 of Raymond et al. (1992). Black circles represent data obtained in the single-target condition in which subjects were told to ignore the target letter. White circles represent data obtained in the dual-target condition in which subjects were told identify the target letter. (Adapted from Raymond, Shapiro, & Arnell 1992.)

AB. Evidence in support of the notion that interference is responsible for the failure to process T2 to a level of report arises from an experiment that will be described subsequently.

Shapiro, Driver, Ward, and Sorensen (1997) presented participants with a modified AB procedure. The new task was to identify three colored words in a stream of black nontarget words. T1 was a white word taken from a list of common words. Pairs of related words were used to provide T2 and T3 on *related* trials. The same words were used as T2 and T3 on *unrelated* trials, but in different pairings. T2 was red, and appeared as the third item after T1, where any AB triggered by T1 should be maximal. T3 was yellow, and appeared as the sixth item after T1, outside the temporal region that usually suffers from the AB caused by T1. The nontargets were drawn from a set of common words. The result of this study relevant to the matter at hand is that T3 performance was better for related pairs than for unrelated pairs on trials when T2 failed to be identified correctly (i.e., trials on which there was an AB). This outcome suggests that T2 was processed, even though it was unable to be reported. (See figure 5.3.)

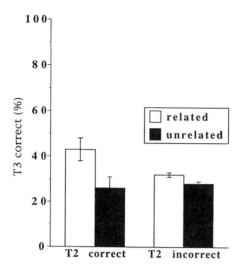

Figure 5.3
Overall percent correct T3 responses, as a function of correct versus incorrect T2 judgments (distinguished along the abscissa), on related versus unrelated trials (light versus dark bars).

In a recent study, Ward and Treisman (1998) also collected evidence that stimuli continue to be processed during the AB. Their unique modification of the basic AB design required participants to report *which* of two possible T2s was presented, after identifying T1. The use of this two-alternative, forced-choice method is innovative in that it provided participants with a reason to *guess* which of the two possible alternatives for T2 was presented in a way not facilitated in previous AB designs. The logic behind such a manipulation is that participants normally may not have sufficient "evidence" to say "present" to T2 when it is inadequately processed. They therefore choose the "safer" alternative and respond "absent." The two-alternative, forced-choice design, on the other hand, "demands" that participants pick one or the other alternative and, given that they assume both alternatives are equally likely, they "guess" on the basis of whatever evidence they have rather than choose the safer "absent" alternative.

Using this design, Ward and Treisman (1998) found that participants' T2 response on T1 correct trials was reliably above chance (though not perfect), suggesting that individuals are able to process stimulus information during the AB. Another manipulation in their experiments is relevant to a point that will be discussed in a subsequent section.

Evidence in support of the other contention relevant to the interference theory—that the AB is due at least in part to interference—comes from a study by Isaak, Shapiro, and Martin (in press; see also Maki, Couture, Frigen, & Lien 1997). In this paper we argued that the magnitude of the effect should reflect (1) the number of items competing for report and (2) the degree of similarity among the competing items. To test this assumption, we employed the no-stream version of the RSVP paradigm, as described by Duncan, Ward, and Shapiro (1994; see also above). T1 and T2 were presented alone, separated by a variable SOA, and each was followed by a mask accounting for four items.

The T1 task was to identify which of two possible white target letters (E and O) was presented. The T2 task was to identify which of a second set of two letters (T and H) was presented. The T1 and T2 masks were a third and fourth set of two-item alternatives, in each case a letter and a false-font pattern mask, the latter chosen to be featurally similar to the letter for which it was serving as a mask. Each possible combination of four items was presented randomly on an equal number of trials. Our conclusion was that the magnitude of the AB was a function of the number of *categorically* similar competitors. Stated another way, there was a positive relationship between the number of letters and the amount of interference with this relationship holding for letters but not for false-font stimuli. The results of this experiment suggest that interference is a contributing factor to the AB.

AB's Relationship to Other Paradigms and Models

Shapiro and Terry (1998) recently described their views on the relationship of the AB to other paradigms and models, including Chun and Potter's two-stage model (Chun & Potter 1995), Seiffert and Di Lollo's views on masking and the AB (Seiffert and Di Lollo 1997), and the potential links to Treisman and colleagues' notions of object files (Kahneman, Treisman, & Gibbs 1992). None of these views has changed substantially, so these issues will not be discussed here, except to say that Chun and Potter's model suggests a notion consistent with the theme of this book, fleeting memories. Their view that T1 is processed to a superficial level waiting on T2 for further (deeper) processing is reminiscent of the book's theme.

Duncan, Ward, and Shapiro (1994; Ward, Duncan, & Shapiro 1996) have made a bold claim that putative serial search processes invoked to describe the outcomes of visual search experiments (see Treisman and Gelade 1980) should be interpreted differently on the basis of evidence collected using the AB paradigm. The reader is referred again to the research reports themselves for further details. Duncan et al. used a modification of the four-item AB paradigm as described above to examine participants' ability to detect targets and, more important, nontargets (i.e., a stimulus item not defined as a "target"), when T1 and T2 were separated by a varying SOA. Moreover, in another departure from conventional AB methods, T1 and T2 were not presented in the same spatial location. The important condition for the purpose of the present discussion is when participants encountered a nontarget as T1, prior to the presentation of T2. In these cases, participants demonstrated an AB. The use of a paradigm meeting the two conditions typically found in the conventional visual search paradigm—(1) nontargets encountered prior to encountering targets and (2) spatially nonoverlapping targets—allowed Duncan et al. to make this claim. The implication of such a claim is far-reaching: It suggests that the approximately 50 msec per item search times typically evidenced in visual search tasks must be the result of a limited parallel mechanism, given the 500 msec dwell time estimate.

Arguments against this point of view have been expressed in a number of recent reports (Chun, Wolfe, & Potter 1996; Moore, Egeth, Berglan, & Luck 1996). Perhaps the best-argued point is that the Duncan et al. paradigm employed masks following T1 and T2, whereas the typical visual search paradigm does not. In support of their contention, Moore et al. found that the absence of masks in a Duncan et al.-type procedure attenuated (but did not eliminate) the AB. The finding that the AB was still present lessens the force of their argument, though the issue of masking is an important one and will be discussed at a later point. Further on the issue of masking, we would like to argue that the multiple items in the typical visual search display may act as *conceptual* masks in a way sufficient to be more like the Duncan et al. paradigm than has been considered previously. An experiment to test this assumption was inadvertently accomplished by Seiffert and Di Lollo (1997). In two experiments, these investigators presented the T1 mask in the same frame as T1, either spatially overlapping (experiment 2) or adjacent (experiment 3). Both conditions revealed a pronounced AB in the absence of a T1 mask. From this outcome we can extrapolate that in a typical visual search paradigm, even though targets are not masked in a conventional way (see discussion below), the presence of other targets in the visual field may act as *conceptual* masks, thus setting the stage for an AB, as is the concern expressed by Duncan et al.

The Role of Masking in the AB Phenomenon

The relationship of the AB to masking is an issue that is receiving a significant amount of interest. This issue has already been discussed in part in the elaboration of the study by Moore, Egeth, Berglan, and Luck (1996) above. Moreover, Shapiro and Terry (1998) discussed certain of these issues (e.g., Seiffert & Di Lollo, 1997) in a chapter on the AB, and the reader is referred to this source for that information. Giesbrecht and Di Lollo (1998) reported that the nature of the T2 task is a key determinant in the magnitude of the observed AB. Specifically, they found that in combination with a T1 task, (1) failure to mask T2 does not yield an AB;[3] (2) pattern masking by camouflage (mask embedded as part of T2) does not yield an AB; yet (3) pattern masking by interruption (mask is spatially overlapping with and follows the stimulus) of T2 does yield an AB. These investigators conclude that a minor modification of the two-stage model (Chun and Potter 1995), taking into account these parameters, is sufficient to account for all AB findings.

Although we not disagree with this conclusion, it is important to point out that the interference theory proposed by Shapiro, Raymond, and Arnell (1994), and as described previously in this chapter, can also explain these outcomes. Such an explanation focuses on the interfering effects of T2 and its mask in combination with T1 and its mask when T2 is required to be retrieved from an overloaded visual short-term memory (VSTM). More specifically, it could be argued that T2 does not become a separable item to add its interference in VSTM when it is either absent (as in Giesbrecht and Di Lollo's conclusion in [1] above) or indistinguishable from T2 (as in [2] above).

Grandison, Ghiradelli, and Egeth (1997) also investigated the role of masking in the AB phenomenon. In their study, these investigators manipulated the nature of the T1 mask. In a series of five studies, they replicated Raymond, Shapiro, and Arnell's (1995, 1992) findings that a T1 mask composed of a dot pattern yields an AB and that the absence of a T1 mask yields no AB, respectively. However, they went on to challenge what they argue is the interference theory's claim that the relationship between the T1 mask and the probe can account for the AB. They found that whereas a white square and a white flashed screen both yielded an AB, a green flashed screen did not.

These data are interesting and bear scrutiny; we will return to them shortly. However, Grandison et al. are somewhat confusing the claims made in the various papers to which they refer. Whereas Shapiro and his colleagues do claim that interference between the various items in VSTM is largely responsible for the AB effect, they do *not* claim that the primary source of this interference is between the T1 mask and the probe. Indeed, the theory is clear in its claim that the primary source of interference is between the T1 and T2 items. Moreover, interference theory has argued that a pattern mask following T1 is important to produce the AB. Raymond et al. (1995) sought merely to qualify the nature of the VSTM interference notion by examining the role of the

T1 mask. Their main conclusion is that the categorical relationship of the T1 mask is important in determining blink magnitude: alphanumeric masks produced greater AB magnitude than either dots or spatially displaced numbers.

To return to Grandison et al. (1997), it is important to note that these investigators replicate the claim made by interference theory that the presence of a T1 mask of some nature is critical to AB production. We are left asking why a white flashed screen as the T1 mask produced an AB but a green flashed screen in the same role did not. We do not have a good answer for this question at present, and believe it warrants further investigation. To speculate for a moment, let us suppose there are two different processes underlying the outcomes produced with each of the flashed T1 masks. The failure of the green flashed mask to produce an AB is consistent with interference theory's claim that a patterned T1 mask is necessary to produce the AB. Perhaps the ability of the white flashed screen to produce an AB is due to some kind of visual transient produced by so powerful a stimulus. But then we are left wondering why the control (ignore T1) condition did not produce a similar outcome. As stated above, this outcome is interesting and deserving of further experimentation.

Ward and Treisman (1998) conducted an experiment on the role of masking in the AB as part of a larger investigation into the notion of conscious processing during the AB interval where accurate verbal report is poor. The results of this study have already been described in this chapter. Of considerable interest is their main finding that when T2's task was changed from the typical detection requirement to that of forced choice (i.e., determining which of two specified targets was presented), performance on T2 improved dramatically, showing no difference from controls. Such a finding is consistent with that reported by Shapiro, Driver, Ward, and Sorensen (1997).

Of particular relevance to our present concerns, in another experiment Ward and Treisman manipulated the type of masking in two experimental conditions. One condition provided participants with the typical AB full-stream method that implements the kind of masking referred to as masking by interruption (see Kahneman 1968) or central masking (Marcel 1983); the T1 mask occurred as the next item in the stream following T1. The second condition removed the T1 mask but degraded T1's discriminability by making the T1 judgment more or less difficult. Such masking is referred to as integration, camouflage, or peripheral masking. Both conditions were presented to the same subjects, who had to perform in the detection and in the forced-choice paradigms. Such a procedure enables the effects of T1 difficulty to be evaluated separately from the effects of masking per se; Ward and

Treisman point out that they had been confounded in previous studies, including those of Shapiro et al. The results of their second experiment revealed that interruption masking caused by the presence of the T1 mask, and not T1 difficulty, is a critical determinant in the magnitude of the AB.

Neuropsychological Issues

Investigations of the primate visual system have suggested that two major functional streams of information emanate from the primary visual cortex (Ungerleider & Mishkin 1982). The dorsal stream is directed to the parietal lobe; the temporal lobe is the target of the ventral stream. Although some researchers have argued that these two cortical pathways are not functionally dissociable (Maunsell & Newsome 1987; Zeki 1993), others have presented evidence to suggest the ventral pathway plays a critical role in object recognition (Ungerleider & Mishkin 1982), whereas the dorsal stream is specialized for representing space or directing spatial attention and movement (Andersen 1987; Husain, 1991; Milner & Goodale 1995).

Which pathway mediates attention for stimuli presented over time, and how does this differ from that mediating attention over space? The role of object perception in RSVP tasks that require T1 and T2 to be identified suggests that cortical representations within the ventral stream mediate the AB. On the other hand, the contribution of the parietal lobe in directing visual attention suggests involvement of the dorsal stream.

Husain, Shapiro, Martin, and Kennard (1997) performed a study in which they sought first to determine whether RSVP paradigms can be used to investigate temporal dynamics of attention in elderly individuals, and second to establish the time course of the AB in stroke patients with unilateral spatial neglect. Visual neglect is a common disorder following stroke. It is most severe after right hemisphere lesions, affecting over 70% of such patients (Stone, Patel, & Greenwood 1993). These individuals are unaware of people or objects to their left and have a poor prognosis for recovery of independent function (Fullerton, Mackenzie, & Stout 1988; Stone, Patel, & Greenwood 1993).

Despite the intense interest in neglect, the mechanisms underlying this disorder remain obscure (Jeannerod 1987; Robertson & Marshall 1993). One prominent theory considers left-sided neglect to be the result of a bias to attend to the right (Kinsbourne 1970). An alternative hypothesis is that neglect patients have a *direction-specific* impairment of disengaging attention from a stimulus on the right when they are required to shift attention to the left (Morrow & Ratcliff 1988; Posner,

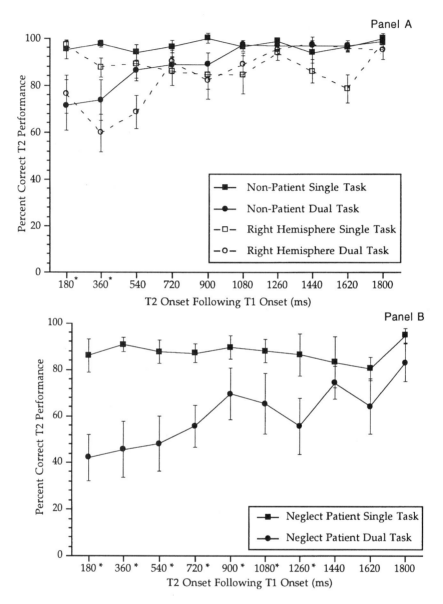

Figure 5.4
(A) Performance of normal individuals without stroke (black symbols) and right hemisphere stroke patients without neglect (white symbols). In both groups, T2 detection on the dual-target task (circles) was significantly different from that on the single-target (squares) task for T1–T2 intervals up to 360 msec (indicated by starred msec designations on the abscissa; p<0.05). Error bars represent standard errors of the mean. T1 was correctly identified on 86% and 81% of dual-target trials by normal volunteers and those

Walker, Friedrich, & Rafal 1984, 1987). Both theories make the fundamental assumption that neglect is an impairment of *spatial* attention. Husain et al. sought to determine if there is a nonspatial component of attention in neglect by measuring the temporal dynamics of attention at one location. The paradigm they used allowed them to measure directly the time required to discriminate an object and release processing capacity for another, when no directional shift of attention was required.

To accommodate the older age of these participants, the rate of stimulus presentation was reduced to 5.5 items per sec. Participants were tested under two conditions in which they saw the same RSVP streams but were required to make different responses. In the dual-response task, they were asked to identify T1 and T2; in the single-response task, they were asked to identify only T2. Each subject performed a total of 320 trials. All patients had visual neglect clinically and on the Mesulam shape cancellation task (Mesulam 1985). The neglect patients found a mean of only 24 targets (range: 6–36) out of 60, all on the right side of the sheet. By comparison, the stroke patients without neglect found a mean of 57 out of 60 targets (range 54–60), without any spatial bias in their omissions.

Husain et al. were able to demonstrate a normal AB in 10 healthy volunteers (mean age=73), as shown by nonneglect data curves in figure 5.4.

Eight patients (mean age=64) with left-sided visual neglect following right parietal or frontal infarcts, as shown in figure 5.5, were then tested. The parietal lesions centered on the inferior parietal lobe, the region most commonly associated with neglect (Vallar & Perani 1986); the frontal lesions occupied the homologue of Broca's area in the right hemisphere, a region that has recently been identified as the lateral frontal area associated with neglect (Husain & Kennard 1996).

The magnitude of the AB was found to be significantly greater and its duration more protracted in both parietal and frontal neglect patients (figure 5.4). When they identified a letter, their awareness of a subsequent letter was diminished for 1.6 sec afterward—an order of magnitude three times that of their healthy counterparts. By contrast, 6 right-hemisphere stroke patients without neglect had normal ABs (data not illustrated).

with stroke, respectively. (B) Performance of patients with visual neglect. Detection of T2 on the dual-target task (circles) was significantly different from that on the single-target task (squares) for T1–T2 intervals less than 1440 msec (indicated by starred ms designations on the abscissa; p<0.05). Furthermore, the magnitude of visual unawareness during this attentional blink was much greater than in stroke patients without neglect or in normal individuals. T1 was correctly identified on 72% of dual-target trials.

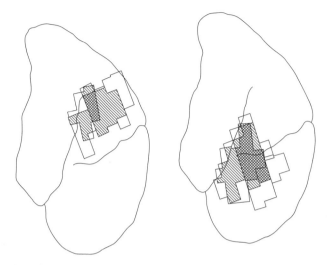

Figure 5.5
Extent of cortical lesions in seven patients with left-side visual neglect. Single hatching represents the region of overlap of 2 lesions; cross-hatching shows the overlap of 3 lesions; solid white is the zone of overlap of 4 lesions. The 2 lesion foci are located in the inferior frontal lobe and hte inferior parietal lobe. One patient suffered a hemorrhage of the basal ganglia without cortical involvement (lesion not shown).

Electrophysiological Approaches

The focusing of attention onto one stimulus frequently leads to slow and/or inaccurate discrimination performance for other stimuli, and it is of fundamental importance to determine whether such effects arise at an early stage of processing, such as stimulus identification, or a late stage of processing, such as short-term memory encoding. This locus-of-selection issue has been examined in many contexts for several decades, but it has been extremely difficult to produce conclusive evidence on the basis of measurements of reaction time and accuracy. The reason for this is straightforward: reaction time and accuracy reflect the combined effects of both early and late processing stages, and it is difficult to determine whether a given change in behavior reflects a modulation of early processes or late processes.

As an alternative, many investigators have recorded the electrophysiological responses elicited by the stimuli instead of—or in addition to—the behavioral responses. These electrophysiological responses provide a continuous, millisecond-by-millisecond measure of processing between a stimulus and a response, thus allowing the experimenter to measure directly the time point at which attention begins to influence the processing of a stimulus. We have recently applied these

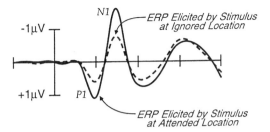

Figure 5.6
Pattern of results from a typical visual ERP attention experiment. In a typical experiment, bars are flashed in a random sequence at locations in the left and right visual fields; most of these bars are a standard size, but smaller deviant bars are occasionally presented. Subjects fixate on a central point and direct attention to the left location on some trial blocks and to the right location on others. Subjects are instructed to press a button whenever a deviant bar is detected on the attended side. As shown here, the P1 and N1 components elicited by a stimulus are larger when attention is directed to the location of that stimulus than when attention is directed to the opposite visual field. By convention, negative is plotted upward.

techniques to the AB paradigm in order to determine whether probes presented during the AB period are identified and then suppressed or, alternatively, the identification process itself is suppressed. Before describing these experiments, however, we will briefly describe the electrophysiological techniques and review previous electrophysiological studies of spatial attention.

The two most common electrophysiological techniques that have been used to study attention are single-unit recordings and event-related potential (ERP) recordings. In single-unit recordings, an electrode is inserted into the brain and used to detect the action potentials emitted by an individual neuron. Although this technique provides extremely precise information about the effects of attention on neural activity, it is obviously limited to use in nonhuman animals. This is especially problematic for a complex task such as the AB paradigm, which would be extremely difficult for a monkey to learn. ERPs, in contrast, reflect the summed postsynaptic potentials of very large numbers of neurons, making them less a specific measure of neural activity, but they can be recorded from the surface of the scalp in normal human subjects. Both techniques offer very high temporal resolution, however, and either technique can therefore be used to determine whether attention operates at an early stage or a late stage.

The pattern of results obtained in a typical ERP study of selective attention is shown in figure 5.6. In this paradigm, subjects continuously maintain fixation on a central point while stimuli are rapidly flashed in random order at a location in the left visual field (LVF) and a

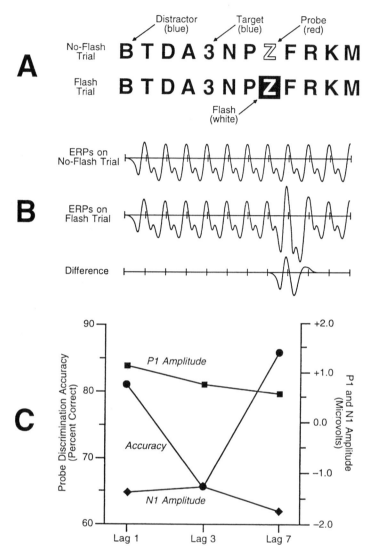

Figure 5.7
Experimental paradigm and results from an AB experiment in which the P1 and N1 components were measured. In panel A, on each trial, a stream of characters was presented at fixation, with an interval of 83 msec between successive stimulus onsets. Most of the characters were blue distractor letters, but one digit was presented on each trial (also in blue). Subjects were required to report at the end of the trial whether this was an odd or even digit. A probe letter was also present on each trial, and was distinguished by being red rather than blue. Subjects were required to report at the end of the trial whether the probe letter was a vowel or a consonant. The probe was presented at lag 1, lag 3, or lag 7 relative to the target. Panel B illustrates the problem of overlapping ERP components in the RSVP paradigm and shows how this problem can be solved by

location in the right visual field (RVF). In some trial blocks, subjects are instructed to attend to the LVF location and to press a button when a predefined target stimulus appears at that location; in other blocks, subjects instead attend to the RVF location and press a button upon detecting targets at that location. This paradigm makes it possible to compare the ERP waveform elicited by the same stimulus when it is attended and when it is ignored, and any differences in these ERP waveforms reflect the operation of attention.

The most fundamental issue in this paradigm is the time at which the waveforms for attended and ignored stimuli begin to differ. If attention influences perceptual processes, then the attended and ignored waveforms should begin to differ at an early latency (e.g., before 150 msec post stimulus). In contrast, if attention does not influence perceptual processes and instead begins to influence processes that follow stimulus identification, then the waveforms elicited by attended and ignored stimuli should be identical until a fairly late time (e.g., after 200 msec post stimulus). As can be seen in figure 5.6, the effects of attention begin within the first 100 msec after stimulus onset and appear to consist of an amplitude enhancement of the initial sensory-evoked ERP responses, the P1 and N1 waves. In addition, the same modulations of P1 and N1 amplitude are observed for target stimuli, for nontarget stimuli that must be discriminated from the target stimuli, and for completely task-irrelevant probe stimuli (Heinze, Luck, Mangun, & Hillyard 1990; Luck, Fan, & Hillyard 1993; Luck, Hillyard, Mouloua, Woldorff, Clark, & Hawkins 1994; Mangun & Hillyard 1990, 1991). Together, these results provide evidence that spatial selective attention begins to operate at an early stage of processing. Similar results have been obtained in single-unit recordings from extrastriate areas of visual cortex (Luck, Chelazzi, Hillyard, & Desimone, 1997).

Although these results provide strong evidence that spatial selective attention can influence perceptual processing, there are two important clarifications that must be noted. First, the finding of attention effects at the level of perception does not preclude the possibility of postperceptual attention effects. Indeed, there is little doubt that it is possible to respond selectively to some stimuli and not to others even when

means of a subtraction technique. The same ERP responses are elicited by the items in the RSVP stream on flash and no-flash trials, but flash trials also contain a response to the flash, which is added to the responses elicited by the RSVP stream. When a flash–no-flash subtraction is performed, the result reflects the response to the flash. Panel C shows probe discrimination accuracy for this experiment, along with the P1 and N1 amplitudes elicited by the flash (these results are based on an average of 14 subjects). Probe discrimination accuracy was substantially lower at lag 3 than at lags 1 and 7, but this was not accompanied by a reduction in P1 or N1 amplitude.

both are clearly perceived. A second, related point is that attention may not operate at a perceptual level under all conditions. For example, if the stimuli are presented at a very slow rate in the paradigm illustrated in figure 5.6, subjects will be able to perceive the stimuli at both locations with little effort, and there will be no reason to limit perceptual processing to the stimuli at one location. Early selection is therefore likely to occur only when the perceptual system is overloaded (e.g., by the presence of many simultaneous or nearly simultaneous stimuli).

In the case of the AB paradigm, there is good reason to believe that the perceptual system is not overloaded, and that the impairment in accuracy for a probe stimulus following the detection of a target stimulus therefore reflects a postperceptual selection mechanism. For example, Potter (1976) has provided evidence that observers are able to extract the essence of complex pictures quite accurately even at rates approaching 10 stimuli per sec, although they are unable to store and/or retain information in working memory at such rates. The letter and digit discrimination tasks typically used in AB experiments presumably are substantially easier than the picture detection task used by Potter, and it therefore seems likely that perceptual abilities are not overloaded in typical AB tasks.

To test this proposal, we recently conducted two experiments in which ERPs were recorded during AB tasks. The first experiment examined the P1 and N1 components that we had previously shown to be modulated by spatial attention. Because the ERP waveform elicited by one stimulus in an RSVP stream is overlapped in time by the ERPs elicited by the previous and subsequent stimuli, it is difficult to isolate the response to the probe stimulus in the standard AB paradigm. We therefore modified the AB paradigm slightly, taking advantage of the fact that voltage fields sum together linearly in a passive conductor like the brain.

Specifically, on half of the trials, a white square was presented behind the probe stimulus, eliciting an ERP response that was added on to the complex response elicited by the RSVP stream. To isolate the response to this task-irrelevant "flash" stimulus, we simply subtracted the waveform obtained on trials without a flash from the waveform obtained on trials with a flash, which yields the response to the flash. This procedure is depicted in figure 5.7, which also illustrates the stimuli used in this experiment. We had previously used a similar technique to assess the effects of spatial attention during visual search, and found that stimuli flashed at the location of the target item elicit larger P1 and N1 peaks than stimuli flashed at the location of a distractor item (Luck et al. 1993; Luck & Hillyard 1995).

Because a large number of trials must be used to obtain an adequate signal-to-noise ratio in ERP recordings, the probe was presented only

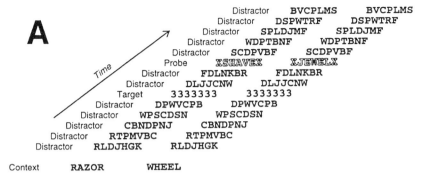

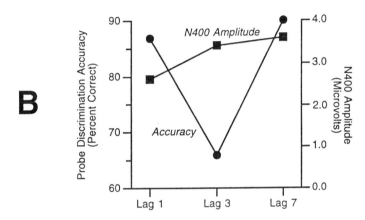

Figure 5.8
Experimental paradigm and results from an AB experiment in which the N400 component was measured. (A) shows the sequence of stimuli. Each trial began with a 1 sec presentation of a context word. This was followed after a 1 sec delay by an RSVP stream of 7-character letter or digit strings, with an interval of 83 msec between successive stimulus onsets. Most of the items in the RSVP stream were arrays of randomly selected consonants, presented in blue. The target was a digit, repeated 7 times to form a 7-character string, and was also presented in blue. The probe was a word, drawn in red rather than blue, and padded with Xs to form a 7-character string. At the end of each trial, subjects were required to report whether the target was an odd or even digit and whether the probe word was semantically related or unrelated to the context word. The probe word was presented at lag 1, lag 3, or lag 7 relative to the target. (B) Probe discrimination accuracy was substantially lower at lag 3 than at lags 1 and 7, but this was not accompanied by a reduction in N400 amplitude (these results are based on an average of 14 subjects).

at lags 1, 3, and 7. As can be seen in figure 5.7C, probe discrimination accuracy was impaired at lag 3 compared with lags 1 and 7, which is the typical AB pattern. However, this impairment in accuracy was not accompanied by a reduction in the amplitude of the P1 and N1 components: these components were the same at lag 3 as at lags 1 and 7. These results indicate that attention does not operate at the same early stage during the AB paradigm as it does during spatial attention paradigms.

Although the results shown in figure 5.7 indicate that the AB does not reflect a suppression of the initial sensory responses, they do not necessarily indicate that the impairment of accuracy during the AB period is entirely postperceptual, because there might be some perceptual process that follows the P1 and N1 components but cannot be observed in ERP recordings. Indeed, there is no particular time point in waveforms such as these at which it is clear that perceptual processing has been completed. To test fully the hypothesis that the AB reflects a postperceptual deficit, it was necessary to provide a clearer marker for the completion of perceptual processing. We therefore conducted a second experiment in which we examined the N400 peak, which can be used to determine whether a word has been identified to the point of meaning extraction. Specifically, the N400 is elicited when a word differs semantically from a previously established semantic context, such as the last word of the sentence "I sat at my computer and wrote a noodle." Because the semantic mismatch between a word and the current semantic context cannot be detected unless the word has been identified, the presence of an N400 peak is an excellent marker of word identification. Consequently, the presence of an N400 peak during the AB interval would provide strong evidence that stimuli presented during this period are fully identified, even though they cannot be accurately reported.

Figure 5.8A shows the paradigm that we used to measure the N400. At the beginning of each trial, a "context word" was presented to establish a semantic context for that trial. After a short delay, the RSVP stream began. This stream consisted mostly of distractor items, each of which was a randomly selected 7-character consonant string. The target item consisted of a string of 7 identical digits, and the probe item consisted of a 3–7 character word, flanked by Xs if necessary to yield a total of 7 characters. At the end of each trial, the subject was required to indicate whether the target was an odd digit or an even digit and whether the probe word was semantically related or unrelated to the context word that had been presented at the beginning of the trial.

To isolate the N400 component from the sensory responses elicited by the character strings, we subtracted the ERP waveform elicited on trials with a probe word that matched the context word from the ERP waveform elicited on trials with a probe word that did not match the context word. The match and mismatch trials were identical except for the semantic relationship between the context word and the probe word, and the subtraction procedure therefore yielded a waveform that reflected the perception of the semantic mismatch. If the AB reflects a suppression of perceptual processing, then the N400 peak in this waveform should also be suppressed during the AB period, as it is for words presented at ignored locations in spatial attention experiments (McCarthy & Nobre 1993; Otten, Rugg, & Doyle 1993). Alternatively, a lack of suppression for the N400 component during the AB period would indicate that perceptual processing is unimpaired, even though the observers are impaired at reporting the probe.

The results from this experiment are summarized in figure 5.8B. As in previous AB experiments, accuracy for the probe task was impaired at lag 3 compared with lags 1 and 7, but there was no sign of a decrease in N400 amplitude at lag 3. These results indicate that at lag 3, subjects were able to perceive the probe words, extract their meanings, and compare them with the context word, even though they were very inaccurate at reporting the semantic relationship between the probe word and the context word at the end of the trial (1–2 sec later). These findings thus provide strong evidence indicating that the AB reflects an impairment in postperceptual processes.

The AB as It Relates to the Topic of this Book

In this final section, we would like to attempt to relate the theme of the book to the topic under discussion in this chapter. "Fleeting memories" makes broad reference to the notion that some memories last for mere fractions of a second. The existence of such a memory form has been postulated for some time by cognitive researchers (e.g., Sperling 1960). Recently, as discussed in this volume and elsewhere, there has been a resurgence of interest in not only the existence of such brief instantiations of memory but also in their disposition. By "disposition" we are referring to the question "When a perceived stimulus fails to be reported, what is its fate?" We hope that our attempts to answer this question are helpful in guiding researchers interested in this issue. Experiments discussed in this chapter strongly support the claim that although the demand to perform two temporally contiguous target tasks raises the second target to "fleeting memory" status (i.e., unavailable for conscious report), its existence seems nevertheless a certainty.

A chapter in Duncan (1996) proposes a model of attention he calls "integrated competition." In this model, Duncan suggests, multiple brain systems compete to represent different objects, but any given object is acted upon by the same multiple systems in a cooperative fashion. He further suggests that the function of such object-based integration is to make object properties available for the control of behavior. As Duncan argues (and we concur), perhaps the attentional blink is the causal by-product of that competitive integration process in an effort to preserve fleeting memories.

Notes

1. Duncan, Ward, and Shapiro (1994). See also Ward, Duncan, and Shapiro (1996).
2. Note that this account may have been dismissed prematurely, particularly if one takes a more encompassing view of the notion of inhibition than may have previously been taken. This issue is discussed by Shapiro and Terry (1998) in detail.
3. A claim made earlier by Lawrence (1971).

References

Andersen, R. A. (1987). Inferior parietal lobule function in spatial perception and visuomotor integration. In F. Plum & V.B. Mountcastle (eds.), *Handbook of Physiology* (vol. 5, pt. 2, pp. 483–518). Bethesda, Md: American Physiological Society.

Broadbent, D. E., & Broadbent, M. H. P. (1987). From detection to identification: Response to multiple targets in rapid serial visual presentation. *Perception & Psychophysics, 42,* 105–113.

Chun, M. M., & Potter, M. C. (1995). A two-stage model for multiple target detection in rapid serial visual presentation. *Journal of Experimental Psychology: Human Perception and Performance, 21,* 109–127.

Chun, M. M., Wolfe, J. M., & Potter, M. C. (1996). Attentional dwell time and serial search. Unpublished manuscript.

Duncan, J. (1996). Co-ordinated brain systems in selective perception and action. In T. Inui and J. L. McClelland (eds.), *Attention and Performance XVI,* pp. 549–578. Cambridge, MA.: MIT Press.

Duncan, J., Ward, R., & Shapiro, K. L. (1994). Direct measurement of attentional dwell time in human vision. *Nature, 369,* 313–315.

Fullerton, K. J., Mackenzie, G., & Stout, R. W. (1988). Prognostic indices in stroke. *Quarterly Journal of Medicine, 250,* 147–162.

Giesbrecht, B. L., & Di Lollo, V. (1998). Beyond the attentional blink: Visual masking by item substitution. *Journal of Experimental Psychology: Human Perception and Performance,* 1454–1466.

Grandison, T. D., Ghiradelli, T. G., & Egeth, H. E. (1997). Beyond similarity: Masking of the target is sufficient to cause the attentional blink. *Perception & Psychophysics, 59,* 266–274.

Heinze, H. J., Luck, S. J., Mangun, G. R., & Hillyard, S. A. (1990). Visual event-related potentials index focused attention within bilateral stimulus arrays. I. Evidence for early selection. *Electroencephalography and Clinical Neurophysiology, 75,* 511–527.

Husain, M. (1991). Visuospatial and visuomotor functions of the posterior parietal lobe.

In J. F. Stein (ed.), *Vision and visual dysfunction* (vol. 13, pp. 12–43). Basingstoke, UK: Macmillan.

Husain, M., & Kennard, C. J. (1996). Visual neglect associated with frontal lobe infarction. *Journal of Neurology, 243,* 652–657.

Husain, M., Shapiro, K. L., Martin, J., & Kennard, C. (1997). Temporal dynamics of visual attention reveal a non-spatial abnormality in spatial neglect. *Nature, 385,* 154–156.

Isaak, M. I., Shapiro, K. L., & Martin, J. (in press). Probe identification errors support an interference model of the attentional blink. *Journal of Experimental Psychology: Human Perception and Performance.*

Jeannerod, M. (ed.). (1987). *Neurophysiological and neuropsychological aspects of spatial neglect.* Amsterdam: North-Holland.

Kahneman, D. (1968). Method, findings, and theory in studies of visual masking. *Psychological Bulletin, 70,* 404–426.

Kahneman, D., Treisman, A., & Gibbs, B. J. (1992). The reviewing of object files: Object-specific integration of information. *Cognitive Psychology, 24,* 175–219.

Kinsbourne, M. A (1970). A model for the mechanism of unilateral neglect of space. *Transactions of the American Neurological Association, 95,* 143–145.

Lawrence, D. H. (1971). Two studies of visual search for word targets with controlled rates of presentation. *Perception & Psychophysics, 10,* 85–89.

Luck, S. J., Chelazzi, L., Hillyard, S. A., & Desimone, R. (1997). Mechanisms of spatial selective attention in areas V1, V2, and V4 of macaque visual cortex. *Journal of Neurophysiology, 77,* 24–42.

Luck, S. J., Fan, S., & Hillyard, S. A. (1993). Attention-related modulation of sensory-evoked brain activity in a visual search task. *Journal of Cognitive Neuroscience, 5,* 188–195.

Luck, S. J., & Hillyard, S. A. (1995). The role of attention in feature detection and conjunction discrimination: An electrophysiological analysis. *International Journal of Neuroscience, 80,* 281–297.

Luck, S. J., Hillyard, S. A., Mouloua, M., Woldorff, M. G., Clark, V. P., & Hawkins, H. L. (1994). Effects of spatial cueing on luminance detectability: Psychophysical and electrophysiological evidence for early selection. *Journal of Experimental Psychology: Human Perception And Performance, 20,* 887–904.

Mangun, G. R., & Hillyard, S. A. (1990). Allocation of visual attention to spatial location: Event-related brain potentials and detection performance. *Perception and Psychophysics, 47,* 532–550.

Mangun, G. R., & Hillyard, S. A. (1991). Modulations of sensory-evoked brain potentials indicate changes in perceptual processing during visual-spatial priming. *Journal of Experimental Psychology: Human Perception and Performance, 17,* 1057–1074.

Maki, W. S., Couture, T., Frigen K., & Lien, D. (1997). Sources of the attentional blink during rapid serial visual presentation: Perceptual interference and retrieval competition. *Journal of Experimental Psychology: Human Perception and Performance, 23,* 1393–1411.

Marcel, A. J. (1983). Conscious and unconscious perception: An approach to the relations between phenomenal experience and perceptual processes. *Cognitive Psychology, 15,* 238–300.

Maunsell, J. H. R., & Newsome, W. T. (1987). Visual processing in monkey extrastriate cortex. *Annual Review of Neuroscience, 10,* 363–401.

McCarthy, G., & Nobre, A. C. (1993). Modulation of semantic processing by spatial selective attention. *Electroencephalography and Clinical Neurophysiology, 88,* 210–219.

Mesulam, M.-M. (1985). *Principles of behavioural neurology. Tests of directed attention and memory.* Philadelphia: F. A. Davis.

Milner, A. D., & Goodale, M. A. (1995). *The visual brain in action.* Oxford: Oxford University Press.

Moore, C. M., Egeth, H., Berglan, L. R., & Luck, S. J. (1996). Are attentional dwell times inconsistent with serial visual search? *Psychonomic Bulletin and Review, 3,* 360–365.

Morrow, L. A., & Ratcliff, G. (1988). The disengagement of covert attention and the neglect syndrome. *Psychobiology, 16,* 261–269.

Otten, L. J., Rugg, M. D., & Doyle, M. C. (1993). Modulation of event-related potentials by word repetition: The role of visual selective attention. *Psychophysiology, 30,* 559–571.

Posner, M. I., Walker, J. A., Friedrich, F. J., & Rafal, R. D. (1984). Effects of parietal injury on covert orienting of attention. *Journal of Neuroscience, 4,* 1863–1874.

Posner, M. I., Walker, J. A., Friedrich, F. J., & Rafal, R. D. (1987). How do the parietal lobes direct covert attention? *Neuropsychologia, 25,* 135–145.

Potter, M. C. (1976). Short-term conceptual memory for pictures. *Journal of Experimental Psychology: Human Learning and Memory, 2,* 509–522.

Raymond, J. E., Shapiro, K. L., & Arnell, K. M. (1992). Temporary suppression of visual processing in an RSVP task: An attentional blink? *Journal of Experimental Psychology: Human Perception and Performance, 18,* 849–860.

Raymond, J. E., Shapiro, K. L., & Arnell, K. M. (1995). Similarity determines the attentional blink. *Journal of Experimental Psychology: Human Perception and Performance, 21,* 653–662.

Robertson, I. H. & Marshall, J. C. (eds.). (1993). *Unilateral neglect: Clinical and experimental studies.* Hillsdale, NJ: Lawrence Erlbaum Associates.

Seiffert, A. E., & Di Lollo, V. (1997). Low-level masking in the attentional blink. *Journal of Experimental Psychology: Human Perception and Performance, 23,* 1061–1073.

Shapiro, K. L., Driver, J., Ward, R. & Sorensen, R. E. (1997). Priming from the attentional blink: A failure to extract visual tokens but not visual types. *Psychological Science, 8,* 95–100.

Shapiro, K. L., & Raymond, J. E. (1994). Temporal allocation of visual attention: Inhibition or interference? In D. Dagenbach and T. Carr (eds.), *Inhibitory processes in attention, memory, and language* (pp. 151–188). New York: Academic Press.

Shapiro, K. L., Raymond, J. E., & Arnell, K. M. (1994). Attention to visual pattern information produces the attentional blink in RSVP. *Journal of Experimental Psychology: Human Perception and Performance, 20,* 357–371.

Shapiro, K. L., & Terry, K. (1998). The eyes have it (but so does the brain). In R. Wright (ed.), *Visual attention.* Oxford: Oxford University Press, 306–329.

Sperling, G. (1960). The information available in brief visual presentations. *Psychological Monographs, 74,* 1–29.

Stone, S. P., Patel, P., & Greenwood, R. J. (1993). Selection of acute stroke patients for treatment of visual neglect. *Journal of Neurology, Neurosurgery, and Psychiatry, 56,* 463–466.

Treisman, A., & Gelade, G. (1980). A feature-integration theory of attention. *Cognitive Psychology, 12,* 97–136.

Ungerleider, L. G., & Mishkin, M. (1982). Two cortical visual systems. In D. Ingle, M. Goodale, & R. Mansfield (eds.), *Analysis of visual behavior* (pp. 549–586). Cambridge, MA: MIT Press.

Vallar, G., & Perani, D. (1986). The anatomy of unilateral neglect after right hemisphere stroke lesions: A clinical CT correlation study in man. *Neuropsychologia, 24,* 609–622.

Ward, R., Duncan, J., & Shapiro, K. L. (1996). The slow time-course of visual attention. *Cognitive Psychology, 30,* 79–109.

Ward, R., & Treisman, A. (1998). Limits to awareness during the attentional blink. Manuscript submitted for review.

Zeki, S. (1993). *A vision of the brain.* Oxford: Blackwell.

Chapter 6

Repetition Blindness for Pictures: Evidence for the Rapid Computation of Abstract Visual Descriptions

Nancy Kanwisher, Carol Yin, and Ewa Wojciulik

What kinds of information do we extract from the first 100-msec glimpse of a picture? Most researchers assume that picture identification, and vision in general, are accomplished by carrying out a sequence of computations in which the retinal image is transformed through a series of increasingly abstract representations. What is the nature of these intermediate representations that are extracted en route to scene and object recognition? Which of them are invariant with respect to location, size, orientation, and viewing angle? Which of them are involved in our conscious experience of the visual world, and which can be derived without ever reaching awareness?

In this paper we use repetition blindness, or RB (Kanwisher 1987) to tackle these questions. In RB, accuracy in reporting two briefly presented visual stimuli is lower when they are identical than when they are different (Kanwisher 1987, 1991a; Mozer 1989; Hochhaus & Marohn 1991; Bavelier & Potter 1992). This effect has been demonstrated in a variety of tasks involving full or partial report of stimuli presented either sequentially (Kanwisher 1987) or simultaneously (Bjork & Murray 1977; Egeth & Santee 1981; Mozer 1989; Kanwisher 1991a). For example, if the word "manager" is presented one letter at a time in rapid serial visual presentation (RSVP) at a rate of 8 letters/ sec, subjects frequently miss the second "a" and so erroneously report seeing "manger" (Kanwisher 1991a).

RB has been taken by Kanwisher and others (e.g., Kanwisher 1987; Mozer 1989; Park & Kanwisher 1994; Chun & Cavanagh 1997) as evidence for a specific difficulty in linking the representation of a repeated visual category or "type" to multiple episodic "tokens" that distinguish each instance. This difficulty represents an actual decrease in sensitivity for detection of the second of two identical items, rather than a difference in response bias or a specific memory problem for repeated items (Park & Kanwisher 1994; Kanwisher, Kim, & Wickens 1996; Hochhaus & Johnston 1996). Difficulties in encoding multiple tokens of the same type are characteristic of "binding problems" that occur in many connectionist networks (Norman 1986; Kanwisher 1990; Mozer 1991). Baylis, Driver, and Rafal (1993) have suggested that the neuroanatomical basis of the type-token distinction may be found in the widely recognized division of primate extrastriate cortex into dorsal and ventral streams, with types extracted primarily in the ventral stream and tokens created for these types in the dorsal stream (or via an interaction of the two streams).

Whatever its neural basis, RB can be useful in characterizing the representations involved in the processing of visual stimuli. Because RB is by definition a phenomenon that is sensitive to the identity of two visual stimuli, it can be used to ask what kind of stimuli are treated as the same by the visual system. For example, in a study of RB for words, Kanwisher & Potter (1990) found that RB occurred for words that were identical or orthographically similar, but not for synonyms. Morphological units were no more likely to produce RB than word fragments that did not carry meaning: RB was about as strong for *barn* and *bar* as for *walks* and *walk*. On the other hand, Kanwisher and Potter found that RB for whole words was not the additive result of RB for individual letters (i.e., subjects did not experience repetition blindness for the *t* in *heart* when it followed *fault* in an RSVP sequence, thereby reporting *hear*). Kanwisher and Potter concluded that when whole words are presented, RB occurs at the level of orthographic letter clusters. Lexical or conceptual identity produced no additional effect, suggesting that meaning is not involved. This evidence for a level of representation that captures letter clusters but not lexical status or word meaning dovetails with other lines of research (McClelland & Rumelhart 1981; Petersen, Fox, Snyder, & Raichle 1990), indicating a role for such intermediate orthographic representations in word recognition.

The present study uses similar logic to investigate repetition blindness for pictures, first reported by Bavelier (1994). Bavelier presented RSVP sequences of three line drawings, intermixed with masking patterns. Subjects were informed about the existence of repetitions, and were asked to report all the pictures they saw immediately after each sequence, reporting an item twice if they saw it twice. The percent of trials in which both of two critical pictures were correctly reported was considerably lower when they were identical than when they were different. Here we ask in what way two pictures must be the same (or similar to one another) for RB to occur between them. Must they be pixel-for-pixel identical, or will RB occur across translations, size changes, rotations in the picture plane, or even rotations in depth? To the extent that RB is undiminished by any of these transformations, we can infer that the underlying representations are invariant with respect to that transformation. Thus, repetition blindness provides a way to characterize the abstractness of the representations that are extracted within the first few hundred milliseconds of viewing a picture. This enterprise is relevant to several different issues in visual cognition.

First, it can provide evidence about the nature of short-term visual memory. Current formulations treat very short-term visual memory as comprised of a number of buffers holding qualitatively different kinds of representations, each lasting for different periods of time (e.g., Potter 1983). However, the representations in these visual buffers presumably are used not only for retaining visual information but also for computing the intermediate results of complex perceptual problems, such as object recognition or scene understanding. Thus a second reason to characterize the visual representations that result from a briefly presented picture is that they may themselves constitute stages in the process of object recognition. Any complete theory of object recognition will have to specify the nature of these intermediate representations, along with the computations necessary to derive each from the preceding one. A third issue addressed by the present experiments concerns the nature of the perceptual representations that can be generated outside of awareness. The sensitivity to repetition manifested by RB implies that the identity of the repeated item was extracted at some level, even though it could not be reported. Thus, repetition blindness constitutes a kind of recognition without awareness of the repeated item, and the present investigation of invariances in RB can tell us about the nature of the inaccessible representations that are computed for the repeated item. In sum, an investigation of RB for pictures might be expected to provide insights into the visual representations involved in (1) short-term visual memory, (2) object recognition, and (3) perception without awareness.

Previous research has approached these questions by using a variety of techniques. Potter (1975, 1976) asked subjects to search for a conceptually defined scene (e.g., "picnic") in an RSVP sequence of pictures; subjects' ability to detect targets accurately at presentation rates of up to 8 pictures/sec or more was taken as evidence for the rapid understanding of briefly presented pictures. In subsequent studies Potter argued that such conceptual codes register very rapidly but are lost almost as quickly if they do not become organized into a meaningful structure or are not detected as a "target" (Potter 1993).

Of particular interest in recent years has been the question of whether viewpoint-invariant representations play a key role in object recognition (Marr 1982), or whether objects are recognized by matching perceptual representations to one of a set of particular views of each object stored in memory (Bulthoff & Edelman 1992; Ullman 1996). While this is currently a highly controversial question (Tarr & Bulthoff 1995), there is considerable evidence that at least some kinds of recognition tasks (e.g., subordinate-level classification) involve viewpoint-specific representations and mechanisms (Bulthoff & Edelman 1992; Logothetis & Pauls 1995). However, there is also some evidence implicating viewpoint-invariant representations in the visual recognition of common objects. Bartram (1976) and Ellis, Allport, Humphreys, and Collis (1989) asked subjects to determine whether two consecutively presented pictures had the same name, and found that although correct "yes" responses were faster when the two pictures were identical, compared with two pictures of the same object photographed from two different angles (the "view benefit"), subjects were also faster when the pictures represented two different views of the same object than two different exemplars (e.g., grand piano, upright piano) of the same basic-level object (the "object benefit"). Ellis et al. further showed that although the view benefit persisted across changes in retinal location, it did not survive a 2-sec ISI, an intervening mask, or a change in size. In contrast, the object benefit was unaffected by these changes. These and other findings were taken as evidence for the existence of two visual codes: (1) rapidly derived nonretinotopic, but size- and viewpoint-specific, representation that is short-lived and susceptible to masking; and (2) a size- and viewpoint-invariant object representation that develops more slowly but is not disrupted by long ISIs or masks.

A different method leading to similar results has been used in some more recent studies by Biederman and his colleagues (Biederman & Cooper 1992; Biederman & Gerhardstein 1993). These experiments used a priming paradigm in which subjects viewed and named pictures that appeared once in each of two consecutive blocks of trials. The amount of priming for a given picture in the second block was not reduced if that picture differed from its counterpart in the first block in size, orientation, translation, or viewpoint (but see Srinivas 1995, experiment 2). This finding has been taken as evidence for representations that are invariant with respect to these transformations. These results are perfectly consistent with those of Ellis et al. (1989), given that the transient viewpoint-specific representations (but not the viewpoint-invariant representations) found by Ellis et al. would have decayed long before the second experimental block.

Thus, both Ellis et al.'s same-name task and Biederman's cross-block priming task provide evidence for the existence of representations that are invariant with respect to changes in retinal position, size, and viewpoint. One concern about the Ellis et al. study is that it is not clear whether the representations used in their matching task are the same as those involved in visual recognition (Lawson & Humphreys 1996). Another concern is that Lawson and Humphreys (1996, experiment 4) failed to replicate Ellis et al.'s (1989) finding that the view benefit was abolished by an intervening mask. Biederman's priming paradigm is open to a different objection. Because typically several minutes elapse between the presentation of the prime and test items, there is no guarantee that the critical intermediate representations involved in object recognition are still available when the test item is presented. Thus, positive evidence of priming is useful, but the lack of evidence for size- or orientation-specific representations may result from the loss of these representations over the intervening period. Indeed, that is exactly what Ellis et al.'s data show: their view benefit was disrupted by as little as 2 secs or one intervening mask.

Neither the same-name nor the priming task described above is relevant to the question of what visual representations are generated for objects that do not enter awareness, as both tasks required subjects to consciously and explicitly process both pictures. Priming studies in normal subjects (Tipper & Driver 1988; Dagenbach, Carr, & Wilhelmson 1989) and neuropsychological patients with neglect (Berti & Rizzolatti 1992) or prosopagnosia (Bruyer, Laterre, Seron, Feyereisne, Strypstein, Pierrard, and Rectem 1983; Bauer 1984) provide some evidence for the extraction of semantic information from pictures that do not reach awareness. However, the interpretation of these studies remains controversial (Farah 1994; Driver 1996). One difficulty in establishing perception without awareness is that the absence of awareness and the presence of perception are usually tested in different trials with different tasks. This leaves such evidence open to the possible objection that different kinds of processing occur in the two cases, with different underlying representations being tapped in the two tasks.

Studies of RB for pictures have several potential advantages over past techniques for investigating the visual representations involved in short-term visual memory, object recognition, and perception without awareness. First, because RB for pictures happens for very short ISIs of 100–200 msec, the effect should be sensitive to visual representations that are extracted on-line in picture processing. Representations that would be too fleeting to last until the second block in a blocked priming paradigm should last long enough to produce RB for a picture presented 200 msec later. Second, Santee and Egeth (1982) have argued that accuracy is a more appropriate dependent measure than reaction time (RT) when studying perceptual phenomena, because RTs are more sensitive to decision-level processing. Finally, for the purpose of studying perception without awarenes, RB has a unique advantage over other techniques: because it is the similarity or identity of the two items that prevents the second one (hereafter C2, for the second critical item) from reaching awareness, we can obtain evidence in the same set of trials both that C2's identity was extracted *and* that it did not reach awareness.

While RB therefore promises to be a useful paradigm for the investigation of visual processing, it is not without shortcomings. First, because all of the list items must be remembered and reported in our task, some of the RB effect may occur because of post-perceptual problems with memory or report of repeated items, as Fagot and Pashler (1995), Armstrong and Mewhort (1995), Whittlesea, Dorken, and Podrouzek (1995), and Whittlesea and Podrouzek (1995) have argued. However, these arguments have been criticized on many grounds (Downing & Kanwisher 1995; Park & Kanwisher 1994), and considerable evidence to the contrary has accumulated. For example, Park and Kanwisher (1994) and Kanwisher, Kim, and Wickens (1996) have shown that RB for letters reflects an actual reduction of sensivity for the detection of repeated, as compared with unrepeated, items, and Kanwisher, Driver, and Machado (1995) have found RB when only a single item is reported (provided the other item has been attended first). Because these tasks require only detection of two items, and because the response is the same in the repeated and unrepeated conditions, the RB effects are very unlikely to be due to forgetting and cannot be due to differences in report bias. In the present experiments, forgetting of items that originally were clearly seen is not likely to be a major factor, because only three items must be reported. These and other findings (Park & Kanwisher 1994; Kanwisher, Driver, & Machado 1995; Hochhaus & Johnston 1996; Chun & Cavanagh 1997) suggest that RB does in fact reflect an on-line perceptual effect rather than some kind of report bias or selective loss of repeated items from memory.

However, there is a second potential problem. Bavelier and Potter (1992) found that RB can occur for visually presented items that are similar only in pronunciation (e.g., EIGHT–ATE and even 8–ATE). Further, Bavelier (1994) has found RB between a word and picture with the same name, even when the two do not have the same meaning (e.g., the word SON and a picture of the sun). These findings spell trouble for any effort to demonstrate invariant *visual* representations: if phonological identity is sufficient for RB, then it would follow trivially that any two pictures with the same name will produce RB, not because invariant visual representations are extracted, but simply because the same phonological code was extracted for each. However, not all repetition blindness is phonologically based. Kanwisher (1991b) demonstrated RB for words that overlapped in orthography but had very little phonological overlap (e.g., right–rig). Other studies have shown

Figure 6.1
Each sequence consisted of 9 rapid serial visual presentations. This sequence was used in experiments 1–5 and 7.

that the codes that produce repetition blindness depend on the task and the subject's attention (Kanwisher 1991a; Kanwisher, Driver, & Machado 1995; Bavelier 1994). For the present study, we reasoned that an experiment using only picture stimuli might not evoke phonological representations. Thus we used only picture stimuli in the experiments reported here (except for experiment 6, which used exclusively words), and we tested for any involvement of purely phonological RB by including picture pairs that were similar only in name (e.g., animal bat, baseball bat). To anticipate, in none of the 6 experiments with picture stimuli did we find any RB for these phonologically identical picture pairs, so we are confident that the effects we report here do not result from phonologically based RB.

Experiment 1

As mentioned above, Bavelier (1994) argues that at least some RB for pictures is mediated by phonological codes. In this experiment we asked whether conditions might exist under which RB for pictures would occur but could not be accounted for by phonological similarity alone. Because the existence of words in Bavelier's stimulus sequences may have led subjects to place more processing emphasis on phonological codes, we used only pictures in our experiment. Thus, subjects viewed RSVP sequences of 2 or 3 consecutive pictures sandwiched between several masking fields; their task was to report all the pictures they saw. This combination of stimulus and task is essentially the same as that used by Bavelier (1994). Performance was compared for report of (1) two identical pictures, (2) two pictures of "different objects" that share the same name but are otherwise unrelated (e.g., baseball bat and animal bat), and (3) two completely unrelated pictures. In an effort to determine whether some kind of low-level visual fusion might underlie RB for pictures, we also varied whether the two critical pictures appeared in a fixed screen location or were displaced laterally from one another.

Different Object Same Name Pairs

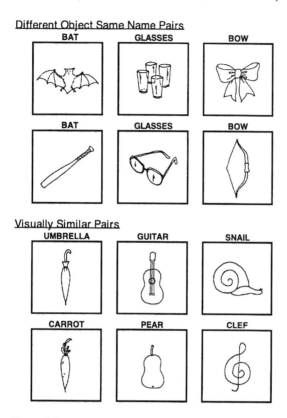

Figure 6.2
Examples of critical items from experiments 1 and 7.

Thirty subjects were run in this experiment, 15 in the "fixed" condition and 15 in the "displaced" condition. The stimuli were line drawings of common objects, either adapted from Snodgrass and Vanderwart (1980) or drawn in their style. Each trial (see figure 6.1) was initiated by the subject's pressing a keyboard button, and consisted of the following sequence displayed in RSVP: (1) a large masking field (presented for 500 msec), (2) 2 random-line masking patterns (100 msec apiece), (3) 3 consecutive pictures (100 msec apiece), (4) 2 random-line patterns (100 msec apiece): and (5) the same large masking field as in (1), presented for 100 msec. Before the experiment began, subjects were given training in naming the pictures (to make sure they would use the same label for each member of the phonologically identical pair). Then the task was explained to subjects: they were told to press the space bar to initiate each trial, watch the sequence, and then report all the pictures they saw. They were explicitly told that some sequences would contain repeated pictures, and if they saw an item twice in a sequence, it was important to say it twice in their response. Subjects performed 8 practice trials, and then the test trials.

The first (C1) and the third (C2) pictures were the critical items, and were either (1) identical (the identical picture), (2) phonologically identical (pictures of different objects with the same name), or (3) completely unrelated (see figure 6.2, set I); there were 24 trials in each condition. The second variable, displacement, had 2 levels and was manipulated between subjects: all pictures in a trial were either centered on the same point in the middle of the screen ("fixed"), or C1 was moved 10 pixels to the left and C2 was moved 10 pixels to the right ("displaced"). While all test trials included 3 consecutive pictures, the experiment also contained 9 filler trials containing only 2 pictures that were intended to discourage subjects from randomly guessing the third picture if they saw only 2 pictures.

Results and Discussion

Table 6.1 presents the data, which were scored in terms of the percent of trials in each condition in which both C1 and C2 were correctly reported. The main effect of the C1–C2 relation was significant— $F(2,56)=58.0$, $p<.001$, but the main effect of displacement and the interaction of these two factors was not significant: $F(1,28)<1$ and $F(2,56)= 1.39$, $p>.10$, respectively. Planned comparisons revealed significant differences between the means for identical and unrelated pictures in both fixed and displaced conditions: $F(1,28)=37.6$, $p<.001$ and $F(1,28)=27.5$, $p<.001$, respectively. The comparisons of phonological and unrelated means were not significant for either the fixed or the displaced condition: $F(1,28)=1.9$, $p>.10$, and $F(1,28)<1$, respectively.

This experiment shows strong RB for identical pictures, but no decrement in performance for pictures of different objects that merely share the same name. Thus the RB for identical pictures cannot be mediated solely by identity in the phonological representations of the pictures (i.e., their names). We suspect that our failure to find phonological RB in a paradigm otherwise similar to Bavelier's is due to the absence of words in our stimulus (which were present in hers) and the resulting greater reliance on visual codes. Further, the fact that RB was not significantly reduced when the two occurrences of the identical picture were displaced by over 10% of the width of the picture argues against an account of the effect in terms of low-level fusion.

Table 6.1
The proportion of trials in which subjects reported both C1 and C2 correctly as a function of the C1–C2 relationship and C2 displacement, experiment 1

Relationship	No Displacement	Displacement
Unrelated	.43	.48
Different object	.49	.47
	NS	NS
Identical	.11	.21
	***	***

The significance of pairwise comparisons between the unrelated condition and the other two conditions for each level of the displacement factor are indicated below each percentage correct.
NS, nonsignificant.
***$p < .001$.

Experiment 2

While experiment 1 rules out both low-level fusion and phonological codes as the basis of picture RB (at least in that experiment), it provides no direct evidence on what kind of representations *do* underlie RB for pictures. In the next experiment we tested whether these representations are invariant with respect to size and orientation within the picture plane by asking whether RB for pictures is reduced when the 2 critical items differ in size, orientation, or both. The stimuli and task for this experiment were much like those used in experiment 1, except that the critical items, C1 and C2, varied in size and orientation. Because we wanted to make sure that phonological codes would not be sufficient to produce RB in this experiment (even though they did not in experiment 1), phonological control trials containing same-name picture pairs (animal bat, baseball bat) were included in this experiment.

Method

Twenty-four new subjects participated in this experiment. Details of the methods were the same as experiment 1, except as follows. Two different sets of trials (interleaved in the same experiment) were used to test (1) the effect of changes in size and orientation on RB, and (2) whether RB occurred for pictures of different objects sharing the same name. As in experiment 1, all test trials contained 3 consecutive pictures, of which the first (C1) and the third (C2) were the critical items. Four versions were made for each of the 16 critical pictures used in the size/orientation trials: large vertical, small vertical, large tilted, and small tilted (see figure 6.3). The picture intervening between C1 and C2 was always large and vertical.

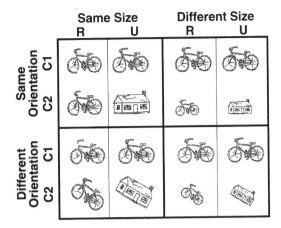

Figure 6.3
Examples of critical items from experiment 2 that differ in (a) size, (b) orientation, and (c) both size and orientation. The "small" stimuli were scaled to be 70% of the original stimulus; the "tilted" stimuli were rotated clockwise by 30°.

For the size/orientation trials, three independent variables were crossed in a 2 x 2 x 2 within-subjects design. The first was the C1/C2 relation: C1 and C2 were either "identical" (the same picture, except for possible differences in size and orientation) or "unrelated" (pictures of different objects). Second, C1 and C2 could be either the same size or different sizes. Third, the critical items could have either the same orientation or different orientations. There were 16 trials in each of the 8 subconditions generated by crossing these 3 factors.

For the phonological control trials, C1 and C2 could be identical (the identical picture, disregarding size and orientation), same-name (pictures of different objects that shared the same name), or unrelated; there were 24 trials for each condition. So that these trials did not stand out from the size/orientation trials, in each condition there were equal numbers of trials in which C1 and C2 were the same in both size and orientation, different in both, same in size and different in orientation, and vice versa.

Finally, 36 filler trials were included in the experiment that contained only 2 pictures.

Results
Separate ANOVAs were run for the size/orientation conditions and the phonologicalcontrol conditions (see table 6.2)

Size/Orientation Trials   A 2 (C1/C2 relation) x 2 (same/different size) x 2 (same/different orientation) repeated-measures ANOVA found sig-

Table 6.2
Mean proportion of trials in which both C1 and C2 were reported correctly, for both the size/orientation trials, and the phonological control stimuli, as a function of size and rotation changes and C1/C2 relationship, experiment 2

Size/Orientation Trials

	Same Size		Different Size	
	Same Or	Diff Or	Same Or	Diff Or
Identical	.34	.27	.33	.22
Unrelated	.55	.51	.50	.45

Phonological Control Stimuli

	Same Size		Different Size	
	Same Or	Diff Or	Same Or	Diff Or
Identical	.38	.29	.30	.35
Same-Name	.49	.29	.37	.46
Unrelated	.51	.17	.32	.49

nificantly lower performance in the identical (29%) than in the unrelated (50%) condition that constitutes RB, $F(1,23)=24.64$, $MSe=22.05$, $p<.001$. Other main effects were higher performance in the same-size than the different-size condition—$F(1,23)=11.90$, $MSe=1.74$, $p=.002$—and higher performance in the same-orientation than in the different-orientation conditions, $F(1,23)=36.58$, $MSe=1.63$, $p<.001$. No interactions were found indicating that RB did not diminish with size or orientation changes: the C1/C2 relation x size interaction was not significant, $F(1,23)<1.2$, $p>.25$; C1/C2 relation x orientation was not significant, $F(1,23)<3,p>.1$. Neither the size x orientation interaction nor the C1/C2 relation x size x orientation interaction was significant; for both, $F<1$.

Phonological Control Trials   A 3 (C1/C2 relation) x 2 (same/different size) x 2 (same/different orientation) repeated-measures ANOVA found no significant main effect of C1/C2 relation, $F(2,46)=2.14$, $p>.12$. However, there was a significant three-way interaction of C1/C2 relation x same/different size x same/different orientation, $F(2,46)=6.45$, $MSe=1.19$, $p<.01$—suggesting that the amount of RB varied across size and orientation conditions. An inspection of table 6.2 shows that this interaction, and the lack of a significant overall RB effect, result from the very low performance in the unrelated conditions for the different size/same orientation and different orientation/same size trials. Because these size/orientation conditions were confounded with particular pictures in these phonological control trials, and because the interaction of RB with size and orientation did *not* occur in the main size/orientation experimental trials, which did not have this confound, we suspect that the interaction resulted from the fact that some of the stimuli in this set became very difficult to recognize when tilted or size-reduced.

Our main question with the phonological control trials was whether RB for repeated pictures can be explained by the sameness of name of the two critical pictures. When particular items produce no RB when repeated, this question does not apply. Therefore we decided to select the two size/orientation cells where RB was found for repeated pictures, to ask whether it was also found for pictures that merely shared the same name. Thus our next analysis looked only at the same size/same orientation and different size/different orientation conditions of the phonological control trials.

Data from these two subconditions were examined in a 2 (identical vs unrelated) x 2 (the two selected subconditions) repeated-measures ANOVA. There was a significant effect of C1/C2 relation, $F(1,23)=$ 5.26, MSe=3, 17, p<.05, no main effect of subcondition, F<1, and no interaction, F<1. Yet analysis of just the same-name and unrelated trials found no significant effect of C1/C2 relation, F<1, showing that phonological similarity alone produced no RB.

This experiment again demonstrates robust RB for identical pictures, and further shows that this effect is not affected by a change in either size or orientation (or both) between the two occurrences of the repeated item. Because no RB was found in this experiment for pictures that were the same only in name, phonological codes alone cannot account for the observed RB. Thus, the codes involved in RB in this experiment are apparently invariant with respect to both size and orientation in the picture plane.

Experiment 3

If the representations involved in RB for pictures are invariant with respect to changes in size and orientation in the picture plane, is it possible that they are invariant even to changes in viewing angle? This question was addressed in the next experiment, which used digitized photographs and photograph-like pictures of common objects seen from different viewpoints. This experiment also tested for RB between two different exemplars of the same kind of object (e.g., upright piano, grand piano). It is usually assumed that there can be no single visual representation for visually different exemplars of the same basic-level object (Biederman & Gerhardstein 1993), and that the only common

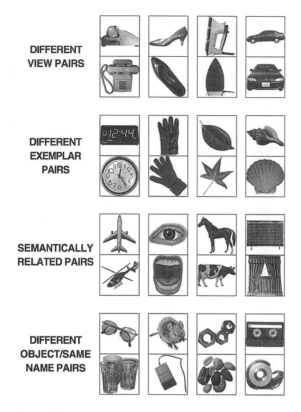

DIFFERENT
VIEW PAIRS

DIFFERENT
EXEMPLAR
PAIRS

SEMANTICALLY
RELATED PAIRS

DIFFERENT
OBJECT/SAME
NAME PAIRS

Figure 6.4
Examples of critical items from (a) the different viewpoint condition, (b) the different exemplar condition, (c) the phonological control condition, and (d) semantic similarity condition. These stimuli were used in experiments 3, 4, and 5.

representation such objects may have is at the level of meaning. However, it is possible that the stored representations of different exemplars of the same basic-level object are somehow linked even within visual memory (Sakai & Miyashita 1991), and if so, that RB may be found between them. As in earlier experiments, we included same-name trials, to make sure that any observed invariances do not result from the involvement of phonological codes.

Method
Twenty new subjects from the pool described above participated in this experiment. Stimuli were digitized 8-bit gray-scale pictures of objects that were either photographed or adapted from the *Macmillan Visual Dictionary* (1992; see figure 6.4). Ten pairs of pictures were different exemplars of a basic-level object (e.g., conch shell and scallop shell),

forming the different exemplar set. Ten pairs of pictures were different viewpoints of a depth-rotated object (different viewpoint set). (For all but three objects, the different viewpoints were the front view of the object and a side or a top view of the object (a 90 degree rotation in depth, along the vertical or horizontal axis, respectively). Three objects (the bucket, shoe, and umbrella) were photographed from the side view and a 45 degree depth rotation). Ten pairs of pictures were of different objects that shared the same name; these pictures were used in the phonological control trials and formed the phonological set. All stimuli were presented upon a white background, and subtended approximately 8 degrees from normal viewing distances.

Design
Because it was impossible to find objects that could appear in all three critical test conditions—different viewpoint, different exemplar, and different object (with the same name)—the effect of each C1/C2 relation was tested with its own set of 10 critical picture pairs bearing that relation. Because different pictures were used for each C1/C2 relation condition, it was important to show that each of the 3 picture sets would produce RB if repeated identically. Thus each of the 3 picture sets was tested not only in the critical test condition for that set (different viewpoint, different exemplar, or same name), but also in an identical/unrelated condition. Thus, C1/C2 relation (identical, unrelated, and test) was crossed with stimulus set (different viewpoint, different exemplar, and different object) in a 3x3 within-subjects design.

In order to make sure subjects were using the correct names for each object, they were first shown all the pictures once (once for each view) with the experimenter naming the picture, then again with the subjects themselves asked to name the picture. Masks containing both lines and regions of different gray levels were used. In all other respects, this experiment was identical to experiment 2.

Results
An omnibus 3 (stimulus set) x 3 (C1/C2 relation) repeated-measures ANOVA found a significant 2-way interaction, $F(4,76)=16.95$, MSe= 4.71, $p<.001$ (see table 6.3). A further analysis tested first for the presence of RB for identical items: a 3 (stimulus set) x 2 (identical/unrelated) repeated-measures ANOVA found that performance was significantly lower in the identical than the unrelated condition: $F(1,19)=28.03$, MSe= 26.40, $p<.001$. Although there was a significant interaction of C1/C2 relation (identical/unrelated) by stimulus set, $F(2,38)4.3$, $p<.05$, RB for identical items was significant for each stimulus set when tested independently (see table 6.3).

Table 6.3
Mean proportion of trials in whch both C1 and C2 were reported correctly as a function of C1/C2 relationship and stimulus type, experiment 3

	Different View	Different Exemplar	Different Object
UN	0.49	0.59	0.58
Test	0.28 ***	0.36 ***	0.63
ID	0.31 **	0.28 ***	0.32 ***

UN = unrelated; ID = identical.
** p<.001. Based on paired, 1-tailed t-tests, df = 19.
*** p<.0001. Based on paired, 1-tailed t-test, df = 19.

RB for the test conditions was analyzed in a 3 (stimulus set) x 2 (test/ unrelated) repeated-measures ANOVA, which found a main effect of lower performance in the test than in the unrelated condition, $F(1,19)=$ 16.14, MSe=12.40, p=.001, as well as a main effect of stimulus set, $F(2,38)=52.95$, MSe=.388, p<.001, and an interaction of the two variables, $F(2,38)=15.90$, MSe=6.24, p<.001. For the different object stimulus set, there was no significant difference between performance in the test and unrelated conditions, $F(1,19)=2.0$, MSe=5.814, p>.15, demonstrating that there was no RB in this experiment for objects that were the same only in name. However, a significantly lower performance for the test than the unrelated condition was also found for both the different view set and the different exemplar set (see table 6.4), demonstrating that RB was significant for two different views of the same object and for two different exemplars of the same basic-level object.

Discussion
In this experiment, RB was undiminished by a rotation in depth. Apparently, the representations involved in RB in this experiment are completely invariant across rotations in depth. It seems unlikely that this RB was based on the visual similarity of the two views, because the different viewpoints of each object were selected to be as visually distinct as possible. And once again, RB was not found between two different objects that shared the same name, so the effect cannot be based on phonological codes. This experiment also found RB for two different exemplars of the same object category.

How can the viewpoint invariance of RB be explained? One possibility is that subjects may have *learned* the association between the two different views during the training that they experienced before the experiment. This possibility seems unlikely because subjects were also trained on both members of the same-name picture pair, and this did not produce any RB. Nevertheless, it would be stronger to demonstrate cross-viewpoint RB in an experiment in which both views were not presented to subjects before the experiment. This was tested in the next experiment.

Experiment 4

This experiment asked whether RB would still be found between two different views of the same object (and between two different exemplars of the same object category) when subjects were trained on only one of those views (or exemplars) before the experiment began. Twenty new subjects were run. All aspects of the procedure were identical to that used in experiment 3 except for the following: subjects were trained on only one view of the different view stimuli, and only one exemplar of the different exemplar stimuli. The particular member of each pair that subjects were trained on was selected by choosing the more difficult item, that is, the item that subjects had reported correctly less often in the unrelated data of experiment 3.

Results
An omnibus 3 (stimulus set) x 3 (C1/C2 relation) repeated-measures ANOVA found a significant two-way interaction, $F(4,76)=11.60$, MSe= 3.81, $p<.0001$ (see table 6.4). As in experiment 3, subsequent 2 x 3 repeated-measures ANOVAs tested for the presence of RB for identical items (by excluding the test condition) and for test items (by excluding the identical items). The RB for identical items in experiment 3 was replicated here: a 3 (stimulus set) x 2 (identical/unrelated) repeated-measures ANOVA showed lower performance in the identical than the in the unrelated condition, $F(1,19)=10.58$, MSe=19.41, $p<.01$. There was an effect of stimulus set, $F(2,38)=11.93$, MSe=3.38, $p<.0001$, and a marginal two-way interaction, $F(2,38)=3.08$, MSe=3.00, $p=.058$. Planned t-tests showed that RB for identical items was significant in each stimulus set condition (see table 6.4). Further, the findings for the test conditions replicated those of experiment 3: a 3 (stimulus set) x 2 (test/ unrelated) repeated-measures ANOVA showed that overall performance in the unrelated condition was better than in the test condition, $F(1,19)=6.71$, MSe=11.21, $p<.05$. There was an effect of stimulus set, $F(2,38)=44.24$, MSe=5.36, $p<.0001$, and an interaction, $F(2,38)=9.57$, MSe=4.0, $p<.001$. Planned t-tests showed that RB was present for different exemplar and different view stimuli, but not for different object stimuli (see table 6.4). Surprisingly, performance was actually lower in the test condition than in the identical condition for the different-view stimulus set, $t(19)=3.0$, $p<.01$.

Table 6.4
Mean percentage of trials in which both C1 and C2 were reported correctly as a function of C1/C2 relationship and stimulus type, experiment 4

	Different View	Different Exemplar	Different Object
UN	.57	.60	.71
Test	.40	.51	.73
	***	†	
ID	.48	.48	.53
	†	*	***

UN = unrelated; ID = identical.
† p = .05. Based on paired, 1-tailed t-tests with df = 19.
* p = .01. Based on paired, 1-tailed t-tests with df = 19.
** p = .001. Based on paired, 1-tailed t-tests with df = 19.
*** p = .0001. Based on paired, 1-tailed t-tests with df = 19.

Discussion

This experiment generally replicated the pattern seen in experiment 3: RB was found both for different views of the same object and for different exemplars of the same object category. Yet in this experiment, subjects were trained before the experiment on only one member of each viewpoint and exemplar pair. Although it is possible that the pairings of objects were learned during the course of the experiment, this seems unlikely. On the other hand, it does seem plausible that the viewpoint-invariant RB observed here is based on the prior linked storage of multiple views of familiar objects posited by several models of object recognition (Tarr & Pinker 1989; Edelman & Bulthoff 1992). Indeed, if simple association of any visual patterns is sufficient to link their visual representations, as Sakai and Miyashita (1991) have argued, then one might account for the RB for both different exemplars of the same object category and different views of the same object in the same way: both effects would be based on associative links between stored visual representations. On this view, the RB for different exemplars might still be accounted for in terms of *visual* representations.

However, the more standard account of effects that transfer across exemplars (Biederman & Gerhardstein 1993; Ellis et al. 1989) is that the processing of these stimuli converges only at a conceptual level. We had assumed when we designed the previous experiments that RB does not occur at a conceptual level, because experiments on words had found no RB for synonyms (Kanwisher & Potter 1990). However, since then Bavelier (1994) has found RB between pictures and words that are semantically related. If RB for pictures can occur at the conceptual level in our experiments, then our earlier findings may not, after all, demonstrate the involvement of visual representations that are invariant across size, orientation, and viewpoint. This possibility was tested in the next experiment.

Experiment 5

What is the basis of the RB for different exemplars observed in experiments 3 and 4? Might the visual system "know" that grand pianos and upright pianos are the same, much as it "knows" that different-depth views of an identical object are the same? Or does the exemplar effect arise instead at a conceptual level, despite the failure to find conceptual RB for words? This experiment was a replication of experiment 3 with the addition of a set of trials designed to test for RB for pictures that were conceptually related only in meaning (e.g., helicopter, airplane).

Method

Thirty new subjects participated in this experiment, which was the same as experiment 3 except in the following respects. A fourth level, semantic similarity, was added to the stimulus-type variable of experiment 3, creating a 4 (stimulus type) x 3 (C1/C2 relation) design. The stimuli for the new condition (see figure 6.4) consisted of pairs of pictures of semantically similar but visually distinct objects (e.g. helicopter, airplane).

Results

An omnibus 4 (stimulus set) x 3 (C1/C2 relation) repeated-measures ANOVA found a significant two-way interaction, $F(6,174)=11.15$, MSe= 2.03, $p<.0001$ (see table 6.5). As in experiments 3 and 4, subsequent 2 x 3 repeated-measures ANOVAs tested for the presence of RB for identical items (by excluding the test condition) and RB for test items (by excluding the identical items). The findings replicate those of experiments 3 and 4 (stimulus set) x 2 (identical/unrelated) repeated-measures ANOVA showed lower performance in the identical than in the unrelated condition, $F(1,29)=53.18$, MSe=5.84, $p<.0001$. There was an effect of stimulus set, $F(3,87)=3.20$, MSe=1.64, $p<.05$, and a two-way interaction, $F(3,87)=7.10$, MSe=1.65, $p<.001$. Planned t-tests showed that RB for identical items was significant in each stimulus set condition (see table 6.5).

RB for the test conditions was analyzed in a 4 (stimulus set) x 2 (test/unrelated) repeated-measures ANOVA; overall performance in the unrelated condition was better than in the test condition, $F(1,29)= 37.72$, MSe=2.45, $p<.0001$. There was an effect of stimulus set, $F(3,87)= 18.71$, MSe=2.34, $p<.0001$, and an interaction, $F(3,87)=10.44$, MSe=2.22,

Table 6.5
Mean proportion of trials in which both C1 and C2 were reported correctly as a function of C1/C2 relationship and stimulus type, experiment 5

	Diff. View	Diff. Exemplar	Semant. Rel.	Diff. Object
UN	.60	.66	.70	.64
Test	.33	.55	.56	.67
	***	***	***	
ID	.44	.34	.41	.49
	***	***	***	**

** p = .001. Based on paired, 1-tailed t-tests with df = 29.
*** p = .0001. Based on paired, 1-tailed t-tests with df = 29.

p<.0001. Planned t-tests showed that RB was present for different exemplar, different view, and semantically related stimuli, but not for different object stimuli (see table 6.5). The surprising result that performance actually was significantly *lower* for different view items in the test (i.e., different view) condition than in the identical condition was confirmed with a post hoc test, t (29)=4.05, p<.001.

Discussion
Once again, RB was undiminished by a rotation in depth. Surprisingly, the effect actually was significantly *larger* between pictures of two different viewpoints of the same object than between two identical pictures. We suspect that this may occur because on some identical trials, subjects may be able to guess the presence of an identically repeated item on the basis of a certain kind of characteristic flicker, a strategy that is not available when two different views of the same item are presented.

Further, RB was found not only for different exemplars of an object type (e.g., grand piano, upright piano) but also—to a similar degree—for objects that were only conceptually related (e.g., airplane, helicopter). Although the RB for exemplars and semantically related objects was weaker than that for different views of the same object, it was highly significant. This raises several questions. First, why was RB found at the level of meaning in this picture experiment, when it had not been found at the level of meaning for words? Second, did all the RB observed so far in this study arise at the conceptual level? If so, the invariances to size, orientation, and depth rotation do not implicate abstract *visual* representations, but simply conceptual representations. We tackled the first question in experiment 6, and the second in experiment 7.

Experiment 6

Although earlier work (Kanwisher & Potter 1990) found no RB for synonyms, experiment 5 found RB for semantically related pictures. Does this represent a stable difference between word and picture stimuli, with semantically based RB happening only for the latter and not the former? Experiment 6 tested this question, using direct picture-to-word translations of the same stimuli used in experiment 5.

Method

Twenty new subjects participated in this experiment. The subset of trials from experiment 5 using the semantically related stimulus set (identical versus unrelated versus test) was translated from pictures into words to create the stimuli for experiment 6. The masks preceding and following the words were strings of eight %s and 10 #s. Thus, the sequence of events in a trial was as follows: %%%%%%%%, ##########, C1 word, intervening word, C2 word, ##########, %%%%%%%%. As in previous experiments, the duration of each item in the sequence was 105 msec. The characters were displayed in lower case in Geneva font (24 point), in white, against a black background, and subtended about 4 degrees of visual angle horizontally from a typical viewing distance of 50 cm. The same procedure used in previous experiments was used here. In addition to the 5 practice trials, all subjects completed 70 trials for this experiment.

Results and Discussion

A one-way, repeated-measures ANOVA found a significant effect of C1/C2 relation, $F(2,38)=88.122$, MSe=9.8921, $p<.001$. Contrasts show that correct report of both C1 and C2 in the identical condition (20.50%) was significantly lower than in either the semantically related condition (80.75%) or the unrelated condition (74%); $F(1,19)=12.2446$, MSe=1.488, $p=.002$. Contrasts also showed that performance in the semantically related condition was significantly higher than in the unrelated condition $F(1,19)=94.29402$, MSe=18.29605, $p<.001$. This shows that there was significant RB for identical words, but a *benefit* for conceptually related words.

Although RB for identical words was very strong in this experiment, no RB was found for the semantically related word pairs that had produced RB when presented in experiment 5 as pictures. Indeed, in the present experiment a significant benefit was found for semantically related word pairs. Thus, there does seem to be a stable difference in RB for words and pictures, with conceptual-level RB occurring in picture experiments but not in word experiments. One possible reason for this

Table 6.6
Mean proportion of trials in which both C1 and C2 were reported correctly as a function of C1/C2 relationship and stimulus type, experiment 7

	Different Object	Visually Similar
UN	.53	.51
Test	.56	.38 **
ID	.26 ***	.16 ***

UN = unrelated; ID = identical.
** p = .001. Based on paired, 1-tailed t-tests with df = 19.
*** p = .0001. Based on paired, 1-tailed t-test with df = 19.

difference is that conceptual representations are necessarily accessed in picture naming, but not in word naming (Potter & Faulconer 1975).

We return now to the question asked earlier: Might all picture RB effects be accounted for in terms of conceptual (rather than abstract visual) representations? If so, then we would expect not to find RB in an experiment with pictures that were visually, but not conceptually, similar. This question was addressed in experiment 7.

Experiment 7

Is visual similarity alone sufficient to produce RB for pictures, or is semantic similarity also necessary? This question was addressed in experiment 7 by testing for RB between two visually similar pictures of conceptually unrelated objects. We used line drawings of common objects, which were subtly altered to increase their similarity to another picture. For example, a drawing of a guitar was altered to look more pearlike, and a drawing of a pear was altered to look more guitarlike (see figure 6.2). These items were tested along with the same-name items from experiment 1.

Method

Fifteen new subjects participated in the experiment. A 3 x 2 within-subjects design was used. The variable of stimulus set had two levels: (1) different objects, consisting of pairs of drawings sharing the same name, and (2) visually similar objects, consisting of pairs of semantically unrelated objects that were drawn to be visually similar. This variable was crossed with the second variable, C1/C2 relation, which had 3 levels: C1 and C2 were either identical, unrelated, or in the test condition. In the test condition, C1 and C2 were different objects sharing the same name for the different object stimulus set, and visually similar objects for the visually similar stimulus set. The stimuli were 24 line drawings depicting real-world objects drawn in the same style as the stimuli used in experiment 1. The procedure in this experiment was identical to that of experiment 1 except in the number and condition of the trials. Each picture was displayed for 105 msec.

Results and Discussion
The data, presented in table 6.6, were scored in terms of the percent of times both C1 and C2 were correctly reported. Data were analyzed with a 2 x 3 within-subjects ANOVA. The main effects of stimulus set and C1/C2 relation, as well as the interaction, were all significant: $F(1,14)=16.3$, $p<.005$; $F(2,28)=30.4$, $p<.0001$; and $F(2,28)=2.3$, $p<.05$, respectively. Planned comparisons showed RB for identical items of both sets: subjects did better on unrelated than identical trials for both the visually similar stimulus set, $F(1,14)=33.9$, $p<.0001$, and the different object stimulus set, $F(1,14)=33.4$, $p<.0001$. However, the partial interaction of unrelated/test x stimulus set was significant, $F(1,14)=5.6$, $p<.05$, suggesting presence of RB for visually similar items but not for phonologically identical ones. Planned comparisons confirmed this statistically: subjects did better on unrelated than test trials for the visually similar items, $F(1,14)=12.3$, $p<.005$, but for the different object items they did equally well on unrelated and test trials, $F(1,14)<1$. Thus, repetition blindness was found in this experiment for identical pictures and for visually similar pictures, but not for pictures that were the same only in name, as observed in earlier experiments.

This experiment shows that while phonological identity was not sufficient to produce RB for two drawings, visual similarity was. Because our visually similar pictures were similar in both global shape and local features, it is not clear exactly which of these is critical to produce the effect. However, the present results do suggest that some kinds of visual representations are involved in RB for pictures, and they further suggest that phonological similarity is not necessary to produce RB for pictures.

However, these implications of RB for visually similar items must remain tentative because an alternative account of the data is possible. Because subjects occasionally reported the wrong member of a visually similar pair (e.g., pear for guitar), it is possible that the RB observed for visually similar pictures is based entirely on such misrecognitions (see also Kanwisher & Potter 1990). If so, then semantic codes could have played a role in producing RB at a stage after misrecognition of one of the critical items. In other words, in a trial containing a pear as C1 and a guitar as C2, subjects may have correctly recognized the pear, but incorrectly recognized the guitar as also a pear. Thus, RB for the guitar could have been based not on the visual similarity of pear and guitar, but on the conceptual similarity of pear and (misrecognized) pear. While this alternative account may sound far-fetched, it remains a logical possibility that cannot at present be ruled out. Thus, while this experiment is suggestive that RB can be based on visual similarity alone, it is not definitive.

General Discussion

The data reported here demonstrate that repetition blindness for pictures is undiminished by changes in size, position, orientation in the picture plane, and viewpoint. In none of these experiments did we observe RB for pictures that were the same only in name, so phonological codes apparently play little or no role in the effects reported here. These data suggest that representations that are completely invariant with respect to changes in size, orientation, and viewpoint are extracted very rapidly by the visual system, and form the basis of RB.

Because of its potential implications for current theories of object recognition, the complete viewpoint invariance of RB for pictures is the most important result reported here. Previous evidence for viewpoint-invariant visual representations has come from blocked priming studies (Biederman & Gerhardstein 1993) and successive same–different matching tasks (Ellis et al. 1989; Srinivas 1995, experiment 2). However, there are potential shortcomings with these techniques. Because several minutes elapse between presentation of the prime and the target in the priming studies, it is not clear that the intermediate representations that mediate recognition of the prime will still be active when the probe is presented, so long-ISI priming may not be sensitive to the representations critical for object recognition (see Tarr & Bulthoff 1995 for other concerns about these studies). Immediate same–different matching paradigms avoid this problem by using intervals of a few seconds or less between the two presentations, but it is unclear whether the representations used in the matching tasks are the same as those involved in visual recognition (Lawson & Humphreys 1996). In the current repetition blindness studies, these problems are mitigated by using a visual recognition task (naming of all pictures presented) and a very brief interval between the two stimulus presentations (105 msec). With this procedure, any intermediate representations that must be accessed for C1 to be recognized should still be active when C2 is presented, and should be in a position to affect processing of C2. Thus the presence of a large RB effect for depth-rotated objects that is at least as great as RB for identical objects provides strong evidence that viewpoint-invariant representations are extracted in a visual recognition task.

Several investigators (e.g., Fagot & Pashler 1995; Armstrong & Mewhort 1995) have suggested that RB may reflect a postperceptual artifact and not a true on-line perceptual effect. In response to these concerns, Park and Kanwisher (1994, experiment 7) and Kanwisher, Kim, and Wickens (1996) devised a detection task that allowed them to demonstrate that the sensitivity (d') for the detection of a target word or letter is lower when it is a repetition than when it is not. Because this reduction in senstivity is found in a simple detection task, it is difficult or impossible to account for it in terms of response biases or the forgetting of repeated items that originally were clearly perceived. Arnell and Jolicoeur (1997) found RB for pictures using detection tasks, as did Muriel Boucart (personal communication, May 1997), suggesting that RB for pictures is also due to a genuine failure to consciously perceive repeated pictures. However, it should be noted that several pilot experiments in our lab and elsewhere (Paul Downing, personal communication, August 30, 1994) have not found repetition blindness for pictures using detection tasks. While this raises some concern, there are several reasons discussed in Kanwisher, Kim, & Wickens (1996) why detection tasks may be overly conservative such that a real repetition blindness effect can manifest itself in full-report but not detection tasks.

Thus the failure to find the effect in detection tasks does not imply that the effect is artifactual. Further, it seems a priori unlikely that the large and robust RB effects seen in all six experiments with pictures reported here, as well as Bavelier's (1994) experiments, are due to report biases or selective forgetting of repeated items. Thus, although we do not yet have a completely satisfying account of why picture RB is found in detection tasks by some investigators (Arnell & Jolicoeur 1997; Boucart, personal communication) but not by others (ourselves and Downing), we think it most likely that the RB effect found in full report of short sequences described here and by Bavelier (1994) nonetheless reflects an on-line perceptual effect and not a postperceptual artifact.

Evidence for the role of viewpoint-invariant representations in object recognition would be important only if those representations can be shown to be *visual*, not phonological or conceptual. (The meaning or name of an object does not change when it is presented from different viewpoints, so conceptual and phonological representations are viewpoint-invariant only in a trivial sense.) We are confident that phonological representations do not play any important role in the RB described here because we failed to find any effect for conceptually distinct objects sharing the same name. The situation is more complex with respect to the role of conceptual representations. Experiments 3–5 found significant RB between two visually different exemplars of the same basic-level object (grand piano, upright piano), and experiment 6 found RB for distinct objects that were merely semantically related (airplane, helicopter).[1] The RB for semantically related pictures raises the question of whether all of the RB observed in the current experiments might be based on semantic representations. If so, the viewpoint invariance demonstrated here would be unsurprising. This hypothesis seems unlikely, given the RB we found for semantically unrelated but visually similar items in experiment 7 and given the fact that Arnell and Jolicoeur (1997) found RB that could not be based on semantic representations because they used novel meaningless pictures as stimuli. Further, in our experiments the RB effect observed for different exemplar pairs and for semantically related pairs is significantly weaker than the RB for identical or depth-rotated picture pairs. (On the other hand, the conceptual similarity is also bound to be weaker between the members of the different exemplar and semantically related pairs than it is for identical pictures or different-view pairs.) Thus, although it is unlikely that all of the RB in the current experiments is based on semantic representations, our current data do not allow us to definitively rule out this hypothesis.

Even if a role of conceptual representations could be ruled out, viewpoint-invariant RB would still not necessarily imply the on-line extraction of object-centered shape representations (Marr 1982). At least two possible alternative accounts would remain. First, recognition could be accomplished by matching perceptual representations to one of many viewpoint-specific representations of that object stored in memory (Bulthoff & Edelman 1992; Ullman 1996). Viewpoint-invariant RB could result from this recognition strategy if the different views are linked such that activation of one automatically leads to activation of the others (Sakai & Miyashita 1991). Second, visual recognition may be accomplished by detecting a small number of distinctive features that are diagnostic of that object and that are themselves highly viewpoint-invariant (Jolicoeur 1990); if so, viewpoint-invariant RB might be based on the activation of these features. On either of these accounts one would expect that the RB would be weaker for different views than for identical pictures: transfer between associated viewpoint-specific representations is not likely to be 100% on the multiple-views account, and features do not overlap completely, as required by the distinctive-features account. Thus neither of these accounts can easily handle the fact that RB was undiminished (in fact, increased!) by a rotation in depth, compared with RB for identical images.

We have made several attempts to distinguish between the object-centered, conceptual, multiple-view, and distinctive-feature accounts of viewpoint-invariant RB. In one experiment designed to minimize the role of conceptual and distinctive-feature representations, subjects were trained on a small set of meaningless three-dimensional shapes, all made from the same white clay and constructed so as to minimize any distinctive features that might be diagnostic of any particular object. However, in subsequent tests we were unable to raise performance off the floor for recognition of these items at the RSVP rates required for RB. We suspect that the kind of visual recognition that is possible in very rapid RSVP sequences may not include the bottom-up extraction of the shapes of objects, but may instead rely on a simpler and faster feature-based strategy. This conjecture is consistent with several recent proposals (Hummel & Stankiewicz 1996; Cavanagh 1991; Sinha & Poggio 1996) that visual recognition may involve two different processes: an initial very rapid (Thorpe, Fize, & Marlot 1996; Kanwisher & DiGirolamo 1995) and fallible, two-dimensional, viewpoint-specific process, and a subsequent slower process entailing a more complete extraction of a viewpoint-invariant representation of the shape of the object. Also consistent with this idea is the fact that the one study (of several attempts) that has managed to attain adequate performance at perception of novel shapes in RSVP sequences used stimuli with highly distinctive visual features (Arnell & Jolicoeur 1997). Importantly, this study found RB for completely novel visual stimuli, opening up the possibility of using this technique in the future to test the multiple stored views and conceptual accounts of the viewpoint-invariant RB reported here.

A second theoretically important question in visual cognition concerns the existence and nature of perception without awareness. As argued in the introduction, RB is unique in its ability to provide evidence, from the very same task and set of trials, both that the critical item was perceived and that it failed to reach awareness. The sensitivity of performance to the sameness or similarity of the two critical items indicates that C2 must have been perceived on at least some trials when it is not reported. The nature of the similarity on which RB depends indicates the level to which the blinded item was processed; RB for semantically related items indicates that at least some semantic information was extracted from the blinded item. The failure of the subject to report the item suggests that it did not reach awareness.[2] Thus the RB method of demonstrating perception without awareness has some advantages over other methods in which one task is used to demonstrate that perception occurred and another is used to show that awareness did not; with the latter technique the processing strategies and internal representations queried in the two tasks may differ.

The criterion for lack of awareness entailed in the present study is similar to the "subjective threshold" criterion of Cheesman and Merikle (1986). As argued above, RB is unlikely to be due to the forgetting of stimuli that originally were clearly perceived (Armstrong & Mewhort 1995; Fagot & Pashler 1995), and instead seems to reflect a failure to consciously perceive those stimuli in the first place. In the limit it may not be possible to distinguish fleeting awareness (lasting a few hundred milliseconds or less) followed by forgetting from the failure to consciously experience an event at all. But intuition suggests that the durability of a perceptual trace is intimately connected to its subjective presence in awareness: a mental wisp that flashes through the mind and is lost within a small fraction of a second does not seem like a clear case of conscious experience. This intuition is built into the token individuation hypothesis (Kanwisher 1987, 1991a), which argues that repetition blindness results from the failure to bring a fleeting type activation into awareness by stably representing the episode in which it was presented. On this view, the present experiments provide a new kind of evidence for the perception and extraction, outside of awareness, of viewpoint-invariant and semantic information from pictures.

Acknowledgments

This research was supported by NIMH grant MH45245 to Nancy Kanwisher, an NSF Graduate Research Fellowship to Carol Yin, and an NSERC fellowship to Ewa Wojciulik. We thank Paul Downing and Steve Hunt for programming assistance; Sue Hillebrand, Boris Lubavin, Dewayne Hayforth, I-Yun Chang, and Liana Machado for running subjects; Eran Zaidel for use of his digitizing equipment in stimulus preparation; and Molly Potter, Russell Epstein, Muriel Boucart, and Veronika Coltheart for comments on the manuscript. Experiments 2, 3, and 5 were reported at the 1993 Association for Research in Vision and Ophthalmology conference. Correspondence concerning this chapter should be addressed to Nancy Kanwisher at the Department of Brain and Cognitive Sciences, MIT (ngk@psyche.mit.edu).

Notes

1. Although the evidence from experiment 6 and from other published studies (Kanwisher & Potter 1990; Altarriba & Soltano 1996) suggests that RB for words cannot be mediated semantically, this area is somewhat controversial (Mackay & Miller 1994; MacKay, Abrams, Pedroza, & Miller 1995).
2. A similar demonstration of perception without awareness was reported by Rafal and Robertson (1995), who showed that a neglect patient who could report the identities

of two objects presented simultaneously on either side of fixation when they were different (e.g., a fork and a spoon, each made of white plastic), nonetheless showed extinction for the object in his "bad" field if it was identical or merely the same category as the stimulus in his "good" field (e.g., a stainless steel fork and a white plastic fork).

References

Altarriba, J., & Soltano, E. G. (1996). Repetition blindness and bilingual memory: Token individuation for translation equivalents. *Memory & Cognition, 24,* 700–711.

Armstrong, I. T., & Mewhort, D. J. K. (1995). Repetition deficit in RSVP displays: Encoding failure or retrieval failure? *Journal of Experimental Psychology: Human Perception and Performance, 21,* 1044–1052.

Arnell, K. M., & Jolicoeur, P. (1997). Repetition blindness for pseudo-object pictures. *Journal of Experimental Psychology. Human Perception and Performance, 23,* 999–1013.

Bartram, D. J. (1976). Levels of coding in picture–picture comparison tasks. *Memory & Cognition, 4,* 593–602.

Bauer, R. M. (1984). Autonomic recognition of names and faces in prosopagnosia: A neuropsychological application of the guilty knowledge test. *Neuropsychologia, 22,* 457–469.

Bavelier, D. (1994). Repetition blindness between visually different items: The case of pictures and words. *Cognition, 51,* 199–236.

Bavelier, D., & Potter, M. (1992). Visual and phonological codes in repetition blindness. *Journal of Experimental Psychology: Human Perception and Performance, 18,* 134–147.

Baylis, G., Driver, J., & Rafal, R. D. (1993). Visual extinction and stimulus repetition. *Journal of Cognitive Neuroscience, 5,* 453–466.

Berti, A., & Rizzolatti, G. (1992). Visual processing without awareness: Evidence from unilateral neglect. *Journal of Cognitive Neuroscience, 4,* 345–351.

Biederman, I., & Cooper, E. E. (1992). Size invariance in visual object priming. *Journal of Experimental Psychology: Human Perception and Performance, 18,* 121–133.

Biederman, I., & Gerhardstein, P. C. (1993). Recognizing depth-rotated objects: Evidence and conditions for three-dimensional viewpoint invariance. *Journal of Experimental Psychology: Human Perception and Performance, 19,* 1162–1182.

Bjork, E. L., & Murray, J. T. (1977). On the nature of input channels in visual processing. *Psychological Review, 84,* 472–484.

Bruyer, R., Laterre, C., Seron, X., Feyereisne, P., Strypstein, E., Pierrard, E., and Rectem, D. (1983). A case of prosopagnosia with some preserved covert remembrance of familiar faces. *Brain and Cognition, 2,* 257–284.

Bulthoff, H. H., & Edelman, S. (1992). Psychophysical support for a two-dimensional view interpolation theory of object recognition. *Proceedings of the National Academy of Sciences, 89,* 60–64.

Cavanagh, P. (1991). What's up in top-down processing? In A. Gorea (ed.), *Representations of vision: Trends and tacit assumptions in vision research* (pp. 295–304). Cambridge: Cambridge University Press.

Cheesman, J., & Merikle, P. M. (1986). Distinguishing conscious from unconscious perceptual processes. *Canadian Journal of Psychology, 40,* 343–367.

Chun, M. M., & Cavanagh, P. (1997). Seeing two as one: Linking apparent motion and repetition blindness. *Psychological Science, 8,* 74–79.

Corbeil, J.-C., & Archambault, A. (eds.). (1992). *The Macmillan visual dictionary.* New York: Macmillan.

Dagenbach, D., Carr, T., & Wilhelmson, A. (1989). Task induced strategies and near threshold priming: Conscious influences on unconscious perception. *Journal of Memory and Language, 28,* 412–443.

Downing, P., & Kanwisher, N. (1995). Types and tokens unscathed: A reply to Whittlesea, Dorken, and Podrouzek (1995) and Whittlesea and Podrouzek (1995). *Journal of Experimental Psychology: Learning, Memory, and Cognition, 21,* 1698–1702.

Driver, J. (1996). What can visual neglect and extinction reveal about the extent of "preattentive" processing? In Kramer A. F. Kramer, M. G. H. Coles & G. D. Logan. (eds.), *Converging operations in the study of visual selective attention* (pp. 193–223). Washington, DC: APA Press.

Edelman, S., & Bulthoff, H. H. (1992). Orientation dependence in the recognition of familiar and novel views of three-dimensional objects. *Vision Research, 32,* 2385–2400.

Egeth, H. E., & Santee, J. L. (1981). Conceptual and perceptual components of interletter inhibition. *Journal of Experimental Psychology: Human Perception and Performance, 7,* 506–517.

Ellis, R., Allport, D. A., Humphreys, G. W., & Collis, J. (1989). Varieties of object constancy. Quartely *Journal of Experimental Psychology, 41A,* 775–796.

Fagot, C., & Pashler, H. (1995). Repetition blindness: Perception or memory failure? *Journal of Experimental Psychology: Human Perception and Performance, 21,* 275–292.

Farah, M. J. (1994). Visual perception and visual awareness after brain damage: A tutorial overview. In C. Umilta & M. Moscovitch (eds.), *Attention and Performance XV* (pp. 37–76). Cambridge, MA: MIT Press.

Hochhaus, L., & Johnston, J. C. (1996). A perceptual repetition blindness effect. *Journal of Experimental Psychology: Human Perception and Performance, 22,* 355–366.

Hochhaus, L., & Marohn, K. M. (1991). Repetition blindness depends on perceptual capture and token individuation failure. *Journal of Experimental Psychology: Human Perception and Performance, 17,* 422–432.

Hummel, J. E., & Stankiewicz, B. J. (1996). An architecture for rapid, hierarchical structural description. In T. Inui & J. McClelland (eds.), *Attention and performance XVI* (pp. 93–121). Cambridge, MA: MIT Press.

Jolicoeur, P. (1990). Identification of disoriented objects: A dual-systems theory. *Mind & Languages, 5,* 387–410.

Kanwisher, N. G. (1987). Repetition blindness: Type recognition without token individuation. *Cognition, 27,* 117–143.

Kanwisher, N. (1990). Binding and type-token problems in human vision. *Proceedings of the Twelfth Annual Conference of the Cognitive Science Society,* 606–613.

Kanwisher, N. (1991a). Repetition blindness and illusory conjunctions: Errors in binding visual types with visual tokens. *Journal of Experimental Psychology: Human Perception and Performance, 17,* 404–421.

Kanwisher, N. (1991b). *Orthographic versus phonological similarity in repetition blindness.* Paper presented at the meeting of the Psychonomics Society, San Francisco, November, 1991.

Kanwisher, N., & DiGirolamo, G. (1995). *Accessing stored representations begins within 155 ms in object recognition.* Paper presented at the meeting of the Psychonomics Society, Los Angeles, November, 1995.

Kanwisher, N., Driver, J., & Machado, L. (1995). Spatial repetition blindness is modulated by selective attention to color and shape. *Cognitive Psychology, 29,* 303–337.

Kanwisher, N., Kim, J., & Wickens, T. (1996). Signal detection analyses of repetition blindness. *Journal of Experimental Psychology: Human Perception and Performance, 22,* 1249–1260.

Kanwisher, N. G., & Potter, M. C. (1990). Repetition blindness: Levels of processing. *Journal of Experimental Psychology: Human Perception and Performance, 16,* 30–47.

Lawson, R., & Humphreys, G. W. (1996). View specificity in object processing: Evidence from picture matching. *Journal of Experimental Psychology: Human Perception and Performance, 22,* 395–416.

Logothetis, N. K., & Pauls, J. (1995). Psychophysical and physiological evidence for viewer-centered object representations in the primate. *Cerebral Cortex, 3,* 270–288.

MacKay, D. G., Abrams, L., Pedroza, M. J., & Miller, M. D. (1996). Cross-language facilitation, semantic blindness, and the relation between language and memory: A reply to Altarriba and Soltano. *Memory & Cognition, 24,* 712–718.

MacKay, D. G., & Miller, M. D. (1994). Semantic blindness: Repeated concepts are difficult to encode and recall under time pressure. *Psychological Science, 5,* 52–55.

Marr, D. (1982). *Vision.* San Francisco: W. H. Freeman.

McClelland, J. L., & Rumelhart, D. E. (1981). An interactive activation model of the effect of context in perception: Part I. An account of basic findings. *Psychological Review, 88,* 375–407.

Mozer, M. C. (1989). Types and tokens in visual letter perception. *Journal of Experimental Psychology: Human Perception and Performance, 15,* 287–303.

Mozer, M. C. (1991). *The perception of multiple objects: A connectionist approach.* Cambridge, MA: MIT Press.

Norman, D. A. (1986). Reflections on cognition and parallel distributed processing. In *Parallel Distributed Processing: Explorations in the Microstructure of Cognition.* Vol. 2: *Psychological and Biological Models.* J. L. McClelland, D. E. Rumelhart, & the PDP Research Group. Cambridge, MA: MIT Press.

Park, J., & Kanwisher, N. (1994). Determinants of repetition blindness. *Journal of Experimental Psychology. Human Perception and Performance, 20,* 500–519.

Petersen, S. E., Fox, P. T., Snyder, A. Z., & Raichle, M. E. (1990). Activation of extrastriate and frontal cortical areas by visual words and word-like stimuli. *Science, 249,* 1041–1044.

Potter, M. C. (1975). Meaning in visual search. *Science, 187,* 965–966.

Potter, M. C. (1976). Short-term conceptual memory for pictures. *Journal of Experimental Psychology: Human Learning and Memory, 2,* 509–522.

Potter, M. C. (1983). Representational buffers: The eye-mind hypothesis in picture perception, reading, and visual search. In K. Rayner (ed.), *Eye movements in reading: Perceptual and language processes* (pp. 413–437). New York: Academic Press.

Potter, M. C. (1993). Very short-term conceptual memory. *Memory & Cognition, 21,* 156–161.

Potter, M. C., & Faulconer, B. A. (1975). Time to understand pictures and words. *Nature, 253,* 437–438.

Rafal, R., & Robertson, L. (1995). The neurology of visual attention. In M. S. Gazzaniga (ed.), *The cognitive neurosciences* (pp. 625–648). Cambridge, MA: MIT Press.

Sakai, K., & Miyashita, Y. (1991). Neural organization for the long-term memory of paired associates. *Nature, 354,* 152–155.

Santee, J. L., & Egeth, H. E. (1982). Do reaction time and accuracy measure the same aspects of letter recognition? *Journal of Experimental Psychology. Human Perception and Performance, 8,* 489–501.

Sinha, P., & Poggio, T. (1996). Role of learning in three-dimensional form perception. *Nature, 384,* 460–462.

Snodgrass, J. G., & Vanderwart, M. (1980). A standardized set of 260 pictures: Norms for name agreement, image agreement, familiarity, and visual complexity. *Journal of Experimental Psychology. Human Learning and Memory, 6,* 174–215.

Srinivas, K. (1995). Representation of rotated objects in explicit and implicit memory. *Journal of Experimental Psychology. Learning, Memory, and Cognition, 21,* 1019–1036.

Tarr, M. J., & Bulthoff, H. H. (1995). Is human object recognition better described by geon structural descriptions or by multiple views? Comment on Biederman & Gerhardstein (1993). *Journal of Experimental Psychology: Human Perception and Performance, 21,* 1494–1505.

Tarr, M. J., & Pinker, S. (1989). Mental rotation and orientation-dependence in shape recognition. *Cognitive Psychology, 21,* 233–282.

Thorpe, S., Fize, D., & Marlot, C. (1996). Speed of processing in the human visual system. *Nature, 381,* 520–522.

Tipper, S. P., & Driver, J. (1988). Negative priming between pictures and words: Evidence for semantic analysis of ignored stimuli. *Memory & Cognition, 16,* 64–70.

Ullman, S. (1996). *High-level vision.* Cambridge, MA: MIT Press.

Whittlesea, B. W. A., & Podrouzek, K. W. (1995). Repeated events in rapid lists: II. Remembering repetitions. *Journal of Experimental Psychology: Learning, Memory, and Cognition, 21,* 1689–1697.

Whittlesea, B. W. A., Dorken, M. D., & Podrouzek, K. W. (1995). Repeated events in rapid lists: I. Encoding and representation. *Journal of Experimental Psychology: Learning, Memory and Cognition, 21,* 1670–1688.

Chapter 7

Role and Nature of Object Representations in Perceiving and Acting

Daphne Bavelier

The swiftness with which humans react to complex new environments is unquestionable. Catching a flying ball; grabbing the phone from among a pile of papers and books; and using a computer are only a few common examples. The ease with which objects in a complex visual environment are perceived and acted upon contrasts with the difficulty in building an artificial system with such skills. While very efficient methods have been developed to recognize the visual features that make up a complex visual scene, such as color, edge orientation, or luminance contrast, an understanding of how these features combine to give rise to a durable and unique percept of the object in view is still superficial. Studies in the field of visual recognition support the view of a dichotomy between a fast, parallel perceptual system that performs a featural analysis of the visual scene, and a slower, more limited visual memory system that is dedicated to keeping track of the objects in view (Kahneman, Treisman, & Gibbs 1992; Kanwisher & Driver 1992; Printzmetal 1995; Treisman 1988, 1991). The importance of such object-specific short-term memory representations (also termed tokens) in cognition is the first topic briefly considered in this chapter. The second part of the chapter discusses the nature of tokens, particularly the type of information that controls the instantiation of tokens as well as the underlying mechanisms of token instantiation (also termed individuation). The last section focuses on brain systems that possibly mediate individuation.

Theories in a number of cognitive domains have recently hypothesized the existence of object-specific representations. For example, a number of experiments have shown that visual attention, when drawn to a part of an object, automatically spreads to the rest of the object (Behrmann, Zemel, & Mozer 1998; Egly, Driver, & Rafal 1994; Kramer & Jacobson 1991). This result has led several authors to propose that object-specific representations are built during visual perception (Duncan 1984; Kahneman et al., 1992; Kanwisher & Driver 1992; Pylyshyn 1989). Reports of object-centered neglect, in which the patient systematically neglects the leftmost part of each of the objects in view (not just the leftmost part of the visual field) also indicate the existence of object-level representations (Humphreys & Riddoch 1994). Studies showing that young infants rely on spatiotemporal information to distinguish between objects further indicate a role for objects early on during cognitive development (Baillargeon 1993; Leslie, Xu, Tremoulet, & Scholl 1998; Spelke 1990).

Object-specific representations are believed to allow appropriate action upon an object even though the relationships between the object, its environment, and the viewer continue to evolve. Imagine you are driving along a busy street and that a biker passes your car. The biker is now ahead of you and disappears behind an unloading truck. You will have no problem perceiving him as the same biker when he reappears a moment later on the sidewalk. Throughout this event, a representation specific to the biker first seen next to your car has been maintained even though he disappeared for a moment behind an occluding truck, and his position relative to you and the environment kept changing. Such a capacity requires a level of visual processing that treats these different visual inputs as arising from a single object. This level is hypothesized to be responsible for the construction and maintenance of object-specific representations during perception. Although the case of occluded objects is extremely striking, the problem of representing objects as they move and change in the environment, as well as with respect to the viewer, is quite general. Imagine you are speeding along the highway and that you detect a police car in your rearview mirror. As the car of interest approaches, you realize that it is not a police car but a vehicle equipped with a ski rack. Throughout this episode, the information about the exact identity and relative position of the vehicle of interest kept evolving; however, the car you first identified as a police car and the vehicle with a ski rack are the same visual object. These examples show that visual analysis requires not only defining the various types of objects in a scene but also keeping track of the objects over time and space. The latter occurs through the establishment and updating of object-specific representations for the objects of interest.

A further understanding of object-specific representation requires determination of what constitutes an object. There is certainly no straightforward answer to an issue that philosophers have debated for centuries; however, a reasonable starting point is that objects are defined by spatiotemporal properties. Within normal bounds of perception, spatiotemporal continuity implies one individual object, while existence at two different locations at the same time enforces two separate objects. In contrast, identity information[1] (i.e., the kind of object) conveys ambiguous information about objects. As illustrated in the police car example, a given object can change perceived identity over time. Vice versa, two separate objects can share the same identity; for example, the chairs in a theater are all identical in kind, but each of them is a separate object. It is interesting to note that young infants appear to rely more readily on spatiotemporal cues than on identity of kind to individuate objects in their visual field (Xu & Carey, 1996). Spatiotemporal continuity has also been shown to facilitate the tracking of moving objects (Pylyshyn 1989; Yantis 1992) as well as the integration of information over time (i.e., object-specific priming; Kahneman et al. 1992). Experimental data and theoretical considerations indicate that spatiotemporal information is one of the strongest cues for the instantiation of new object representations. By this view, spatiotemporal discontinuity acts as a trigger for individuation. Such a role for spatiotemporal information is supported by the phenomenon of repetition blindness (RB).

Repetition blindness, first described by Kanwisher (1987), is the failure to see or recall the second of two identical items in rapid serial visual presentation (RSVP) (Bavelier 1992; Kanwisher 1986). A similar failure to see or recall two different items is also observed when items are simultaneously flashed for a very short period of time (Kanwisher 1991; Luo & Caramazza 1996). Under these limited viewing conditions, the relative temporal order and/or spatial location of presentation of the items becomes more difficult to process. This is illustrated, for example, by illusory conjunctions (spatial or temporal) (Keele, Cohen, Ivry, Liotti, & Yee 1988; Treisman & Schmidt 1982) or by poor report of temporal order and/or spatial location. Under fast viewing conditions, the spatiotemporal information, which is usually relied upon to segregate the visual scene into separate objects, appears to be of poor quality. Accordingly, when two identical objects are flashed under limited viewing conditions, subjects often report seeing only one of them (repetition blindness). As the time of presentation increases, subjects' ability to individuate the two separate objects increases.

Can this effect be explained by an increased difficulty in processing under limited viewing conditions? If it were the case, the identity of the items should not matter. On the contrary, under limited viewing conditions, subjects are much worse at individuating two identical objects than two different objects. This comparison is the prime index of repetition blindness. Such difference between identical and different items is consistent with the hypothesis that under fast presentation, the indexation of items in space and time is hindered. Spatiotemporal information cannot be used efficiently to individuate objects. As a result, the most reliable cue for individuation appears to be identity.

Objects are, then, less accurately individuated when identical than when different. Thus, the phenomenon of repetition blindness (i.e., the difference in performance when processing two identical versus two different stimuli) provides a tool for studying the conditions under which individuation fails or succeeds. The study of the nature of the information that leads to RB, and of the mechanisms underlying RB, along with the neural events mediating RB will increase our understanding of individuation.

Identity-Based Individuation: Study of the RB Phenomenon

Repetition blindness is the failure to see or recall the second of two visually identical or similar items. This phenomenon is observed when two items are simultaneously flashed for a brief moment (spatial RB) or when the items are presented in rapid serial visual presentation (temporal RB). Spatial and temporal RB are believed to result from the same mechanism, a failure to individuate each of the items as a separate object. RB was first reported by Kanwisher (1987), who proposed a two-stage model of visual encoding in which the visual input activates its corresponding perceptual code (i.e., a mental representation that is accessed during perception), and then a token of that perceptual code is instantiated. The token is a specific representation of the event or object available in episodic memory for further processing (such as recall of the object's identity or preparation of a hand movement to grasp the object). In this model, RB is attributed to the inability to instantiate a second new token from a perceptual code that has just been involved in individuation. Thus, when RB occurs, only the first instance is represented episodically. The original hypothesis assumed that a condition for RB was the presentation of two identical visual events. RB between visually similar but not identical words, such as *cap* and *cape* (Bavelier & Segui 1990; Kanwisher & Potter 1990), established that RB occurs not only for identical words but also for pairs of similarly spelled words. While visual identity is sufficient for RB, it may not be necessary. The next section considers what role identity information plays in individuation.

Our working hypothesis is that individuation is a graded process during which information from various perceptual levels is integrated into a common episodic representation. By lying at the junction between perception and short-term memory, individuation is neither a perceptual process nor a memory process, but shares properties of both. Accordingly, RB, as an index of individuation, should be dependent upon properties of the perceptual system as well as of the short-term memory system.

Nature of the Information That Leads to RB

RB was initially observed between identical words and was quickly expanded to visually similar but nonidentical words. This last observation led to a closer investigation of the nature of the information that leads to RB. Is RB between *cape* and *cap* due to the misreading of *cap* as *cape* at the perceptual level (Kanwisher & Potter 1990)? This account predicts that RB should be restricted to cases in which the two critical items (hereafter referred to as C1 [first critical item] and C2 [second critical item]) are perceived as visually identical. If that is so, RB should not generalize to visually dissimilar items. We challenged this view through a number of studies. In all subsequent experiments described in this chapter, we assessed the size of RB by comparing task performance when C1 and C2 were related (repeated condition) against task performance when C1 and C2 were unrelated (not-repeated condition). For example, subjects may recall C2 on 85 percent of the not-repeated trials, but only 50 percent of the repeated trials; this would be a sizable RB effect of 35 percent.

We observed robust RB between uppercase and lowercase letters (Bavelier & Potter 1992) consistent with previous results that RB between letters or words is indifferent to case (Kanwisher 1986). We demonstrated RB between visually different items in corresponding systems that were more distinct, such as Arabic (9) and verbal (*nine*) digits (Bavelier & Potter 1992). The presence of RB between differently formatted numbers indicates that RB is not restricted to visually similar or identical items. 9 and *nine* are identical along two different dimensions: conceptual and phonological. The conceptual hypothesis posits that RB between 9 and *nine* occurred because they share a common conceptual type. The phonological hypothesis claims that RB between 9 and *nine* is due to their common phonological representation. Although support for either of these accounts was initially scarce, there are now a number of studies that support a role for nonvisual codes in RB.

We confirmed RB between homophones (won/one) by using the presentation of short RSVP lists as well as sentences (Bavelier & Potter 1992). The comparison of RB between homophone pairs (*won/one*) and nonhomophone control pairs matched for orthographic overlap (*get/ age*) established that this effect was due to the shared phonology and not merely to the large orthographic overlap between members of homophone pairs (table 7.1). Thus, phonological identity plays a role in RB. These results also indicate that visual identity is not necessary for RB. It is important to note, however, that identical pairs always produced a substantially larger RB effect than visually different items. These results suggest that at least 3 different codes participate in individuation: visual, orthographic, and phonological codes. We further

Table 7.1
RB effect as measured by the percent trials in which C1 and C2 were both recalled in
the not-repeated trials minus the repeated trials

	Homophones		Orthographic Controls	
Spelling	Identical (won/won)	Different (one/won)	Identical (get/get)	Different (age/get)
RB effect	28.5	16.5	38.5	5

Note: C1 = first instance; C2 = second instance.
From Bavelier & Potter, 1992.

investigated the level of processing at which each code becomes involved in individuation, as well as the manner in which these codes interact with each other during individuation. We showed that visual and phonological codes do not play equivalent roles. For example, Bavelier, Prasada, and Segui (1994) tested the relative contribution of orthographic and phonological codes in the manifestation of RB by using pairs of words that differed by one letter but were phonologically dissimilar (e.g., *reach/react*) or differed by one phoneme but were orthographically dissimilar (e.g., *great/freight*). RB between orthographically similar/phonologically dissimilar items (*reach/react*) was robust and of a size comparable with that observed between identical items. RB between orthographically dissimilar/phonologically similar items was also observed; its size was, however, reduced (table 7.2). Hence, orthographic similarity led to an RB effect of a size comparable with that found between identical items, while phonological similarity led only to reduced RB. This pattern of results confirms the predominant role of visual similarity in RB. In the presence of orthographically similar items, phonological information barely influences RB. Yet, when using orthographically dissimilar items, phonological similarity alone can lead to a weaker but reliable RB.

The overwhelming effect of orthographic similarity in RB suggests that little recovery can occur once RB has been induced at the orthographic/visual level. However, if no RB occurs at the orthographic level, it can still be induced at a higher level of processing, such as the phonological one. Thus, orthographic information and phonological information play distinct and nonadditive roles in RB. These results are consistent with the view of individuation as a dynamic process (as different codes become available in the perceptual system) with two principal stages: the instantiation of a new token or memory trace, which would primarily depend upon the detection of two visually separate events, and the stabilization of that new token in memory by appropriate binding of other information concerning the event. In this

Table 7.2
RB effect as measured by the percent trials in which C1 and C2 were both recalled in the not-repeated trials minus the repeated trials

	Identical (doctor/doctor)		Orthographic (reach/react)		Phonological (great/freight)	
SOA	Short	Long	Short	Long	Short	Long
RB effect	39	8	32	15	7	19

Notes: C1 = first instance; C2 = second instance.
Short SOA = 200 msec; long SOA = 300 msec.
From Bavelier et al., 1994.

framework, RB can occur because of a failure to instantiate a new token or a failure to stabilize a newly established token in memory. We hypothesize that orthographic and visually based RB arises from the former, while the reliable phonological RB between items as visually different as freight/great comes from the latter. This point is addressed further in the section "Mechanism Underlying Individuation," subsection "Building Object-Specific Representation." In summary, we propose that visual, orthographic, and phonological information contribute to individuation, albeit at different levels of processing.

This line of research was pursued by investigating the role of other information in RB. For example, we tested the status of morphological information in RB. Morphological information has been shown to influence word processing in a number of studies using priming, reading, production, detection, or recognition (Henderson 1985; Taft 1991). Does morphological similarity also contribute to RB? Bavelier et al. (1994) constructed pairs of morphologically related words (verbs in their present and past forms were used; e.g., *edit/edited*). For each pair of verbs, a pair of orthographic controls was constructed that shared the same orthographic relationship as the original pair (e.g., *wand/wander* for *edit/edited*). The amount of orthographic overlap was varied by including pairs of irregular verbs (*take/took*) and their controls (*bake/book*). RB between identical repetitions of these different types of words was used as a baseline. RB was observed for all identical pairs; the size of the effect was comparable across the different kinds of stimuli (regular verbs, irregular verbs and orthographic controls). As in previous experiments, RB between identical items was stronger than RB between related pairs (table 7.3). However, the amount of RB between morphologically related pairs and their orthographic control did not differ. Hence, the size of RB was the same whether the target words were morphologically related or just orthographic controls. Moreover, a post hoc analysis of the items based on the degree of orthographic

Table 7.3
RB effect as measured by the percent trials in which C1 and C2 were both recalled in
the not-repeated trials minus the repeated trials

	Verbs		Orthographic Controls	
	Identical	Related	Identical	Related
Regulars	(edit/edit)	(edited/edit)	(wand/wand)	(wander/wand)
RB effect	34	11	24	18
Irregulars	(took/took)	(take/took)	(book/book)	(bake/book)
RB effect	25	3	39	9

Note: C1 = first instance; C2 = second instance.
From Bavelier et al. 1994.

overlap indicated that orthographic overlap primarily determined the
presence of RB. Morphological relationships in this experiment did not
increase RB; rather, the manifestation of RB was chiefly dependent on
the degree of orthographic and phonological overlap between the
words. This study demonstrates that some dimensions play a greater
role than others in the manifestation of RB. In the kind of experiments
described here, orthographic and/or phonological similarity led to
robust RB, while semantic or morphological similarity was not a precursor of reliable RB.

A possible conclusion from these studies is that only a subset of the
codes activated during perception can influence the manifestation of
RB. There are, however, alternative accounts. In particular, we have
proposed that any codes accessed during perception can potentially
affect the manifestation of RB; whether a code affects RB depends on
the perceptual status of the code and the memory requirements of the
task. We hypothesized that codes accessed during recognition are most
likely to influence RB if they are readily available upon presentation,
if they are known to be efficient for encoding information in memory,
and if they are recruited by the task at hand. In this view, the absence of
RB between morphologically related items in the experiment described
above may result from the combination of the following facts: morphological information was irrelevant, and it is not the most readily
retrieved information during word processing. By this account, visual
information plays a leading role in the manifestation of RB because it
is readily retrieved during perception and is critical to the segmentation
of the scene into separate objects. Phonological information plays a
role in RB because it is important for the stabilization of information
in short-term memory, especially during recall tasks. This view also
predicts that other dimensions may play a role in RB if enhanced by

experimental conditions. Accordingly, we found that semantic information can influence the manifestation of RB when the use of semantic codes is enhanced (Bavelier 1994, experiment 4; MacKay & Miller 1993).

The next two sections review evidence that RB is a function of the codes activated upon presentation and those important to guide the behavior required by the task. How this view of RB impacts on the further understanding of individuation is also discussed.

Role of the Organization of Perceptual Information on the Manifestation of RB

It is clear from the data reviewed above that perceptual information, and in particular visual similarity, guides the manifestation of RB. However, the effects considered so far mainly document the kind of perceptual information that is important in RB. In this section, we review evidence that the finer organization of perceptual processing also affects RB. Word recognition is of special interest in testing the role of perceptual organization in RB because extensive work is now available describing the organization and timing of orthographic, phonological, and semantic activation upon word presentation. Orthographic representations are assumed, for example, to be initially organized along letter clusters (i.e., graphemes) whose activations combine to activate full orthographic representations (Humphreys, Evett, & Quinlan 1990; McClelland & Rumelhart 1981; Mozer 1989). During this activation process, words that share orthographic clusters with the presented word may also become activated and compete with the target word for recognition. The organization of word recognition in such orthographic neighborhoods has been actively investigated (Ferrand & Grainger 1992; Forster & Davis 1991; Forster & Shen 1996; Rapp 1992; Sears, Hino, & Lupker 1995; Segui & Grainger 1992). In particular, the spreading of activation within a neighborhood has been found to be dependent on relative frequency of the words within that neighborhood. When a target word is orthographically similar to a frequent word (e.g., *blur* similar to *blue*), it is harder to recognize than a word of equivalent frequency that does not have any high-frequency neighbors (Grainger 1990; Grainger, O'Regan, Jacobs, & Segui 1989; Segui & Grainger 1990).

If the orthographic representations involved in RB are similar to the ones involved in early word recognition, factors known to affect the relative timing of the activation in word recognition studies (such as relative frequency) should also interact with RB. We found that relative frequency, particularly C1 frequency, has a sizable effect on the size of RB between orthographic neighbors (Bavelier et al. 1994). Repetition blindness for high-frequency C1s (*like/lime*) was larger than for low-

Table 7.4
RB effect as measured by the percent trials in which C1 and C2 were both recalled in
the not-repeated trials minus the repeated trials

	C1 HF – C2 LF		C1 LF – C2 HF	
SOA	Short	Long	Short	Long
RB effect	32	30	11	22

Notes: C1 = first instance; C2 = second instance.
HF = high frequency; LF = low frequency.
Short SOA = 200 msec; long SOA = 300 msec.
From Bavelier et al. 1994.

frequency C1s (*lice/lime*), while the frequency of C2 did not significantly affect RB (table 7.4). These results are consistent with the findings in priming studies that high-frequency words hinder the processing of their orthographic neighbors more quickly than do low-frequency words (Segui & Grainger 1990). Accordingly, at the short SOA, RB was stronger for high-frequency C1s than for low-frequency C1s. Furthermore, the size of RB when C1 was low-frequency increased as SOA increased. Thus, the SOA at which maximum RB is observed, is longer for low-frequency C1 than for high-frequency C1. These results fit well with the proposal from word recognition experiments that high-frequency C1s rapidly hinder the processing of their neighbors, while hindrance from low-frequency C1s takes longer to develop. These findings support the claim that orthographic RB is dependent on the dynamics of the activation within orthographic neighborhoods during word recognition. It is important to note that the effect of C1 frequency on RB is restricted to the use of neighbors. The same amount of RB was observed between identical pairs of high-frequency words such as *like/like* and low-frequency words such as *lice/lice* (Bavelier et al. 1994). Hence, RB is not sensitive to the frequency of C1 per se, but to the relative frequency organization of orthographic neighborhoods.

As the orthographic neighborhood organization revealed by word recognition studies affected the manifestation of RB between words, so the organization of word recognition along phonological neighborhoods also influenced RB. Previous literature has shown that the nature of the relationships between orthographic and phonological codes reliably influences word recognition. In particular, words that belong to the same orthographic neighborhood (i.e., the *have-mave-cave-save-wave* etc. cohort) benefit from their friends (similarly pronounced words, *save-wave*) but compete with their enemies (differently pronounced words, *save-have*) (Ferrand & Grainger 1992; Jared, McRae, & Seidenberg 1990; Lesch & Pollatsek 1993; Lukatela, Carello, & Turvey 1990;

Perfetti & Bell 1991). In particular, Jared et al. (1990) have established longer naming times for words with high-frequency enemies than for those with low-frequency enemies, and for words with low-frequency friends than for those with high-frequency friends. This pattern of facilitation and competition can be shown to affect the size of RB. The results of Jared et al. (1990) predict greater RB when C1 is a high-frequency enemy of C2 than when it is a low-frequency enemy, as well as greater RB when C1 is a low-frequency friend of C2 than when it is a high-frequency friend. We investigated RB when the two critical items were friends or enemies. In accordance with reports from Jared et al. (1990), the experiment revealed a triple interaction between repeatedness, friend/enemy (e.g., same/different pronunciation), and C1 frequency. This interaction was due to greater RB from high-frequency C1s between enemies, whereas RB tended to be greater for low-frequency C1s between friends. Thus, the organization of phonological neighborhoods revealed by word recognition experiments correctly predicted the pattern of RB. Interestingly, the amount of RB was equivalent between same and different pronunciation trials. As in previous experiments, the manipulation of phonological similarity when words are highly visually similar appeared to have little effect on the size of RB. These studies show that RB between words is affected by the organization of word recognition into neighborhoods and the dynamics of the activation within these neighborhoods. These results support the view that the orthographic and phonological representations involved in RB are similar to those mediating the early stages of word recognition.

The observation that individuation is influenced by the fine-grained organization of early perceptual levels is consistent with the idea that individuation is a perceptual process. The next section presents evidence that individuation is also a memory process, as it is sensitive to the properties of episodic memory and the requirements of the task.

Role of the Properties of Episodic Memory on the Manifestation of RB
Upon presentation of an object, various codes become activated within the perceptual system; codes that correspond to the same spatiotemporal entity get bound together to form a representation unique to the object in view. This binding of perceptual information enables information about the presented item to be indexed and organized in memory to guide future behavior. Under conditions of fast presentation, it is assumed that only a fraction of the perceptually retrieved information has time to become stabilized in episodic memory. In line with previous literature, we proposed that saliency of the codes and task requirements mostly determine the nature of the information stabilized in episodic

memory. Therefore, RB should be sensitive not only to the salience of perceptual codes but also to the nature of the codes the task requires for its execution.

It is interesting to consider the case of phonological information in this framework. Indeed, phonological representations play a key role in RB between visually different items, not only because they are one of the activated codes common to both items but also because phonological codes are the preferred dimension for encoding information in episodic memory when a verbal recall task follows (Baddeley 1986). In this view, phonological RB occurs because C2 phonological information is not available for individuation. Upon the presentation of C2, a token for C2 is instantiated. However, since C2 phonological representation has just been associated with the C1 token, it fails to be individuated in the C2 token. As a result, the strength of the C2 token in memory is weakened, rendering it more vulnerable to loss. This view predicts a reliable effect of phonological similarity in RB for a recall task. It also suggests that task requirements may alter the role of phonological similarity in RB. If the task requires codes other than phonological to be encoded in object-specific representations, the role of phonological information in RB should diminish. We tested these predictions in a series of experiments using line drawings and words (Bavelier 1994).

The perceptual codes initially activated by line drawings and words are believed to differ. While words are known to first activate their corresponding orthographic representation, line drawings are believed to first contact their semantic/conceptual representation (Potter & Faulconer 1975; Theios & Amrhein 1989). The case of words and pictures is interesting to consider because these items clearly differ in the visual dimension. If RB relied purely on perceptual similarity, little RB should be observed between items that are so perceptually different. However, we found reliable RB between pictures and words, using short lists or sentences (Bavelier 1992, 1994). How is it that RB is still observed between items that are strikingly visually different and that lead, upon presentation, to very different sequences of activation in the perceptual system? We suggest that RB between a line drawing and its corresponding name is mostly mediated by the identity of their phonological representations. Accordingly, we found RB between pictures and words that differ on all dimensions (visual, orthographic, semantic) but the phonological one. For example, Bavelier (1992, experiment 2) observed RB between items such as the line drawing of a ball and the written word *bawl* when using verbal recall of RSVP sentences. Furthermore, the size of RB between pictures and words varied as a function of task requirements. Reduced RB between the line drawing of a ball and the written word *bawl* was found when the task diminished

Table 7.5
RB effect as measured by the percent trials in which C1 and C2 were both recalled in the not-repeated trials minus the repeated trials

	Phonological Task			Visual Task		
	pw	wp	M	pw	wp	M
RB effect	21	10	15	13	0	6

Notes: pw = C1 picture and C2 word; wp = C1 word and C2 picture.
Phonological task = recall of word and picture's name; visual task = recall of name as well as visual format of presentation (i.e. word vs. picture).
From Bavelier, 1994.

the contribution of phonological information in the stabilization of information in memory (Bavelier 1994).

In a more direct test of the role of task requirements, we tested the size of RB between line drawings and words as task requirements varied. RB was expected to be strongest when the task forced C1 and C2 to be encoded along similar codes, but reduced if the task required C1 and C2 to be encoded in memory using some codes that differ. In a key experiment, we presented subjects with a short RSVP list of line drawings and words. We asked subjects to recall the name of the words or line drawings presented for half of the experiment (termed phonological task). In the other half, we asked subjects to report not only the names of the line drawings and words they saw, but also their format by stating for each item whether it was a word or a picture (termed visual task). RB between a picture and its corresponding word was found to be sizably larger in the phonological task than in the visual task (table 7.5). Hence, RB is not solely a function of the items presented, but also is altered by the dimensions required to be encoded in memory.

This property was confirmed in a very different setting by Kanwisher, Driver, and Machado (1995). These authors presented subjects with two simultaneously flashed colored shapes. In one representative condition, subjects were first told to determine the color of the item on the left. If blue, they had to recall the color of the item on the right. If not blue, they had to recall the shape of the item on the right. Hence, in these experiments the nature of the information to encode was determined by the perceived color of C1. When color information had to be encoded for C2 (if C1 was blue), only color similarity predicted the amount of RB. However, when shape information had to be encoded for C2 (if C1 was not blue), reliable RB was observed only when both dimensions were identical (table 7.6). This pattern of results is consistent with the

Table 7.6
Percent trials in which C1 and C2 were both recalled

	Task Demands for C1 and C2							
	Color-Color				Color-Shape			
Color	Same		Diff.		Same		Diff.	
Shape	Same	Diff.	Same	Diff.	Same	Diff.	Same	Diff.
	53	52	76	75	57	70	69	73

Notes: Average values across the 4 experiments presented by Kanwisher et al. (1995). In the color-color trials, RB is a function of color similarity between C1 and C2, independent of shape information. In the color-shape trials, RB is observed only when C1 and C2 have the same color and the same shape.
From Kanwisher et al. 1995.

proposal that similarity/dissimilarity along the encoded dimension(s) sizably influences the manifestation of RB. The pattern of results described by these authors can be naturally accounted for in the framework developed here, given one additional assumption: once a dimension has been set by the task requirements to be individuated, this dimension will participate in the individuation of *all* the items presented. Since the color of C1 had to be encoded on every trial, color information always participated in the individuation of C1 as well as of C2. When shape was not an important dimension, it was ignored for both items, leading to color-based RB. However, when shape was the relevant dimension for C2, subjects could not help attending to shape for C1 as well. Consequently, in these trials, individuation relied on individuating color and shape information. If C1 and C2 were not identical, their individuation would rely on encoding in memory at least one code that differed. In our view, RB should be reduced or even suppressed when two items are encoded using some dimensions that differ. Consistent with this prediction, during trials in which color and shape had to be encoded, robust RB was observed only when items were identical in color and shape.

The proposal that RB lies at the junction between perception and memory predicts that it should be sensitive to the perceptual properties of the stimuli as well as to manipulations that affect the nature of the information to be encoded in episodic memory. In accordance with these predictions, RB was found to be sensitive to the nature and organization of the perceptual representations contacted by the items presented, as well as the properties of the initial encoding in short-term memory. The next section turns to the underlying mechanisms of individuation. In particular, the study of RB can shed light on how identity information is used to individuate different events in the absence of reliable spatiotemporal labels.

Mechanisms Underlying Individuation

Individuation is dependent on the efficient registration of perceptual information into a stable object-specific representation. The mechanisms on which individuation relies have, however, not been made explicit. Our working hypothesis is that the same individuation mechanism applies independently of the kind of perceptual information that has to be registered (visual, orthographic, phonologic, color-based, shape-based, etc.). Indeed, individuating the first occurrence from the second raises the same problem at all levels of representation. However, the resulting effects of an individuation failure should differ, depending on the level of processing at which individuation failed.

An RB Mechanism

Some aspects of visual perception require spatially invariant and temporally invariant recognition processes. For example, such processes are necessary to ensure reliable recognition of an object in different environments (e.g., a chair in the kitchen vs. a chair in the garden). Alternatively, representations that are unique to the objects in view have to be constructed to guide immediate behavior. How can general knowledge and occurrence-specific representations be implemented within the same system? At present only a few formalizations allow for general and event-specific representations within the same structure (Hinton 1990; Smolensky 1990). The manner in which these approaches may account for RB has, unfortunately, not been thoroughly investigated (Zemel & Behrmann 1996). It is for future research to investigate whether RB can be understood as resulting from the conflicting representational demands of visual processing.

A complementary approach has been to frame RB as a problem of detecting similar signals of unknown time of arrival and duration (Bavelier & Jordan 1992). In this model, the parsing of the visual flow into separate events is formalized as a signal detection problem. RB arises from the conflicting constraints of integrating information over time (in order to increase the signal-to-noise ratio) and segregating the continuous and fluctuating pattern of activation into separate events (in order to organize knowledge for further processing). As indicated at the beginning of the chapter, segmentation of the sensory inputs is a necessary basis for various cognitive abilities (counting, verbal recall, reasoning, visual selection etc). The model assumes that upon presentation of an item, the activation level of its corresponding codes will increase and then slowly decrease back to resting level; rise and fall of activation are controlled by two independent time constants. New events are detected when the difference between the smaller activation value since the last detection and the present activation value exceeds a fixed threshold (T) (figure 7.1). In this model, if an item is presented only briefly (100 msec), the activation will not saturate, but with longer duration (300 msec) the activation will eventually saturate. This model correctly captures the findings that RB decreases for a longer presentation of C2, and that the amount of RB between identical items decreases as the time elapsed between C1 and C2 increases (Luo & Caramazza 1996; Park & Kanwisher 1994). This model also captures the disrupting effects of pre- and postmasking on recognition. In general, the known temporal characteristics of RB and masked priming between identical items are naturally embodied in this model (Bavelier & Jordan 1992).

Furthermore, this model can also account for the effects of neighborhood on RB. The size of RB is determined in this model by the difference between the smallest activation level following the detection of C1 and the highest activation value following the presentation of C2. This difference is controlled by three main factors: the time elapsed between C1 and C2, the dynamics of the activation of C1, and the dynamics of the activation of C2. The first two factors primarily affect the minimum value reached after C1 detection, while the last factor mainly controls the highest activation value reached after C2 presentation. When the dynamics of the activation of C2 are modified by the presentation of C1, the pattern of RB is affected. As discussed above, research from word recognition suggests that high-frequency words hinder the processing of their neighbors more rapidly than do low-frequency words. Hence, if the time elapsed between C1 and its neighbor C2 is very short, the processing of C2 will be hindered when preceded by a high-frequency C1. On the contrary, if C1 is low frequency, activation from C2 will have time to build up before being hindered by C1. As more time is allowed between C1 and C2, C2 will eventually be presented while the hindering effect from the low-frequency C1 is maximal, leading to maximal RB. Neighborhood interactions affect the pattern of RB because they affect the highest activation value reached after C2 presentation. Bavelier and Jordan's model (1992) can capture these findings by implementing the inhibition and/or facilitation occurring within the orthographic and phonological neighborhoods in the model. The model can then account for the findings that RB between some neighboring words is stronger at long than at short SOAs, while RB between identical items always diminishes as SOA increases.

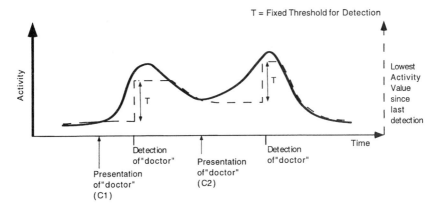

Figure 7.1
Illustration of the time course of the activation for the orthographic code corresponding to "doctor" during the presentation of a short list containing two separate occurrences of "doctor" (solid line). The dotted line indexes the behavior of the detection mechanism implemented by Bavelier and Jordan (1992). Successful detection is achieved when the difference between the present level of activation and the lowest level of activation since the last detection is greater than a fixed detection threshold.

Thus, although the interaction between SOA and type of RB may appear paradoxical at first glance, it does not imply two different RB mechanisms (Chialant & Caramazza 1997). Rather, the paradox vanishes when the dynamics of word activation are considered.

In the model, RB arises from a failure to segregate the activation due to C2 from that which is due to C1. It can be viewed as an explicit implementation and extension of the initial RB account (i.e., the fact that the same type cannot be individuated twice in a short amount of time; Kanwisher 1987). The model has the advantage of readily capturing the dynamic properties of the perceptual system and the individuation process. For instance, the role of the organization of perceptual representations is easily integrated via the dynamics of the activation of C1 and C2. There is, however, a key difference between the present proposal and previous accounts of RB. In the present framework, individuation does not occur just once for a unique level of representation; rather, the various codes activated upon presentation of an item are individuated at different times according to the spreading of activation within the perceptual system and the requirements of the task. Hence, the successful establishment of an object-specific representation is assumed to be a graded, dynamic process. The next section addresses the consequences of this new framework for our understanding of individuation.

Building Object-Specific Representation

The previous section considered a detection mechanism that would account for RB in terms of a difficulty in segregating activation due to C2 from that due to C1. How can this mechanism account for the various properties of RB reviewed above? The individuation mechanism previously described is an all-or-nothing phenomenon: either C2 activation is seen as separate from C1 or it is not. The key difference from previous proposals is that this mechanism is applied at several different levels of representation during recognition. For example, upon presentation of a word, visual information would be individuated, followed by orthographic, phonological, and eventually semantic information. In this view, the establishment of an object-specific representation is a graded process during which various forms of perceptual information concerning the object are individuated and then integrated into a single representation. By this account, RB occurs when no C2-specific representation is available to mediate the response selection demanded by the task. This could occur because upon the presentation of C2, no C2-specific representation was ever initiated or because a C2-specific representation was initially set up but failed to be further stabilized in memory. Our working hypothesis is that the former is most common in cases of visually based RB, while the latter constitutes the core of RB between visually different items, in particular phonological RB.

Visual information is the first perceptual information available after the presentation of an item and is therefore the first to be individuated. This allows visual information to play a critical role in deciding whether or not a new memory representation specific to C2 should be instantiated. The status of visual information for the instantiation of object-specific representation is illustrated by the importance of visual information in RB. RB between visually identical or similar items is always strongest; it shows little sensitivity to dissimilarity along nonvisual codes (such as phonological code or semantic code); and it is barely affected by changes in task requirements (Bavelier et al. 1994; Kanwisher et al. 1995; Yin, Wojciulik, & Kanwisher 1993). Moreover, visual dissimilarity has been shown to reduce significantly the size of RB (Bavelier 1992, 1994; Kanwisher et al. 1995; Yin et al. 1993). These properties indicate that visual information is instrumental for instantiating new tokens. In accordance with these findings, it is hypothesized that the presentation of visually different items (such as a picture and a word) leads to the instantiation of two separate tokens. In such cases, RB is proposed to arise from a failure to stabilize an opened token in memory. In this view, individuation of nonvisual information, such as phonological or semantic, significantly contributes to the stabilization of tokens in memory. If phonological information fails to be registered in a token, the corresponding token will be less stable, and subsequently subject to loss. This view also accounts for the finding that the dimensions along which RB between visually different items is observed varies as a function of task requirements. Indeed, under the fast conditions of presentation used in RB experiments, there is not enough time to individuate all the information related to each item; rather, only the information required by the task demands tends to be individuated. Consequently, the size of RB varies depending on whether the items are similar or different along the encoded dimension(s). In summary, visual RB differs from phonological RB by the level of processing at which individuation fails. However, in either case, the individuation failure is due to a common mechanism, that is, a failure to individuate C2 information from C1 information.

For the purpose of simplicity, we have stressed the distinction between two stages in individuation: an initial stage, during which a new token or memory trace is instantiated, and a stabilization stage, during which the newly established memory trace is stabilized in STM. This distinction is highly arbitrary. We favor the view that individuation is a dynamic and continuous process that relies on similar mechanisms at all levels of processing. There is at present no reason to hypothesize that opening a new token requires different binding mechanisms than does stabilizing an open token. Future research may indicate differences between the binding mechanisms at different levels of processing. It is clear, however, that the failure to individuate C2 from C1 will always remain a possible precursor to individuation failure, whatever the level of processing considered. We presently favor the view that the key difference between different kinds of RB is the time at which individuation fails during the establishment of a token, rather than the mechanisms leading to that failure.

It is important to stress the difference between the loss of a token or memory trace advocated in phonological RB and the loss of a memory trace as described in the classical short-term memory literature (Fagot & Pashler 1995) . The latter refers to STM confusion effects, also termed acoustic similarity effect and Ranschburg effect (Baddeley 1966; Conrad 1964; Wickelgren 1965, 1966). This is the observation that the immediate ordered recall of items is weaker when they are similar rather than dissimilar in sound. Hence, it is harder to memorize *can, map, tan, man* than *cat, pen, day, fir*. This effect is assumed to occur while items are maintained in memory. Whereas STM confusion is believed to occur after each of the items presented has had ample time to be fully encoded in memory, phonological RB is hypothesized to arise from a failure to initially encode phonological information in the

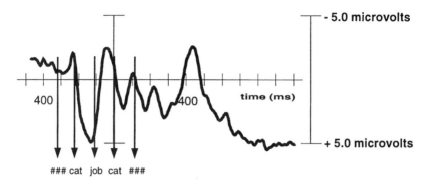

Figure 7.2
Stimulus sequence and corresponding ERP. The upper trace shows the morphology of the ERP as subjects viewed the following sequence of items: mask, C1 (*cat*), an intermediary word (*job*), C2 (*cat*), mask. Arrows indicate the time of presentation of each item.

C2 memory trace. Hence, STM confusion effects imply that phonological information has been encoded in memory for each of the items presented. On the contrary, in phonological RB it is assumed that C2 phonological information fails to be registered in memory.

We have just reviewed how the study of the parameters that affect RB help shed light on individuation and its underlying mechanisms. The next section turns to the consideration of the neural systems that may mediate individuation.

Neural Events Related to Individuation

Present knowledge of the cortical organization of visual functions suggests that processing of location information is mediated by the parietal cortex, processing of visual forms and object identity is mediated within the temporal lobe, and processing of temporal information is mediated by frontal structures. As discussed, individuation or the establishment of representations specific to the objects in view consists of integrating these sources of information. The study of how such integration may be implemented at the neural level is in its infancy. The understanding of individuation as a dynamic process (requiring the integration of different sources of perceptual information and their consolidation in short-term memory) points to the study of the time course of neural activity as a fruitful source of information. As the primary step toward investigating the neural bases of individuation, we combined the study of RB with event-related brain potentials (ERP). The ERP technique allows recordings to be made from the surface of the scalp, monitoring the electrical activity generated by neurons while a cognitive or sensory

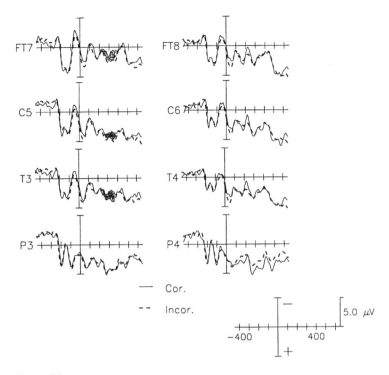

Figure 7.3
ERP for repeated trials as RB occurred (incorrect trials) or did not occur (correct trials)

task is being performed. The spatial resolution of the technique is on the order of several millimeters, allowing gross localization of function; furthermore, it has excellent time resolution, allowing the tracking of neural events as they unfold in real time.

We recorded ERPs while subjects viewed a shortly presented list of words (117 msec per item, no ISI; figure 7.2). We assessed the neural indices and timing of RB by comparing trials in which RB occurred (i.e., individuation failed) against trials during which RB was absent (i.e., individuation was successful). The proposal that RB occurs at the bridge between perception and short-term memory processes predicts a certain time window for the effect. In particular, the RB effect (i.e., the difference between the trials with and without RB) should appear after basic perceptual processes have been completed and higher-level visual processes engaged, but before short-term memory maintenance has been recruited. These constraints predict that the RB effect should fall between 150–200 msec and 400 msec. Indeed, studies of the timing of visual processing in humans suggest that elaborate aspects of object recognition may be engaged as early as 150–200 msec (Anllo-Vento &

Repeated Trials   **Not Repeated Trials**

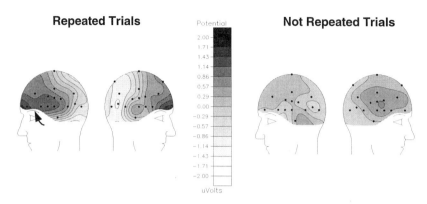

Figure 7.4
Potential differences between incorrect and correct trials 220 to 400msec after the presentation of C2. The scalp distribution of this potential difference is shown on the left for repeated trials; the left frontal positivity observed for RB trials can be seen by the darkening of the map over the left frontal electrodes. The difference map for not-repeated trials is shown on the right. The difference in scalp distribution between repeated and not-repeated trials shows that the effects observed for repeated trials cannot be accounted for in terms of general differences between incorrect and correct trials.

Hillyard 1996; Thorpe, Fize, & Marlot 1996). Furthermore, rehearsal in STM seems best indexed by a slow negative component that is clearly marked 600 msec after the stimuli and develops no earlier than 400 msec (Ruchkin, Canoune, Johnson, & Ritter 1995).

Subjects viewed short RSVP lists of words; half of the trials included a repetition. After the presentation of each list, subjects were asked to recall as accurately as possible the words presented. Trials in which subjects failed to report the second occurrence of the repeated word (i.e., trials in which RB occurred) were contrasted with those in which they correctly recalled all the presented words (i.e., trials without RB). The main differences between these two conditions occurred as early as 200 msec after the onset of C2. Trials with RB elicited a larger positive component over the left anterior temporal sites, and trials in which individuation was successful tended to elicit a larger positive component over right parieto-occipital sites (figure 7.3). To confirm that this effect is due to a failure of the individuation process rather than an obligatory effect of correctness, unrepeated trials were analyzed as a function of correctness. Between 220 msec and 400 msec, the ERPs elicited by nonrepeated trials as a function of correctness did not differ, indicating that the difference observed between trials with and without RB cannot be accounted for merely in terms of correctness (figure 7.4). Thus, as early as 200 msec after the presentation of C2, neural events associated with C2 processing differ significantly on whether C2 will be subject to RB or not.

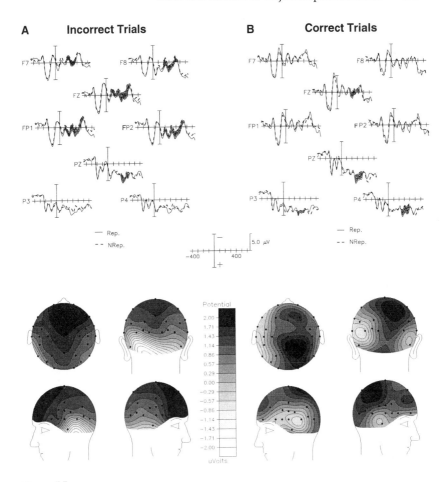

Figure 7.5
ERPs and potential differences for trials in which the incorrectness can be attributed to
RB. (A) ERPs for incorrect trials as a function of whether the omission is primarily due
to RB (repeated trials) or not (not-repeated trials). The scalp distribution of the repeated
versus not repeated difference is shown below, and indicates a frontal effect. (B) ERPs
and scalp potential distribution for correct trials as a function of repeatedness. The
comparison of the effect of repeatedness in correct and incorrect trials clearly indicates
different morphology and distribution.

The hypothesis that the failure to recall a repeated item in this paradigm arises predominantly from a failure of the individuation stage also predicts that ERP traces in trials in which the word is omitted because of the repetition should differ from those in which the word is omitted because of other reasons. The comparison of trials in which the word is omitted because of its repetition (trials in which the incorrectness is predominantly due to RB) against trials in which the word is omitted because of other reasons (nonrepeated trials that are incorrect) reveals a significant difference as soon as 220 msec that extends to 400 msec (figure 7.5a). This effect cannot be accounted for by an effect of repeatedness because it was not present when comparing correct trials as a function of repeatedness (figure 7.5b).

The timing of these effects is consistent with the view that RB occurs at the bridge between perception and memory processes (for a similar conclusion, see also Schendan, Kanwisher, & Kutas 1997). It fits well with previous reports in the ERP literature about encoding in STM. These studies suggest that processes that make an item memorable for future behavior are active as early as 250–300 msec (Neville, Kutas, Chesney, & Schmidt 1986; Paller 1990; Rugg 1995). It is important to note that this early timing of the RB effect challenges any account of RB as an STM confusion effect after items have been fully encoded in memory.

Although future research on the neural bases of individuation is certainly needed, it is interesting to consider the kind of syndrome one may expect if individuation were to fail. Since individuation requires the proper integration of spatial, temporal, and identity information, impairments in encoding any of these dimensions should affect individuation abilities. Such deficits should be especially visible when only the missing information can be used to support individuation. There are a few studies in the neuropsychology literature that strongly support this point. For example, parietal patients (who have difficulty encoding spatial location) should be impaired when integrating the spatial location of objects during individuation. If so, these patients should show RB-like symptoms even at slow rates of presentation. A study by Baylis, Driver, and Rafal (1993) confirms this prediction. Parietal patients, when asked to recall two letters presented simultaneously on the right and left of fixation, tend to omit the letter in their neglected field, a phenomenon known as extinction. Interestingly, these patients were found to exhibit greater extinction when the letters were identical than when they were different, even though the letters were presented for a long period of time. This finding is consistent with the idea that proper tagging of information in space is critical for successful individuation when the items cannot be individuated on the basis of their identity. When only spatial information was available to distinguish between the two visual events, parietal patients were worse than when identity was also available. Along the same line, frontal patients, who are impaired at encoding temporal information, should show RB when sequences of items are presented slowly at the same location. Indeed, under such conditions, the only distinguishing information between C1 and C2 on the repeated trials is the temporal information.

Individuation may also fail if the processes underlying individuation are themselves impaired. Significant impairments of the individuation process may be less interesting because they should result in profound disruption of cognitive abilities. It should, however, be possible to reveal mild impairments of individuation by looking for failure to encode two or more stimuli in short term memory under limited viewing conditions. Patients with a mixed pattern of perceptual and short-term memory deficits, such as patients with simultagnosia, extinction, or problems when working with two or more objects (Attig, Jacquy, Uytdenhoef, & Roland 1993; Benson, Davis, & Snyder 1988) are potential candidates for such investigation.

Conclusion

At present RB seems best understood as an encoding phenomenon occurring at the interface between perception and memory while memory traces for objects in the visual field are set up. We confirmed the role of perceptual processes in RB by showing that RB is sensitive to the fine organization of perceptual levels. We established the role of STM properties in RB by showing that RB can be influenced by the preferred encoding in STM. These properties of RB suggest that tokens are to be seen as dynamical entities that are built over time as a function of the activation in the perceptual system and the task demands. The characteristics of tokens revealed by this work support the view that tokens play a critical role in filtering and organizing the flow of perceptual information in representations adequate to guide future action.

Acknowledgments

We are especially indebted to Sandeep Prasada and Alexandre Pouget for stimulating discussions related to this chapter. We thank Andrea Tomann and David Higgs for help with manuscript preparation. This work was supported by a McDonnell Pew Foundation for Cognitive Neuroscience grant to Daphne Bavelier and an NINDS grant (DC00128) to Helen Neville.

Note

1. We use "identity" to refer to objects' identity in kind. For example, two chairs will be said to share the same identity.

References

Anllo-Vento, L., & Hillyard, S. A. (1996). Selective attention to the color and direction of moving stimuli: Electrophysiological correlates of hierarchical feature selection. *Perception & Psychophysics, 58*(2), 191–206.

Attig, E., Jacquy, J., Uytdenhoef, P., & Roland, H. (1993). Progressive focal degenerative disease of the posterior associative cortex. *Canadian Journal of Neurological Science, 20*, 154–157.

Baddeley, A. (1996). Short term memory for word sequences as a function of acoustic, semantic, and formal similarity. *Quarterly Journal of Experimental Psychology, 18*, 362–365.

Baddeley, A. (1986). *Working memory.* Oxford: Clarendon Press.

Baillargeon, R. (1993). The object concept revisited. In C. Granrud (ed.), *Visual perception in cognition and infancy.* Hillsdale, NJ: Lawrence Erlbaum Associates.

Bavelier, D. (1992). *Phonological repetition blindness.* Ph.D. dissertation, Massachusetts Institute of Technology.

Bavelier, D. (1994). Repetition blindness between visually different items: The case of pictures and words. *Cognition, 51*, 199–236.

Bavelier, D., & Jordan, M. I. (1992). A dynamic model of word recognition. In C. L. Giles, S. J. Hanson, & J. D. Cowan (eds.), *Advances in neural information processing Systems* (Vol. 5, pp. 879–886). San Mateo, CA: Morgan Kaufman.

Bavelier, D., & Potter, M. C. (1992). Visual and phonological codes in repetition blindness. *Journal of Experimental Psychology: Human Perception and Performance, 18*(1), 134–147.

Bavelier, D., Prasada, S., & Segui, J. (1994). Repetition blindness between words: Nature of the orthographic and phonological representations involved. *Journal of Experimental Psychology: Learning, Memory and Cognition, 20*(6), 1437–1455.

Bavelier, D., & Segui, J. (1990). Perceptual integration and repetition blindness in sentence processing. Unpublished manuscript.

Baylis, G. C., Driver, J., & Rafal, R. D. (1993). Visual extinction and stimulus repetition. *Journal of Cognitive Neuroscience, 5*, 453–466.

Behrmann, M., Zemel, R. S., & Mozer, M. C. (1998). Object-based segmentation and occlusion: Evidence from normal subjects and a computational model. *Journal of Experimental Psychology: Human Perception and Performance, 24*, 1011–1036.

Benson, R., Davis, C., & Snyder, C. R. R. (1988). Posterior cortical atrophy. *Archives of Neurology, 45*(7), 789–793.

Chialant, D., & Caramazza, A. (1997). Identity and similarity factors in repetition blindness: Implications for lexical processing. *Cognition, 63*(1), 79–119.

Conrad, R. (1964). Acoustic confusion in immediate memory. *British Journal of Psychology, 55*, 75–84.

Duncan, J. (1984). Selective attention and the organization of visual information. *Journal of Experimental Psychology: General, 113*(4), 501–517.

Egly, R., Driver, J., & Rafal, R. D. (1994). Shifting visual attention between objects and locations: Evidence from normal and parietal lesion subjects. *Journal of Experimental Psychology: General, 123*(2), 161–177.

Fagot, C., & Pashler, H. (1995). Repetition blindness: Perception or memory failure? *Journal of Experimental Psychology: Human Perception and Performance, 21*(2), 275–292.

Ferrand, L., & Grainger, J. (1992). Phonology and orthography in visual word recognition: Evidence from masked non-word priming. *Quarterly Journal of Experimental Psychology, 45A*(3), 353–372.

Forster, K. I., & Davis, C. (1991). The density constraint on form-priming in the naming task: Interference effects from a masked prime. *Journal of Memory and Language, 30,* 1–25.

Forster, K. I., & Shen, D. (1996). No enemies in the neighborhood: Absence of inhibitory neighborhood effects in lexical decision and semantic categorization. *Journal of Experimental Psychology: Learning, Memory, and Cognition, 22*(3), 696–713.

Grainger, J. (1990). Word frequency and neighborhood frequency effects in lexical decision and naming. *Journal of Memory and Language, 29,* 228–244.

Grainger, J., O'Regan, J. K., Jacobs, A. M., & Segui, J. (1989). On the role of competing word units in visual word recognition: The neighborhood frequency effect. *Perception & Psychophysics, 45*(3), 189–195.

Henderson, L. (1985). Toward a psychology of morphemes. In A. W. Ellis (ed.), *Process in the psychology of language* (vol. 1, pp. 15–72). Hillsdale, NJ: Lawrence Erlbaum Associates.

Hinton, G. E. (1990). Mapping part–whole hierarchies into connectionist networks. *Artificial Intelligence, 46,* 47–75.

Humphreys, G. W., Evett, L. J., & Quinlan, P. T. (1990). Orthographic processing in visual word identification. *Cognitive Psychology, 22,* 517–560.

Humphreys, G. W., & Riddoch, M. J. (1994). Attention to within-object and between-object spatial representations: Multiple sites for visual selection. *Cognitive Neuropsychology, 11*(2), 207–241.

Jared, D., McRae, K., & Seidenberg, M. S. (1990). The basis of consistency effects in word naming. *Journal of Memory and Language, 29,* 687–715.

Kahneman, D., Treisman, A. M., & Gibbs, B. J. (1992). The reviewing of object files: Object-specific integration of information. *Cognitive Psychology, 24,* 175–219.

Kanwisher, N. G. (1986). Repetition blindness: Type recognition without token individuation. Ph.D. dissertation, Massachusetts Institute of Technology.

Kanwisher, N. G. (1987). Repetition blindness: Type recognition without token individuation. *Cognition, 27,* 117–143.

Kanwisher, N. G. (1991). Repetition blindness and illusory conjunctions: Errors in binding visual types with visual tokens. *Journal of Experimental Psychology: Human Perception and Performance, 17,* 404–421.

Kanwisher, N. G., & Driver, J. (1992). Objects, attributes, and visual attention: Which, what, and where. *Psychological Science, 1*(1), 26–31.

Kanwisher, N. G., Driver, J., & Machado, L. (1995). Spatial repetition blindness is modulated by selective attention to color and shape. *Cognitive Psychology, 29,* 303–337.

Kanwisher, N. G., & Potter, M. C. (1990). Repetition blindness: Levels of processing. *Journal of Experimental Psychology: Human Perception and Performance, 16,* 30–47.

Keele, S. W., Cohen, A., Ivry, R., Liotti, M., & Yee, P. (1988). Tests of a temporal theory of attentional binding. *Journal of Experimental Psychology: Human Perception and Performance, 14*(3), 444–452.

Kramer, A. F., & Jacobson, A. (1991). Perceptual organization and focused attention: The role of objects and proximity in visual processing. *Perception & Psychophysics, 50*(3), 267–284.

Lesch, M. F., & Pollatsek, A. (1993). Automatic access of semantic information by phonological codes in visual word recognition. *Journal of Experimental Psychology: Learning, Memory, and Cognition, 19*(2), 285–294.

Leslie, A. M., Xu, F., Tremoulet, P. D., & Scholl, B. J. (1998). Indexing and the object concept: Developing "what" and "where" systems. *Trends in Cognitive Science, 2*(1), 10–18.

Lukatela, G., Carello, C., & Turvey, M. T. (1990). Phonemic priming with words and pseudowords. *European Journal of Cognitive Psychology, 2*, 375–394.

Luo, C. R., & Caramazza, A. (1996). Temporal and spatial repetition blindness: Effects of presentation mode and repetition lag on the perception of repeated items. *Journal of Experimental Psychology: Human Perception and Performance, 22*(1), 95–113.

MacKay, D. G., & Miller, M. D. (1993). Semantic blindness: Repeated concepts are difficult to encode and recall under time pressure. *Psychological Science, 5*, 52–55.

McClelland, J. L., & Rumelhart, D. E. (1981). An interactive activation model of context effects in letter perception: I. An account of basic findings. *Psychological Review, 88*, 375–407.

Mozer, M. C. (1989). Types and tokens in visual letter perception. *Journal of Experimental Psychology: Human Perception and Performance, 15*(2), 287–303.

Neville, H. J., Kutas, M., Chesney, G., & Schmidt, A. L. (1986). Event-related brain potentials during initial encoding and recognition memory of congruous and incongruous words. *Journal of Memory and Language, 25*, 75–92.

Paller, K. A. (1990). Recall and stem-completion have different electrophysiological correlates and are modified differently by directed forgetting. *Journal of Experimental Psychology: Learning, Memory and Cognition, 16*, 1021–1032.

Park, J., & Kanwisher, N. G. (1994). Determinants of repetition blindness. *Journal of Experimental Psychology: Human Perception and Performance, 20*, 500–519.

Perfetti, C. A., & Bell, L. C. (1991). Phonemic activation during the first 40 ms of word identification: Evidence from backward masking and priming. *Journal of Memory and Language, 30*, 473–485.

Potter, M. C., & Faulconer, B. A. (1975). Time to understand pictures and words. *Nature, 253*, 437–438.

Printzmetal, W. (1995). Visual feature integration in a world of objects. *Current Directions in Psychological Science, 4*(3), 90–94.

Pylyshyn, Z. W. (1989). The role of location indexes in spatial perception: A sketch of the FINST spatial-index model. *Cognition, 32*, 65–97.

Rapp, B. C. (1992). The nature of sublexical orthographic organization: The bigram trough hypothesis examined. *Journal of Memory and Language, 31*, 33–53.

Ruchkin, D. S., Canoune, H. L., Johnson, R., & Ritter, W. (1995). Working memory and preparation elicit different patterns of slow wave event-related brain potentials. *Psychophysiology, 32*(4), 399–410.

Rugg, M. D. (1995). Event-related potential studies of human memory. In M. S. Gazzaniga (ed.), *The cognitive neurosciences.* Cambridge, MA: MIT Press.

Schendan, H. E., Kanwisher, N. G., & Kutas, M. (1997). Early brain potentials link repetition blindness, priming and novelty detection. *Neuroreport, 8*(8), 1943–1948.

Sears, C. R., Hino, Y., & Lupker, S. J. (1995). Neighborhood size and neighborhood frequency effects in word recognition. *Journal of Experimental Psychology: Human Perception and Performance, 21*(4), 876–900.

Segui, J., & Grainger, J. (1990). Priming word recognition with orthographic neighbors: Effects of relative prime–target frequency. *Journal of Experimental Psychology: Human Perception and Performance, 16*(1), 65–76.

Segui, J., & Grainger, J. (1992). Neighbourhood frequency and stimulus frequency effects: Two different but related phenomena? In J. Alegria, D. Holender, J. J. deMorais, & M. Radeau (eds.), *Analytic approaches to human cognition* (pp. 183–192). Amsterdam: Elsevier.

Smolensky, P. (1990). Tensor product variable binding and the representation of symbolic structures in connectionist systems. In *Artificial intelligence* (vol. 46, pp. 159–216). Amsterdam: Elsevier Science Publishers.

Spelke, E. S. (1990). Principles of object perception. *Cognitive Science, 14*, 29–56.

Taft, M. (1991). *Reading and the mental lexicon*. Hillsdale, NJ: Lawrence Erlbaum Associates.

Theios, J., & Amrhein, P. C. (1989). Theoretical analysis of the cognitive processing of lexical and pictoral stimuli: Reading, naming, and visual and conceptual comparisons. *Psychological Review, 96*(1), 5–24.

Thorpe, S., Fize, D., & Marlot, C. (1996). Speed of processing in the human visual system. *Nature, 381*, 520–522.

Treisman, A. M. (1988). Features and objects: The fourteenth Bartlett memorial lecture. *Quarterly Journal of Experimental Psychology, 40A*(2), 201–237.

Treisman, A. M. (1991). The perception of features and objects. In A. Baddeley & L. Weiskrantz (eds.), *Attention: selection, awareness, and control. A tribute to Donald Broadbent* (pp. 1–51). Oxford: Oxford University Press.

Treisman, A. M., & Schmidt, H. (1982). Illusory conjunctions in the perception of objects. *Cognitive Psychology, 14*, 107–141.

Wickelgren, W. A. (1965). Short term memory for repeated and non-repeated items. *Quarterly Journal of Experimental Psychology, 17*, 14–25.

Wickelgren, W. A. (1966). Associative intrusions in short-term recall. *Journal of Experimental Psychology: 24*, 295–340.

Xu, F., & Carey, S. (1996). Infants' metaphysics: The case of numerical identity. *Cognitive Psychology, 30*, 111–153.

Yantis, S. (1992). Multielement visual tracking: Attention and perceptual organization. *Cognitive Psychology, 24*, 295–340.

Yin, C., Wojciulik, E., & Kanwisher, N. G. (1993 May). *Codes mediating repetition blindness for pictures: Phonological, visual or conceptual?* Poster paper presented at the 3rd annual West Coast Attention Conference.

Zemel, R. S., & Behrmann, M. (1996 April). *A computational unification of object and spatial attention*. Paper presented at the 3rd meeting of the Cognitive Neuroscience Society, San Francisco.

Chapter 8

Phonological Codes in Reading Comprehension, Short-Term Memory, and Memory for Rapid Visual Sequences

Veronika Coltheart

Evidence of phonological coding has frequently been reported in studies of reading comprehension and short-term memory, and various questions have been asked about phonological codes in reading and memory tasks. How are phonological codes obtained from written words? Are the phonological codes observed in reading tasks the same as those supporting recall in memory tasks? What function, or functions, do these phonological codes serve? More recently, since the demonstrations of phonological repetition blindness (Bavelier & Potter 1992), further questions can be posed. What is the relationship between phonological codes affecting phonological repetition blindness and those which are influential in word recognition and short-term memory paradigms?

This chapter will review evidence concerning the role of phonological coding in reading comprehension, in short-term memory list recall, in recall of words presented at fast RSVP rates of up to 10 words per second, and in phonological repetition blindness.

Phonological Codes in Reading Comprehension

Single-Word Comprehension

The role of phonological representations in single-word comprehension has been assessed in semantic categorization tasks in which inappropriate homophones have been used (Banks, Oka, & Shugarman 1981; Coltheart, Avons, Masterson, & Laxon 1991; Jared & Seidenberg 1991; Van Orden 1987; Van Orden, Johnston, & Hale 1988). In these experiments, a semantic category (e.g., A PART OF THE BODY) was briefly presented, and subjects had to decide whether the word that followed was a member of the category. The incidence of false positive responses to homophone foils (PART OF BODY: HARE) was higher than to orthographic control words (PART OF THE BODY: HARP). These results led Van Orden and his colleagues (Van Orden 1987; Van Orden et al. 1988) to conclude that phonological codes mediate comprehension of single written words.

A second question considered in this research has concerned the procedure by which the phonological representation is obtained. A contrast is drawn between a lexical lookup process and a nonlexical assembly of phonology through the use of letter-sound rules (Coltheart 1978; Coltheart, Curtis, Atkins, & Haller 1993). The operation of these alternative procedures was assessed by presenting real-word and pseudo homophones (nonwords that sound like real words). Van Orden et al. (1988) presented both types of foils to subjects in a categorization experiment and concluded, on the basis of similar error rates on real and nonword homophone foils, that assembled phonology is required to access word meanings. However, other experiments have found higher error rates for real-word homophone foils than for pseudo homophones (Coltheart et al. 1991; Coltheart, Patterson, & Leahy 1994).

Various findings challenge strong conclusions about the obligatory role of phonology in access to meaning. In categorization experiments, orthographic similarity of exemplar to homophone foil (e.g., HAIR/HARE) is matched to the orthographic similarity of exemplar to control foil (HAIR/HARP). In English, the degree of orthographic overlap between pairs of homophones varies quite widely, with some pairs differing in only one letter (DEER/DEAR) and others having low orthographic similarity (EIGHT/ATE). The level of orthographic similarity between foil and exemplar determines whether a homophone effect occurs. When both homophone and control foils have high orthographic overlap with the exemplar (as in exemplar MEAT, foils MEET/MELT), the homophone effect is large, whereas when orthographic overlap is lower (ROSE, ROWS/ROBS), the homophone effect is small (Van Orden 1987) or nonsignificant (Coltheart et al 1994; Jared & Seidenberg 1991). A significant homophone effect for othographically dissimilar foils has been demonstrated only under conditions of backward pattern masking of the target word (Van Orden 1987, experiment 2), and this result, which has yet to be replicated, was obtained with a very small stimulus set. Thus, the evidence indicates that the activation of a homophone of the presented word will occur only if the presented word is sufficiently orthographically similar to its homophone.

The size and nature of the semantic category also determine the extent to which homophone effects occur. Van Orden (1987) used narrow, specific, small categories like PART OF A MOUNTAIN (exemplar PEAK, foils PEEK/PECK) and obtained the homophone effect for both high- and low-frequency foil words. With much broader categories (such as LIVING THING or OBJECT), the homophone effects in Jared and Seidenberg (1991) were restricted to low-frequency foils. Category size probably reflects the extent of priming of relevant category instances by prior presentation of the category name: PART OF A HORSE'S EQUIPMENT is likely to activate correct exemplars when few exist (BRIDLE, STIRRUP, SADDLE, . . .). Then, if the subsequent target word is BRIDAL, its phonological representation will match one that is already active. By contrast, the large number of LIVING THINGS reduces the probability of significant pretarget activation of any specific instance. Consequently, the use of highly specific categories with small sets of exemplars has provided an exaggerated estimate of the extent of phonological effects in written word comprehension.

Lexical frequency of the exemplar also determines the size of the homophone effect (Jared & Seidenberg 1991; Van Orden 1987). Jared and Seidenberg (1991) found, for the category LIVING THINGS, that there was a significant homophone effect for foils like FLEE (correct exemplar FLEA, a low-frequency word) but not for foils like HOARSE (correct exemplar HORSE, a high-frequency word). Both of the *foil* words are of low frequency here. The exemplar frequency effect might reflect lack of knowledge of the word's spelling. Error rates are likely to be increased when subjects are uncertain about the correct spelling of homophonic words. The subjects may lack fully specified orthographic representations of the words presented. For example, 15% of the *non-word* homophones (e.g., SUTE) used by Van Orden et al. (1988) were accepted as real words in an untimed lexical decision task.

Instructions to the subject regarding misspelled target words determine whether homophone effects occur (Coltheart et al. 1991). If subjects are not told to reject misspellings, they may assume that these were unintentional typing errors by the experimenter. Furthermore, the fact that misspellings of common words frequently occur in brand names and shop signs (e.g., LITE ALE, NITE-N-DAY, KLEEN MAID) may encourage a greater tolerance of incorrect spelling.

In our studies (Coltheart et al. 1994), spelling knowledge was assessed, and we demonstrated that the homophone effect is not merely caused by uncertainty about a word's correct spelling. However, such uncertainties produce inflated estimates of phonological effects. Incomplete knowledge of orthography could lead to errors on low-frequency homophones; for instance, a subject may recall that there is a word for a weather phenomenon (sleet) and have a phonological representation linked to the appropriate semantic representation, but may have no orthographic representation of it. Such a subject would be at chance if asked to select the correct spelling from SLEAT and SLEET. After our categorization experiments (Coltheart et al. 1994), we tested homophone spelling knowledge of each critical exemplar, and discarded errors in the categorization data corresponding to an error in the spelling knowledge test. The problems presented by spelling uncertainty are illustrated by the following anecdote. I corresponded with a psycholinguist some time ago about phonological effects and used the following example of a typical stimulus, A TYPE OF JEWELRY: BROACH. He replied that he could not see what was wrong with this example until he read my references to BROOCH a few lines later. He then recognized BROOCH and recalled it as a word with irregular spelling-to-sound correspondence. In this case, spelling of the exemplar was known, but the word was so infrequently encountered in print that a phonologically appropriate spelling was accepted as correct. Thus, it is imperative to ensure that subjects understand task requirements and to assess their knowledge of the critical words' spellings and meanings. Few studies have done so. Failure to do this is likely to lead to overestimates of the contribution of phonological codes to written word comprehension.

Sentence and Phrase Comprehension
The contribution of phonological codes to sentence and phrase comprehension has been studied for a longer period. Investigators used a variety of reading tasks to investigate phonological coding. An early study by Kolers (1966) examined speeded oral reading of mixed French and English text by French–English bilinguals. Kolers observed frequent translation errors; for instance, "His horse, followed de deux bassets, faisait la terre resonner under its even tread" was read aloud as "His horse, suivi by deux hounds. . . ." He concluded that semantic representations were accessed prior to access to phonological representations. Potter (personal communication) has noted that the result can better be explained by the Potter–Lombardi sentence regeneration theory, in which a sentence is represented propositionally and then expressed from that base—a person reading aloud is usually reading ahead and representing meaning, which could easily lead to the translations Kolers observed.

A different conclusion can be drawn from experiments that required acceptability judgments for phrases (Baron 1973) or sentences (Doctor & Coltheart 1980; Treiman, Freyd, & Baron 1983). In these tasks the sentence or phrase contains a homophone of an appropriate word, and the sentence or phrase is semantically unacceptable but *sounds* right. Various experiments (Coltheart et al. 1991; Coltheart, Laxon, Rickard, & Elton 1988; Doctor & Coltheart 1980; Treiman et al. 1983) demonstrated a significantly higher rate of false positive errors for incorrect sentences with homophones of an appropriate word (e.g., *The none says her prayers.*) than for sentences with an incorrect word of equivalent orthographic similarity to the appropriate word (e.g., *The nine says her prayers.*) Some studies (Coltheart et al. 1988; Treiman et al. 1983) showed that the phonological effects were not simply due to subjects' imperfect knowledge of homophone meanings and spellings. Thus, the phrase and sentence acceptability tasks provide evidence of some degree of phonological involvement in reading comprehension.

The phonological effects are found for exception words such as *through*, as well as for words that are regular in spelling-to-sound correspondence, such as *throne* (Coltheart, Avons, & Trollope 1990; Coltheart et al. 1991). Furthermore, there appears to be no reliable correlation between error rate and orthographic similarity between the foil and appropriate homophone: *through* and *threw* are less similar than are pairs like *week* and *weak*. When sentences contain nonword homophones of the appropriate word, such as *bloo*, significant phonological effects are not reliably found and error rates are low (Coltheart et al. 1990, 1991). Theories of word recognition that incorporate localized representations, such as an orthographic input lexicon (Coltheart, Curtis, Atkins, & Haller 1993), characterize phonological effects that are confined to real-word foils as postlexical.

Perhaps the phonological effects in sentence-evaluation tasks arise at later stages, such as those required for sentence comprehension; phonological codes may not be required for the comprehension of single printed words. In sentence reading, the phonological code may be a later, postlexical representation that maintains information in a phonological short-term store (Baddeley 1986). The later phonological code may provide a backup representation for sentence comprehension while syntactic and/or semantic analyses are performed. It should be noted that neuropsychological and normal data have suggested that a phonological code may be required only at late (postsyntactic) stages in the comprehension of longer sentences containing many propositions (Waters, Caplan, & Hildebrandt 1987). Consistent with this idea of a late phonological representation, it has also been found that these effects are abolished by concurrent irrelevant articulation, as are phonological effects in short-term memory tasks (Coltheart et al. 1990). Thus, if concurrent articulation abolishes phonological effects in both sentence evaluation and short-term memory, and the latter is obviously postlexical, then the former is likely to be, too.

Conclusions

This review of phonological effects indicates some similarities and differences in the pattern of effects obtained in single-word comprehension and sentence comprehension. In both, phonological effects are manifested in increased error rates but not in reliable increases in decision times. In single-word comprehension, phonological effects are obtained only when foils and homophone exemplars are orthographically very similar, and increased error rates are sometimes observed with pseudo homophone foils. In contrast, in sentence comprehension, phonological effects are confined to real-world homophones, and the orthographic similarity between the foil and appropriate homophone appears to be unimportant. These differences suggest that different phonological codes arise in word and sentence comprehension. However, both may be the result of automatic processes that serve no useful role in reading comprehension but cannot be inhibited.

Phonological Coding in Short-Term Memory

Next I consider the role of phonological coding in short-term memory. Since the time of Wundt at the turn of the twentieth century, we have known that there are limits on our immediate memory span for short lists of unrelated letters, digits, words, and objects, when these lists are presented at a rate of about 1 second per item and when the lists are recalled in order of presentation. Conrad (1964) demonstrated that for visually presented consonant lists, memory errors resemble acoustic confusions arising in a listening task. Subsequently, Baddeley (1966) showed that phonologically similar words are harder to recall than are dissimilar-sounding words. These results led to the formulation of theories that postulated the existence of a short-term memory store with a rehearsal process used to retain briefly presented stimuli (Atkinson & Shiffrin 1968; Waugh & Norman 1965). Later, Baddeley and Hitch (1974) developed a theory of short-term working memory consisting of a central executive system served by two slave systems: the visuospatial sketchpad and the phonological loop. The phonological loop (Baddeley 1986), which consists of a phonological short-term store and a rehearsal process, is the system used for the recall of rapidly presented lists. Visually presented items are registered in the phonological short-term store after they have been phonologically recoded (in the case of written words) or after their names have been retrieved (in the case of objects or pictures of them). The phonological short-term store was assumed to be limited in capacity and duration, so that memory traces required maintenance by rehearsal. Evidence consistent with this theoretical account consists of several reliable findings.

The Phonological Similarity Effect and Concurrent Articulation

Lists of phonologically similar items (letters, words, or pictures with similar names) are recalled less accurately than are lists of dissimilar items (e.g., Baddeley 1966; Schiano & Watkins 1981; Wickelgren 1965). For visually presented lists, this phonological similarity effect is removed if subjects are required to engage in repetitive, irrelevant articulation (saying "the, the, the, . . ." or "1, 2, 3, 4, 5, 1, 2, 3, 4, 5, . . .") when the list is shown (e.g., Coltheart 1993b; Murray 1968). Baddeley (1986) argued that concurrent articulation disrupts both phonological recoding and rehearsal. Given that, with auditory presentation, the phonological similarity effect survives concurrent articulation, Baddeley (1986) argued that the locus of the phonological similarity effect is the phonological short-term store, and that concurrent articulation has prevented access of visual items to this store.

The Word-Length Effect and Concurrent Articulation
The finding that lists of short words are better recalled than are lists of long words is termed the word-length effect (Baddeley, Thomson, & Buchanan 1975; Coltheart et al. 1990). This effect is removed by concurrent articulation (for both visual and auditory lists). Baddeley et al. (1975) found a positive correlation between memory performance and speech rate for the list words, and argued that the word-length effect was caused by a limited-capacity rehearsal loop. Thus, fewer long than short words can be rehearsed. The relevant word-length variable may be the number of phonemes/syllables, or it may be the duration of the utterance (Baddeley & Andrade 1994; Caplan & Waters 1994).

The Operation of the Rehearsal Process
The rehearsal process, formerly termed articulatory rehearsal, was assumed to involve articulatory mechanisms and to take place in real time at a rate comparable with that of overt speech. Evidence for this view of rehearsal comes from attempts to measure overt speech rate for the words used to constitute short and long word lists. Speech rate has typically been measured by timing speeded repeated articulations of the words used in the memory tasks (Baddeley et al. 1975). A further assumption has been that covert speech proceeds at the same rate as overt speech, a view that appears to depend on the results of a single paper by Landauer (1962). Later studies by Anderson (1982), MacKay (1981), and Marshall and Cartwright (1978, 1980) all found that inner speech is faster than overt speech. The difference between the two rates seems to be on the order of 15–25%. The idea that the rehearsal loop's capacity is equivalent to the amount of speech that can be articulated in 1.5–2 sec appears to arise from the finding of a significant positive correlation between speech rate and memory span (Baddeley et al. 1975), but such a correlation does not imply that the rates are equal.

Lists of Limited or Unlimited Word Pools
Many experimenters investigating short-term memory have used a small set of items from which lists were chosen. This procedure was

introduced by Conrad (1964) and subsequently used by Baddeley (1966) in most of the studies that followed. In Baddeley's (1966) experiments, sets of 8 or 10 words were used (8 or 10 similar words and 8 or 10 dissimilar words), and lists were repeatedly sampled from these small word sets. Furthermore, the subjects were familiarized with these word sets, which were often visible throughout the task. The rationale, occasionally mentioned, seems to have been the assumption that short-term working memory is specialized for the encoding of order information, and that demands of item encoding should be minimized. This restricts what we can say about short-term memory in situations where the same small set of items must repeatedly be recalled.

A few experiments have used tasks in which words were new for every list. La Pointe and Engle (1990) contrasted performance on repeatedly sampled lists with that on lists of unrepeated words, and manipulated word length and concurrent articulation. They replicated the effect of word length and concurrent articulation on lists from small subsets of words: short words were better recalled than were long words, an advantage that was removed by concurrent articulation. The word-length effect was also obtained when lists were composed of new words on every trial, but the word-length effect *survived* concurrent articulation. As noted by Neath and Nairne (1995), this result is hard to reconcile with any current theory of short-term working memory.

It could be argued that item encoding is more difficult for long than for short words, that fewer long than short words can be rehearsed, and that fewer long words can be transferred to a limited-capacity output buffer. Consequently, the reduced recall for long words might arise from limits on encoding, rehearsal, *and* output storage and processes. However, when words are repeatedly sampled from a small, familiar set, item encoding might be achieved by registering the first letter or syllable of long words, or some element smaller than the entire word. An abbreviated code is less likely to suffice when words are new and unpredictable on every trial. Thus, the word-length effect might arise chiefly from rehearsal and output processes when words are repeatedly selected from a small pool. These processes are disrupted by concurrent articulation, and the word-length effect is removed. In contrast, when words are new on every trial, encoding processes make substantial contributions to the word-length effect, and encoding processes are not (or are less) disrupted by concurrent articulation. Hence a word-length effect remains with concurrent articulation.

The results obtained when unlimited word pools are used to select phonologically similar and dissimilar lists are as follows (Coltheart 1993b). When words are new on every trial, the phonological similarity effect is obtained; concurrent articulation removes this effect (as it does for limited word pool lists). Thus, both phonological similarity and word-length affect recall when fresh words are presented in every list, and *item* as well as order encoding is required.

Recall of Rapidly Presented Visual Sequences and Repetition Blindness

The research of Forster (1970) and Potter (1976) demonstrated that sentences or pictures shown at the rate of about 10 items per second can be comprehended. Such lists appear to leave only fleeting memories, but sentences of 12 or more words can be recalled. This contrasts with the very inferior recall of unrelated word lists shown at such fast rates (Potter 1984, cited in Potter 1993). Potter (1993) argued that words and pictures are capable of rapidly activating semantic and conceptual representations, along with scene- and sentence-parsing mechanisms, in long-term memory. These temporarily active representations can be regarded as a form of very short-term conceptual memory. (A comprehensive account of very short-term conceptual memory is presented in chapter 2 of this volume.)

There are a number of phenomena observed at fast rates of visual presentation that are not found at the slower rates typical of short-term memory tasks in which items are shown at the rate of 1 per second. At much faster rates of 8–10 items per second, the attentional blink (Raymond, Shapiro, & Arnell 1992) and repetition blindness (Kanwisher 1987) are observed. The attentional blink refers to a reduced accuracy in the detection of a second target in a list when it occurs soon after the first target (see chapter 5 in this volume). Repetition blindness refers to reduced accuracy when reporting both occurrences of a repeated list item, with the second occurrence usually being omitted (see chapter 6 in this volume). Different forms of explanation have been offered for these two types of phenomena. The repetition blindness phenomenon is particularly interesting because it occurs when the critical items are orthographically similar (but not identical) and when they are phonologically identical but differ orthographically, as noted earlier (Bavelier & Potter 1992). It is also interesting in that the task demand is similar to that in short-term memory experiments, as subjects are asked to recall the list shown. Furthermore, concurrent articulation had no effect on either recall or repetition blindness with lists shown at 117 msec per item. It has been argued that rehearsal is not possible at these fast rates of presentation (Bavelier & Potter 1992).

Even if rehearsal proceeds faster than the rates of overt speech, as discussed earlier, it seems reasonable to claim that presentation rates of 8–10 items per second are too fast for rehearsal. For visually presented lists to be rehearsed, the words must be recognized, their phonological forms must be retrieved, inner speech forms must be generated, and the "inner speech" must be "heard" by the "inner ear." It does not seem likely that these processes can occur when words are presented at rates of 8–10 per second.

Support for this view is provided by the evidence of phonological and orthographic repetition blindness exhibited when stimuli are successively presented at fast rates (Bavelier & Potter 1992). People have difficulty in reporting an item that is phonologically identical to an earlier stimulus. This difficulty rapidly diminishes over a period of about half a second, and does not occur at the much slower presentation rates of standard short-term memory tasks. If the phonological codes that are the basis for short-term memory recall cannot readily be established at rates of 8–10 words per second, how is recall achieved and why does phonological repetition blindness occur? The fact that repetition blindness and recall were unaffected by concurrent articulation in Bavelier and Potter's (1992) study supports the view that recall of rapidly presented stimuli is not mediated by the phonological codes arising in short-term memory tasks as a consequence of rehearsal. Bavelier and Potter (1992) proposed that it arises from an early phonological code used in the initial registration of an item in STM (tokenizing). They noted Besner and Davelaar's (1982) distinction between phonological codes in word recognition and those used to maintain items in short-term memory. Establishment of the former appeared to be unaffected by concurrent articulation, which appeared to disrupt the short-term memory codes (Besner 1987).

If phonological effects in short-term memory arise from phonological coding and rehearsal processes that can occur only at slower rates of presentation, these effects might not occur at fast rates of presentation. The next section reports the results of experiments that studied phonological similarity effects on recall of rapidly presented lists.

Phonological Similarity and RSVP List Recall
We conducted three experiments (Coltheart & Langdon 1995, 1998) that aimed to establish the temporal conditions under which phonological similarity effects occurred. The first experiment investigated whether phonological similarity affected recall when lists were presented at both fast (9 words and 4 words per second) and more conventional short-term memory rates (2 words per second). Lists of 5 words were selected from large word pools. The rationale was that the conditions would resemble those which occur when lists of words, pictures, and sentences are shown at fast rates. As in Baddeley's (1966) experiments, the words were 3 letters long and similar words contained *a*, such as *map, cat, map, pat*. Dissimilar words matched the similar ones in word

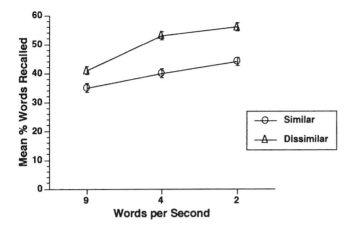

Figure 8.1
Mean percentage of words recalled (with standard error bars) from phonologically similar
and dissimilar lists shown at different rates. (Based on Coltheart & Langdon 1998.)

frequency, used all the vowels, and had a more varied set of consonants,
for example, *mop, vet, cow, pen, day.* The subjects had to complete written
recall of the lists in order of presentation.

The mean percentage of words recalled in correct order is shown
for the two types of lists and for each of the three presentation rates in
figure 8.1. Significantly fewer words were recalled from phonologically
similar lists (39.5%) than from dissimilar lists (50%). Increasing presentation time improved recall from 38% of list words at 9 words per
second to 50% of list words at 2 words per second. The phonological
similarity effect (6%) was significant at the fastest rate, but was significantly smaller than at the slower rates (13%). Recall was also scored
with order disregarded, and phonological similarity still significantly
impaired recall (49% versus 57% words recalled). Thus, the phonological similarity effect was not merely the consequence of scoring item-
order information.

A second experiment investigated the influence of presentation rate
and manipulated recall instructions. The effects of free and serial recall
instructions were compared. The presentation rates were 9, 6, and 4
words per second, and instructions were manipulated as a between-
subjects factor.

The mean percent correct recall for free and serial recall instructions
and the three rates of presentation are shown in figure 8.2. List recall
was significantly higher under free recall instructions (50% of words)
than under serial recall instructions (42% of words), but instruction

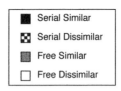

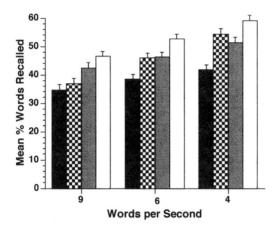

Figure 8.2
Mean percentage of words recalled (with standard error bars) from phonologically similar and dissimilar lists shown at different rates with serial and free recall instructions. (Based on Coltheart & Langdon 1998.)

type did not interact with phonological similarity or presentation rate. Phonologically similar lists were significantly less well recalled than were dissimilar lists: 42% versus 49%. Increasing presentation time significantly improved recall from 40% at the fastest rate to 52% at 4 words per second. The phonological similarity effect was not significant (3%) at the fastest rate, but was significant at the slower rates (7% and 10%, respectively).

The results of both experiments showed that phonological similarity impaired recall at much faster rates of presentation than those used in short-term memory research. The difficulty in recalling phonologically similar lists was also demonstrated by a significantly higher level of omissions in recall for these lists in both experiments.

The phonological similarity effect was not produced by the requirement for order information as it occurred with free recall. In fact, the instructions did not interact significantly with either phonological similarity or rate of presentation. The higher recall scores obtained when item order was disregarded chiefly occurred because, although

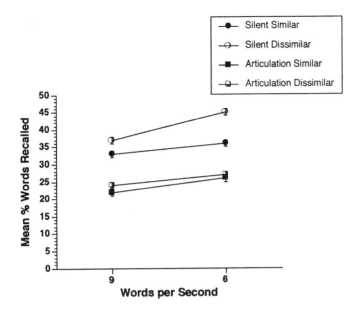

Figure 8.3
Mean percentage of words recalled (with standard error bars) from phonologically similar and dissimilar lists shown at different rates in silent or concurrent articulation condition. (Based on Coltheart & Langdon 1998.)

words were typically recalled in presentation order, the subjects often did not correctly indicate the location of omitted items.

Thus, phonological coding is possible even when lists are presented at rates about 6 to 9 times those used in short-term memory research. The effect of phonological similarity increased with slower rates of presentation, but the size of the effect, 12–13% at 4 words per second, was similar to that found with the standard 1 second presentation rate of 14% (Coltheart 1993b).

A third experiment investigated effects of concurrent irrelevant articulation on recall of lists of phonologically similar and dissimilar words shown at two fast rates of presentation (9 and 6 words per second). The results are shown in figure 8.3. Phonological similarity significantly reduced recall. Recall was significantly better at the slower rate than at the faster rate. Concurrent articulation also significantly reduced recall. The interaction between phonological similarity and the articulation condition was significant, and arose because phonological similarity significantly impaired recall *only* in the silent condition and not in the articulation condition.

The results of these experiments demonstrated a significant detrimental effect of phonological similarity when lists are presented in the normal silent condition. When subjects had to engage in irrelevant concurrent articulation, recall was reduced and there was no longer a significant effect of phonological similarity of list items. These results are typically observed when lists are presented at the much slower rate of 1 item per second in short-term memory tasks (e.g., Coltheart 1993b; Murray 1968).

However, dissimilar list recall is much higher at the slower rate of 1 word per second (83% in Coltheart 1993b). The low levels of recall of dissimilar lists shown at fast rates suggest that there are limits on the rate at which phonological and other representations can be activated and stabilized to support recall. The fact that phonological similarity further reduced recall indicates that the phonological representations established at fast rates are not qualitatively different from those generated when the slower STM rates are used. Support for this suggestion is provided by the effects of irrelevant concurrent articulation in the third experiment: it reduced recall and removed the phonological similarity effect. As already noted, the detrimental effects of phonological similarity and the effects of concurrent articulation are not simply due to the requirement of correct order in recall. When free recall criteria were used, the same detrimental effects of phonological similarity and concurrent articulation were observed.

The main difference between recall for lists shown at fast rates and those shown at slower rates are in the incidence of intrusions and omissions. At fast rates, recall is characterized by frequent omissions that increase as a function of phonological similarity and presentation rate, and in the articulation condition. At slower presentation rates, omissions are less common and intrusions are more likely to occur. Intrusions were infrequent with fast rates, and were unaffected by the articulation condition. They were, however, more common for phonologically similar lists and for the slower presentation rate. Intrusions are likely to be the result of combinations of phonologically similar traces, and slower rates of presentation are more likely than faster rates to increase the probability of the establishment of memory traces, even of weak or partial representations.

It has already been argued that rehearsal is unlikely to occur when lists are shown at the fast rates of 6 and 9 words per sec, used in the experiments described above. What are the mechanisms by which concurrent irrelevant articulation reduces recall? Gupta and MacWhinney (1995) argued that concurrent irrelevant articulation reduces both general processing capacity and articulatory resources, and causes interference with phonological traces through the production of irrelevant sounds (speech). Furthermore, the auditory interference could be external (hearing one's own speech) and/or could arise internally through bone conduction. Gupta and MacWhinney (1995) report evidence implicating *all* of these processes.

Returning to the effects of concurrent articulation on recall of rapidly presented lists, it could be argued that concurrent articulation lowered overall recall by increasing general processing demands and by causing external auditory interference. However, heard irrelevant speech does not remove the phonological similarity effect for lists presented visually at a rate of 1 word per second (Boyle & Coltheart 1996). Consequently, the removal of the phonological similarity effect by concurrent articulation in the experiment mentioned above may be due to the disruption of phonological output processes and/or storage. In any event, these experiments with fast RSVP rates have indicated phonological similarity effects comparable to those found in short-term memory paradigms.

Word Length and RSVP List Recall
As stated earlier, word length is a potent influence on short-term memory recall. Short (monosyllabic) words are better recalled than are long (polysyllabic) words (Baddeley et al. 1975). The effects of word length were studied in two experiments using lists presented at fast rates (Coltheart & Langdon, 1998). Large word pools were used to construct lists. The effects of free and serial recall instructions were investigated.

Mean percentages of words recalled at different rates of list presentation and with serial and free recall instructions are shown in figure 8.4. Recall scores were significantly higher with free recall instructions and scoring than with serial recall instructions and scoring: 66% and 48%. Short words were significantly more likely to be recalled than were long words: 63% vs. 50%. Recall improved significantly with a slower rate of presentation, from 47% at 9 words per second to 65% at 4 words per second. The word-length effect was significantly smaller at the fastest rate (9%) than at the slower rates (14% and 16%, respectively). Subjects were more likely to omit words when recalling lists of long words (36%) than when recalling lists of short words (22%). Omissions were also more frequent with faster rates of presentation: 38% versus 20% at 4 words per second.

This experiment clearly showed that lists of long words were harder to recall than were lists of short words: the word-length effect. This effect occurred even at the fastest rate of presentation (9 words per second). It affected performance with free recall instructions as well as with serial recall instructions. The increase in recall at slower rates occurred for both serial and free recall instructions.

Previously, the word-length effect on recall was attributed to limits on the rehearsal process (Baddeley et al. 1975), although this explanation has been questioned. A second experiment investigated the effects

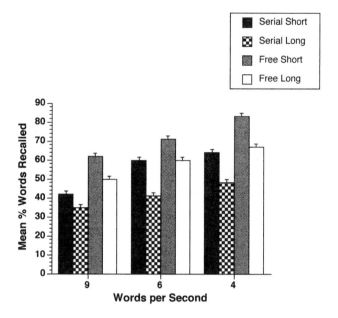

Figure 8.4
Mean percentage of words recalled (with standard error bars) from lists of short and long words shown at different rates with serial and free recall instructions. (Based on Coltheart & Langdon 1998.)

of concurrent articulation on the recall of short and long words. Lists were shown at 6 and 9 words per second in normal, silent conditions and when subjects were engaged in concurrent irrelevant articulation.

Mean percentages of words recalled in correct serial position are shown in figure 8.5. Recall of lists of short words (41%) significantly exceeded recall of lists of long words (36%). The slower rate of presentation significantly increased recall from 36% to 41%. Concurrent articulation reduced recall from 46% to 32%. There was a significant interaction between concurrent articulation, presentation rate, and word length: word-length effects were significant only in the silent conditions and were larger at 6 words per second than at 9 words per second: 14% and 7%, respectively. Recall was also scored without regard to order, and a similar pattern of results was found.

The incidence of omissions was significantly higher after concurrent articulation (45%) than in the silent condition (36%); with fast presentation rate, 43% versus 38%; and with long words, 46% versus 34%. Recall intrusion rates were unaffected by articulation and presentation rate, but were significantly higher for lists of short words (10%) than for lists of long words (5%).

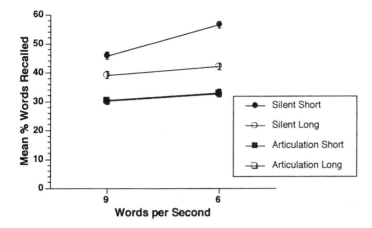

Figure 8.5
Mean percentage of words recalled (with standard error bars) from lists shown at different rates in silent or concurrent articulation condition. (Based on Coltheart & Langdon 1998.)

The results of these two experiments showed that word length affected recall in the silent condition at both fast rates of presentation, and that the advantage of short over long words increased with the slower presentation rate. Concurrent articulation both reduced recall and removed the advantage of short words. These effects have been reported at rates of 1 word per second and 1 word per 2 seconds in research on short-term memory when words are repeatedly used in lists and item encoding is minimized. It has already been argued that rehearsal is unlikely to occur when lists are shown at the fast rates of 6 and 9 words per second. At such rates, limitations on encoding as well as on output processes are likely to cause the word-length effect. Concurrent articulation may have interfered with encoding through its general, dual task demands, as well as through its more specific effects on output processing and storage.

Conclusions
The RSVP experiments described above demonstrated that it is difficult to recall lists of words when they are presented at fast rates of 6–9 words per second. Recall dropped to about 50% of the level attained when lists are presented at 1 word per second. Despite this, there was evidence to indicate that phonological codes were established at 9 words per second, and at 4 words per second the phonological similarity effect was comparable in magnitude with that found at 1 word per second. Furthermore, concurrent articulation eliminated the phonological similarity effect, as it did at slow rates of presentation.

Word length of list items also affected recall even at the fastest rates, and the word-length effect increased in magnitude with slower presentation rates. Again, concurrent articulation removed the word-length effect, as it does in STM tasks. These results are more striking, given that they occurred when lists words were new on every trial and not repeatedly selected from small, familiarized sets. Thus, the effects of phonological similarity and word length are not confined to recall situations that minimize item encoding and simply require retention of item order. Moreover, the phonological similarity and word-length effects were observed when order was not a requirement, and free recall instructions and scoring criteria are used. The findings indicate that phonological coding has a pervasive role in supporting item recall in immediate memory tasks using very fast presentation rates and constantly changing items. This indicates a continuity between processes supporting recall at fast RSVP rates and those of the much slower standard STM tasks. However, phonological representations are not likely to be the only ones supporting recall. Semantic, conceptual, and orthographic representations are also likely to support recall, which, even at the fastest rates used in these experiments, did not decrease to 0 with phonologically similar words.

Recall of Rapidly Presented Pictures

Phonological similarity effects on STM recall have been found when subjects are asked to recall short lists of pictures whose names are similar or dissimilar (Schiano & Watkins 1981). This phonological similarity effect is removed by concurrent articulation. Robyn Langdon and I (1998) investigated the phonological similarity effect for picture lists shown at fast (8 per second) and slower (1 per second) STM rates.

Research on picture naming by Potter and Faulconer (1975) showed that people are slower to name pictures than they are to name words. Moreover, for pictures shown at RSVP rates, Intraub (1979) showed that the time to name pictures did not predict their likelihood of being recognized. Consequently, fast rates of presentation might not permit retrieval of their names and, hence, phonological coding. The subjects were presented with lists of 5 pictures selected from the Snodgrass and Vanderwart (1984) set, with a few drawn by R. Langdon, that had similar or dissimilar monosyllabic names. All the similar names in a list shared their vowel phoneme and had some consonant phonemes shared with other names, for instance, *duck, cup, gun, jug, glove*. Four sets of 5 lists of 5 pictures were selected, each set sharing a vowel phoneme (*a* as in *hat*, *e* as in *bed*, *o* as in *dog*, and *u* as in *cup*). Four sets of 5 lists of 5 pictures having dissimilar names were also selected, such

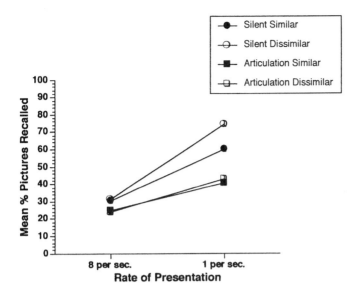

Figure 8.6
Mean percentage of pictures recalled (with standard error bars) from lists with phonologi-cally similar and dissimilar names shown at different rates in silent or concurrent articula-tion condition.

as *phone, leaf, ring*. The selected pictures had similar and dissimilar names that were matched in word frequency, orthographic neighbor-hood size (N), and length (number of letters). The pictures were initially presented twice in a picture-naming task to establish that subjects recognized the pictures and to ensure that they gave the names appro-priate to the condition in which they were used in the subsequent lists. The experimenter corrected any alternative names given by subjects and asked them to use the designated name.

The lists were then presented at one of two rates: 8 per second and 1 per second. Half the lists at each rate were presented in silent condi-tions and half while the subject engaged in concurrent articulation (counting from 1 to 5 repeatedly). Lists were blocked by rate and articulation condition, with 5 lists with similar names and 5 with dissim-ilar names within each block. Order of lists within blocks was random-ized, and order of blocks was counterbalanced across subjects. Recall was written in booklets.

The results are shown in figure 8.6, which presents mean percentages of pictures recalled in each condition. Analyses of the data indicated significantly higher recall at the slower presentation rate (55% versus 28%), and a significant reduction in recall in the concurrent articula-

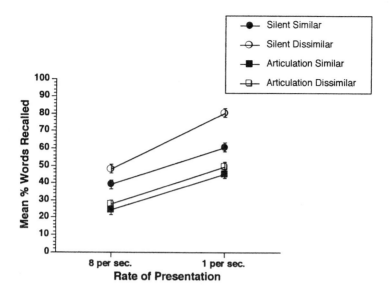

Figure 8.7
Mean percentage of picture names recalled (with standard error bars) from lists with
phonologically similar and dissimilar names shown at different rates in silent or concurrent articulation conditions.

tion condition (from 49% to 33%). Pictures with similar names were
significantly harder to recall (60%) than those with dissimilar names
(75%) only in the silent condition when shown at 1 per second. At the
fast rate, phonological similarity of picture names did not affect recall,
nor was there any effect on recall in the concurrent articulation condition.

This experiment showed that phonological similarity of their names
did not affect recall of pictures when they were shown at fast rates.
We attributed this to the difficulty of retrieving names when pictures
were shown at fast rates. However, it is possible that the level of
similarity of the names may not have been sufficient to generate an
effect at fast rates of presentation. Consequently, we conducted a second experiment in which a new set of subjects was presented lists of
the written names of the pictures shown at the same rates of 8 per
second and 1 per second. As in the previous experiment, concurrent
articulation was also manipulated.

The results are presented in figure 8.7, which shows that the level
of recall was higher than it was for the pictures corresponding to the
names. Recall increased at the slower rate (from 35% to 59%), and
phonological similarity reduced recall at both fast and slow rates of

presentation in the silent condition. Concurrent articulation reduced recall and removed the phonological similarity effect. Thus, performance on the picture names shown at fast rates was comparable with that on the other phonologically similar and dissimilar lists studied in the experiments reported earlier in this chapter.

Taken together, the results of these two experiments on memory for pictures of their written names show that evidence of phonological coding is not obtained with fast presentation when the names of list items cannot be retrieved in the time available before the next item appears. Consequently, fleeting memories established at fast presentation rates of up to 10 items per second may be based on phonological codes, but only if the items' names can be retrieved at those rates. Such retrieval is possible for monosyllabic written words but not for pictures of common objects.

Phonological Repetition Blindness

Although there appears to be a continuity in the effects of phonological similarity, word length, and concurrent articulation at fast and slow presentation rates, some phenomena, such as repetition blindness, occur at fast visual presentation rates but not at the slow (1 word per second) rates used to assess short-term memory span. Kanwisher (1987) found that when a sentence contained a repeated word, subjects had difficulty in recalling both words, with the second one more commonly omitted. This phenomenon was observed with lists as well as with sentences, and when the repeated items were words, letters, or numbers. Orthographic similarity between a pair of words was sufficient to cause some degree of repetition blindness as well. Kanwisher (1987) proposed the following account. RSVP stimuli activate their type nodes in long-term memory. Episodes are recorded by the establishment of token nodes representing serial order and other forms of contextual information. A process of token individuation links type and token nodes. Repetition blindness was assumed to occur through a failure of token individuation. When a type node has been assigned to a token, it is briefly unavailable for a second token individuation (see chapter 6 in this volume for Kanwisher et al.'s current theoretical account).

Repetition blindness is not confined to identical or orthographically similar stimuli. Bavelier and Potter (1992) demonstrated the existence of phonological repetition blindness. When sentences contained a pair of homophones (e.g., Last night Bob ate the eight cookies in the box.), recall of the second homophone was reduced compared with recall of an orthographically and phonologically unrelated word in control sentences. Phonological repetition blindness was also found when homophones were presented in short lists shown at fast rates (8–10 words per second). When concurrent articulation of "da da da da ..." was required during sentence presentation, recall of the noncritical words remained at about 90%, and the extent of repetition blindness was unaffected. This led Bavelier and Potter (1992) to conclude that phonological repetition blindness involves an "early" phonological code used in registration of items in STM, rather than a later code generated by short-term memory rehearsal. However, their experiments obtained repetition blindness using homophone pairs of *low* orthographic similarity, such as *one/won* and *ate/eight*. Thus, the phenomenon of phonological repetition blindness, like the phonological effects in sentence comprehension, is not dependent on a high level of orthographic similarity between homophones, whereas phonological effects in word recognition and comprehension *are* usually dependent on high levels of orthographic similarity between homophone/pseudo homophone pairs.

It has been argued that repetition blindness arises from a failure of token individuation (Kanwisher 1987) or, in the case of phonological repetition blindness, registration of phonological codes in STM (Bavelier & Potter 1992). If concurrent articulation does not interfere with the phonological encoding of individual words, then it is unlikely to affect phonological repetition blindness. The fact that it also had no effect on sentence recall indicates that semantic access and sentence parsing mechanisms do not depend on the articulatory resources that are required for concurrent articulation.

Homophone Effects with RSVP Sentences
The following experiments (Coltheart 1993a) investigated the relationship between phonological codes invoked during sentence reading and those causing repetition blindness. The first investigated whether phonological effects occur at faster rates of sentence presentation when words are presented sequentially. The second investigated the effects of concurrent articulation on recall of RSVP sentences.

A set of 80 6-word sentences, half of which were acceptable English and half of which were semantically and/or syntactically unacceptable, were devised. Half of the unacceptable sentences *sounded* acceptable but contained an inappropriate homophone (e.g., The none says her prayers aloud.) and half sounded unacceptable and contained a word orthographically matched to the homophone that should have been used (e.g., The nine was in church today.) The sentences were adapted from those used in experiment 1 of Coltheart et al. (1991). Two versions of the unacceptable sentences were constructed. In the second, the assignment of homophone and control word to sentence frame was

Table 8.1
Mean percent errors in evaluation of unacceptable sentences presented at RSVP rates and simultaneously

Presentation Rate	Homophone	Control
7 words/second	23	17
4 words/second	14	10
Simultaneous	15	8

reversed. Thus, the examples above appeared as *The none was in church today.* and *The nine says her prayers aloud.*

The unacceptable homophones and orthographic control words were matched on word frequency, length, and orthographic similarity. The unacceptable word occurred equally often at the beginning, middle, and end of a sentence. The acceptable sentences also contained a homophone or a word orthographically similar to it, but these were correctly used, and were different from the homophone and control words used in the unacceptable sentence sets.

Sentences were shown sequentially, 1 word at a time, in the center of a computer screen at either 4 words or 7 words per second in 2 RSVP conditions. Each sentence was preceded by the word *Ready*, followed by a blank screen. In the third condition, all words appeared simultaneously on the screen in one line. The subjects were instructed to read and decide whether each was an acceptable English sentence whose words were appropriate and correctly spelled.

Mean percent of errors for unacceptable sentences are shown in table 8.1. Analyses showed that the error rate for sentences with homophones (that *sounded* right) was significantly higher than the error rate for sentences with orthographic controls (that sounded wrong). Presentation rate also significantly affected decision accuracy: error rates were significantly higher at 7 words per second than at 4 words per second. Error rates at 4 words per second did not differ significantly from error rates for simultaneously presented sentences whose reading rate was subject-paced. The error rate for acceptable sentences was also affected by presentation rate, with the highest error rate for 7 words per second (13%) and lower rates at 4 words per second (9%), which did not differ significantly from the error rate for simultaneously presented sentences (6%).

The results of this experiment showed that subjects have difficulty in evaluating unacceptable sentences with homophones that sound right, and that this difficulty is manifested in increased error rates. Although accuracy was lower at 7 words per second, the homophone

Table 8.2
Mean percent errors in sentence evaluation for unacceptable sentences presented at 7 words per second in silent and concurrent irrelevant articulation conditions

Condition	Homophone	Control
Silent	18	13
Concurrent articulation	22	26

effect was present. Thus, the phonological code that causes errors in sentence evaluation was present at the typical rate at which repetition blindness is observed. Bavelier & Potter (1992) found that repetition blindness was unaffected by concurrent articulation, and they concluded that repetition blindness is caused by an early phonological code that is used in word recognition and to establish an initial registration of an event in short-term memory. In contrast, phonological codes in short-term memory tasks and in printed sentence evaluation are abolished by concurrent articulation

Concurrent Articulation and Sentence Evaluation
The second experiment examined the effects of concurrent articulation on the evaluation of sentences shown at 7 words per second. A set of 120 acceptable and unacceptable 6-word sentences was presented to subjects in silent conditions or while they performed a concurrent articulation task (repetitive counting).

Mean error rates are presented in table 8.2. Concurrent articulation significantly increased errors on unacceptable sentences, and there was a significant interaction between homophony and concurrent task. There was a significant homophone effect in the silent condition, but during concurrent articulation this effect was removed. Concurrent articulation had no effect on accuracy of decisions as to acceptable sentences (mean errors equal to 10% in both conditions).

Thus, when subjects were required to read and comprehend sentences shown word by word at a rapid rate, phonological codes caused errors in sentence evaluation. If subjects performed a concurrent irrelevant articulation task during reading, then the phonological code was removed, as it is when subjects read sentences shown under normal conditions (Coltheart et al. 1990). Thus, the sentence evaluation task appears to invoke a phonological code that, like short-term memory codes, is susceptible to concurrent articulation.

The finding that concurrent articulation did not impair performance on acceptable sentences has also been obtained when sentence words are presented simultaneously (Coltheart et al. 1990). This suggests that

Table 8.3
Mean percentage joint recall of words 1 and 2 and mean percentage total recall for
sentences with repeated words, pairs of homophones, and controls shown at 7 words
per second in silent and concurrent articulation conditions

| | Type of Repetition | | | |
| | Same thrown/thrown | | Homophone sword/soared | |
	Repeated	Control	Repeated	Control
Mean % joint recall of words 1 & 2				
Silent	30	41	25	40
Concurrent articulation	20	20	16	24
Mean % recall of all words				
Silent	80	81	82	83
Concurrent articulation	73	70	75	72
Mean % recall of all words of filler acceptable sentences				
Silent		95		
Concurrent articulation		91		

a phonological code is consulted primarily when an anomaly is encountered and extra processing of a sentence, backtracking, or reanalysis is
needed.

Recall of Sentences with Repeated Words and Homophone Pairs
Two further experiments aimed to discover whether repetition blindness occurred with the sorts of sentences used in the sentence evaluation
task, and whether concurrent articulation affected sentence recall and
repetition blindness. In the first experiment, phonological repetition
blindness was studied by adding a homophone of an earlier word in
unacceptable sentences similar to those used in sentence evaluation.
Phonological repetition blindness was contrasted with the effects of
repeating an identical word from the sentence, and the effects of concurrent articulation were examined. Control sentences were also
included.

Sentences were shown 1 word at a time at 7 words per second. The
subjects were informed that some sentences had inappropriate words,
or words in the wrong order, and might contain repeated words, and
were asked to write down each sentence exactly as they saw it after
its presentation. The incidence of repetition blindness was assessed by
calculating the number of trials on which *both* of the critical target words
were recalled. Recall of both the repeated-word and the unrepeated

(control) sentences indicated that homophone substitutions sometimes occurred—for instance, "The flower fell off the bush," where *flower* has been substituted for *flour* by the subject. In fact, recall often showed a tendency to omit or reorder words so that the sentence became acceptable.

The mean percents of sentences on which *both* target words were recalled are shown in table 8.3. Analysis of these scores showed that the 2 target words were less likely to be recalled when sentences contained a repetition than when they did not. These omissions did not differ for the two types of repetition: same word or homophone of earlier word. Concurrent articulation lowered recall, and there was a trend for a larger repetition effect in silent conditions than during articulation.

Overall recall of sentences (see table 8.3) was reduced by concurrent articulation. Recall of the acceptable filler sentences was significantly higher than that of the various types of unacceptable sentences, whose recall (80–83%) did not differ significantly. The interaction between sentence type and concurrent articulation was also significant, and arose because articulation impaired recall of unacceptable sentences but not of the acceptable filler sentences.

In this experiment, a repetition blindness effect had occurred: subjects were less likely to report both members of a pair of words that were identical (*thrown/thrown*) or that were homophones (*soared/sword*) than they were to report unrepeated pairs. The repetition effect for a pair of homophones did not differ significantly from that for a pair of identical words. Bavelier and Potter (1992) had found a larger repetition effect for repeated identical words than for homophones. The difference may be due to the fact that Bavelier and Potter's (1992) homophone pairs were more orthographically dissimilar (e.g., *eight/ate*) than those used in the experiment reported here. Other research has shown that orthographic as well as phonological similarity contributes to repetition blindness (Kanwisher 1987; Bavelier 1994).

However, concurrent articulation both impaired recall and appeared to reduce the repetition blindness effect. Similar results have been found in sentence evaluation tasks in which accuracy is reduced and phonological effects are abolished. In sentence evaluation tasks these effects were observed with *unacceptable* sentences, and performance on *acceptable* sentences was unaffected by concurrent articulation. The repetition effect had been explored with unacceptable sentences in order to permit a more direct comparison with the data on phonological effects in sentence evaluation. Additionally, repetition blindness has been reported for both word lists and sentences (Bavelier and Potter 1992; Kanwisher 1987). However, unacceptable sentences may involve an extra processing load for the reader who is attempting to parse and integrate the words on-line as they are presented.

The second experiment, therefore, investigated concurrent articulation and repetition effects with both acceptable *and* unacceptable sentences. Since the major purposes of the experiment was to explore phonological repetition blindness, the repeated target word pairs were homophones (*through/threw*). Eighty 7-word sentences were adapted from sentences used in the sentence evaluation tasks. There were 5 types:

1. Unacceptable sentence with homophone repetition (e.g., He *through* away *threw* the old rubbish).
2. Unacceptable control sentence (e.g., She *pact* the *threw* old coat away).
3. Acceptable sentence with homophone repetition (e.g., Rebels have *thrown* the king's *throne* away).
4. Acceptable control sentences (e.g., Impostors were *flung* from the *throne* previously).
5. Acceptable filler sentences (e.g., They went on a long *cruise* recently.

Note that target word 1 in the unacceptable control sentence (*pact*) was also a homophone of a word that would have been appropriate in the sentence (*packed*), and that for both homophone and control sentences, if target word 2 is omitted, the sentence *sounds* acceptable (He *through/pact* away the old rubbish.).

The effect of repetition was, again, assessed by comparing the incidence of joint recall of *both* target words for homophone pair and control sentences. The mean percentages are shown in table 8.4. Analysis of recall of both word 1 and word 2 indicated that repetition significantly reduced recall (35% and 48% for repeated and unrepeated pairs). Recall of word pairs from acceptable sentences (58%) was significantly higher than recall of pairs from unacceptable sentences (25%). Concurrent articulation impaired recall (36% vs 47%). There was a significant interaction between repetition and sentence acceptability because the repetition effect was significantly larger for acceptable sentences (19%) than it was for unacceptable sentences (7%). Finally, the interaction between concurrent articulation and sentence acceptability was also significant: concurrent articulation reduced recall of word pairs from *acceptable* sentences (by 16%), but for unacceptable sentences the difference in recall of target word pairs (5%) only approached significance.

The mean overall recall score for all words in a sentence is shown for each condition in table 8.4. Analysis of these scores indicated that

Table 8.4
Mean percentage joint recall of words 1 and 2 and mean percentage total recall for sentences with homophones and controls shown at 7 words per second in silent and concurrent articulation conditions

	Sentence Type			
	Unacceptable		Acceptable	
	Repeated	Control	Repeated	Control
Mean % recall of W1 & W2				
Silent	22	33	58	74
Concurrent articulation	20	24	39	60
Mean % recall of all words				
Silent	80	78	85	88
Concurrent articulation	76	74	78	80

repetition did not affect overall recall. Acceptable sentences were better recalled than were unacceptable sentences. Concurrent articulation impaired recall; however, even for unacceptable sentences, 75% of words were recalled. Finally, the interaction between sentence acceptability and articulation was significant. Concurrent articulation significantly impaired recall of both acceptable and unacceptable sentences, but its effect was larger for acceptable sentences.

Inspection of the recall data indicated that subjects tended to "regularize" both types of unacceptable sentences. In recall, sentences were transformed into an acceptable form through reordering and word substitutions (e.g., "The reign wet the rain ground outside." became "The ground was wet from the rain outside."). An analysis of the incidence of these types of "regularized" recalls showed that they were significantly more frequent during concurrent articulation (35%) than in silence (27%). The incidence of these responses did not differ for sentences with and without repetitions, nor was the interaction between articulation and repetition significant. An even higher percentage of recalls was phonologically acceptable but retained an inappropriate homophone (e.g., "The due glittered on rain the petals." was transformed to "The due glittered on the petals."). Again, the transformations were more frequent in the articulation condition (68%) than in the silent one (62%). These paraphrasings and regularizations of sentences are reminiscent of recall of sentences by conductive aphasics who have a very reduced memory span (Saffran & Marin 1975, chapter 9).

The results of this experiment indicated clear evidence of phonological repetition blindness. Subjects were less able to recall both members of a pair of words such as *through/threw* than they were to recall control pairs such as *pact/threw*. This repetition blindness occurred both when sentences were acceptable and when they were unacceptable. Interestingly, the repetition blindness was greater for acceptable sentences that became unacceptable when the repeated word was omitted (e.g., "The king was thrown from his _____ previously .") than it was for unacceptable sentences. However, the recall of the critical word pairs in unacceptable sentences was much lower than recall of these pairs in acceptable sentences. Again, as in the previous experiment, concurrent articulation impaired recall. Concurrent articulation had a greater effect on recall of word pairs from acceptable sentences than on recall from unacceptable sentences. However, concurrent articulation did *not* interact with repetition blindness.

Thus, repetition blindness appears to have occurred during concurrent articulation as well as during silent reading, as it did in Bavelier and Potter's (1992) study, which used only acceptable sentences. If the effects of homophone substitution and repetition blindness reflect the functioning of a rapidly activated phonological code, then the derivation of this code appears to be unaffected by concurrent articulation. Both the list recall and the repetition blindness paradigms require subjects to generate and maintain 2 or more similar phonological representations. Concurrent articulation disrupts this process, as does a fast presentation rate. Phonological repetition blindness does not appear to arise through an early lexical access code. If it did, then, as noted earlier, repetition blindness would be unlikely to occur with orthographically very dissimilar homophones such as *eight/ate* and with Arabic numerals and words (*3/three*). Thus, there are probably no fundamental differences among the phonological representations that reduce recall of list words, provoke errors in evaluation of unacceptable sentences, and cause repetition blindness.

At the same time, it is apparent that phonological codes are not the only ones subserving list and sentence recall. Orthographic and semantic representations are also invoked during RSVP tasks. In the sentence recall experiments reported above, transformations of the unacceptable sentences to acceptable forms were common, and supported Potter's (1993) postulation of a very fleeting conceptual memory that can be used to comprehend sentences presented at fast RSVP rates and that must be used to reconstruct the sentence in recall.

In the experiments I have reported so far, phonological repetition blindness was assessed by the usual method of asking subjects to recall words presented at fast rates. In the experiments described below, attempts were made to investigate effects of homophone repetition in tasks that did not require recall, as well as in those which did.

Phonological Repetition Blindness and Semantic Categorization

The following 4 experiments investigated phonological and ortho-graphic repetition blindness. The first experiment investigated whether repetition blindness occurred for phonologically identical or ortho-graphically related words, and whether orthographic similarity affected repetition blindness, using the normal recall method. Subjects had to recall sequences of 4 rapidly presented words. The critical words (word 1 and word 2) were the first and third words in each list. There were 6 types of trials: word 1 was a homophone of word 2, or word 1 was orthographically related to word 2, or word 1 and word 2 were unrelated; these critical word pairs also varied in their level of ortho-graphic similarity (high versus low). The predictions were that repeti-tion blindness would occur for homophone pairs and orthographically related pairs, and that the magnitude of repetition blindness would vary with orthographic similarity.

In the second experiment, recall was not required. Instead, this exper-iment examined whether subjects were able to access semantic informa-tion about the second word and to decide whether the list included a member of a previously designated semantic category (e.g., PART OF THE BODY). On the trials of interest, word 2 was a category exemplar and word 1 and other list words were not. If repetition blindness occurs through limitations on retrieval processes supporting recall (a Ranschburg effect), then categorization accuracy should not be affected by the prior occurrence of the related word 1.

As in Bavelier and Potter's experiments, lists consisted of 4 words plus 3 symbol sequences (&&&&&); subjects had to recall the words but not the symbols in the first experiment. Items used for the critical word 1 and word 2 for both experiments were based on a pool of 68 orthographically highly similar and 68 orthographically less similar homophone pairs. For the highly similar set, the mean orthographic similarity (OS) between homophones of a pair was .74 (e.g., *bred/bread*), whereas the mean OS for the less similar homophone pairs was .44 (e.g., *knows/nose*). One member of each pair was an exemplar of an easily described category, such as PART OF THE BODY, while the other was unrelated to that category (e.g., *knows/nose*). For each homo-phone pair, another word was selected to be as orthographically similar to the exemplar as the homophone was. Thus, there were 68 ortho-graphic controls for the highly similar homophone pairs (e.g., *bead* for *bread*) and 68 orthographic controls for the less similar homophone pairs (e.g., *snows* for *nose*). The sets of homophones and orthographic controls were matched on word frequency. For the baseline condition, a final set of 136 words was selected so as to be orthographically dissimilar to the exemplar but matched in word frequency to the homophones and orthographic controls.

Versions of the experiment were constructed so that the critical word 2 was preceded by its homophonic mate, its orthographic control, or an unrelated word in different versions. No subject saw a homophone more than once, and in the recall experiment, each subject saw a total of 102 lists with 17 lists in each of the 6 conditions described in table 8.5. Trials began with a blank screen with a central fixation X shown for 715 msec, then a blank screen for 429 msec, followed by four words and three symbol strings presented for 129 msec each. Finally, a blank screen appeared and remained on view during subjects' recall. The two critical words (word 1 and word 2) were always separated by an unrelated word and a symbol string. One or 2 symbol strings always preceded word 1. Another unrelated word, or an unrelated word and another symbol string, followed word 2. This allowed word 1 and word 2 to be in fixed positions relative to each other while varying where word 1 and word 2 appeared in a list. Written recall was required.

Repetition blindness was assessed by scoring the number of trials on which *both* critical words were recalled. The mean percentages are shown for each condition in table 8.5. The effects reported were significant by items as well as by subjects. Recall of the critical words differed significantly as a function of type of word pair. Evidence for phonological repetition blindness is provided by the fact that recall of homophone pairs (15%) was significantly worse than recall of orthographically related pairs (20%). Additionally, there was reliable evidence for orthographic repetition blindness: orthographically related pairs of words were significantly less well recalled than were unrelated pairs of words (20% vs. 44%).

This recall experiment yielded evidence of both phonological and orthographic repetition blindness. As stated above, the second experiment did not require recall. Instead, the same lists were preceded by a category description appropriate for each list. Subjects were asked to decide whether the sequence contained a word belonging to the category stated before the list, such as A FOUR-FOOTED ANIMAL or A FOOD. Difficulty in detecting an exemplar preceded by a similar word would be evidence of repetition blindness.

In the categorization experiment, there were 8 conditions. In addition to the 6 conditions in the recall experiment, 2 conditions assessed the extent to which false alarms to the inappropriate homophone (word 1) occurred. Thus, there were trials in which the inappropriate homophone was word 1 and no exemplars were presented. On experimental "Yes" trials, the category exemplar was the third word and was pre-

Table 8.5
Mean percentage joint recall of words 1 and 2 for lists with related and unrelated words

Orthographic similarity of words 1 and 2	Relationship of Word 1 to Word 2		
		Orthographically	
	Homophone	Related	Unrelated
Low	15	24	45
High	14	17	44
Mean	15	20	44

ceded by either no related words or by 1 of the 4 types listed below as the first list word:

1. An orthographically similar homophone (*dear/deer*)
2. An orthographically similar control word (*deep/deer*)
3. An orthographically dissimilar homophone (*knows/nose*)
4. An orthographically dissimilar control word (*knots/nose*)

On experimental "No" trials, there was an inappropriate homophone of an exemplar (e.g., *bred* or *knows*. On the remaining negative instance trials, none of the words was related to the category. All the negative instance trials consisted of words and symbol strings, as did the positive trials.

Forty new subjects from the same population participated in the categorization experiment. The subjects' knowledge of the correct spellings of the lower-frequency homophones used as category exemplars was tested after the experimental task, and those with poor knowledge of spelling were excluded. All subjects had spelling test scores greater than or equal to 90% correct.

The two pools of 68 word sets were each divided into 4 subsets of 17 experimental lists that included the following:

1. Both homophones
2. An orthographically related word and a homophone exemplar
3. A homophone exemplar only
4. A homophone foil only.

Four versions of the lists were prepared so that critical words appeared only once in each. An additional 23 filler positive trials were constructed, and the exemplar appeared as first, second, or fourth word in these trials. Finally, 91 negative instance trials were also constructed. These, too, consisted of 4 word and 3 symbol sequences, as did the positive trials. Thus, in total there were 125 positive and 125 negative instance trials.

The presentation conditions were the same as in the previous experiment, with the following changes to trial structure. Trials began with a blank screen with a central fixation X for 715 msec, then a blank screen for 429 msec, followed by the category label for 2431 msec and another blank screen for 429 msec. The list of 4 words plus three symbol strings was shown for 129 msec each, as before, and a blank screen for 3100 msec was present in the intertrial interval.

Categorization accuracy for each condition is shown in table 8.6. Hit rates were significantly reduced when the word preceding the exemplar was a homophone or an orthographically similar word. The interaction between type of preceding word and orthographic similarity was also significant. For word pairs high in orthographic similarity, exemplars preceded by a homophone or an orthographically related word were more likely to be missed than were exemplars preceded by an unrelated word. For word pairs low in orthographic similarity, only exemplars preceded by homophones were missed more often than were those preceded by unrelated words. Thus, phonological identity is sufficient to reduce detection of a subsequent word in a categorization task. Orthographic similarity reduces exemplar detection only if the level of similarity is high.

False Alarms for Sequences of Negative Instances
The mean percentages of false alarms on negative trials containing homophones highly similar or less similar to their exemplar mates, along with false alarms to trials with unrelated words only, are shown in table 8.7. Significant differences in false alarms occurred for different types of foils. More false alarms occurred for homophone foils that were highly orthographically similar to an exemplar than for those less orthographically similar, and more false alarms occurred for low-similarity homophones than for unrelated words.

This experiment showed that when subjects are required to read a rapidly presented list and to decide whether any of the words belong to a previously designated category, they are less likely to detect an exemplar that is preceded by a homophone or an orthographically very similar word. This is evidence for phonological and orthographic repetition blindness in a task that does not require recall or report of list items. It is interesting that this reduction in exemplar detection was found in conditions provoking false alarms. When the inappropriate homophones were presented as the first word in the list, they provoked significantly more false alarms than did lists of unrelated negative

Table 8.6
Mean percentages of hit rates for sequences with positive instances

Orthographic Similarity of Words 1 and 2	Type of Related Preceding Word		
	Homophone	Orthographic Control	Unrelated
Low	63	72	76
High	63	64	76
Mean	63	68	76

instances. Thus, it seems likely that the miss rates for lists with homophone pairs underestimate the true levels of phonological repetition blindness, especially for very similar homophone pairs.

The results support explanations of repetition blindness that assume phonological repetition blindness occurs as the result of failure of encoding processes. They could also be accommodated by a type activation/token individuation account if it is assumed that successful semantic categorization requires token individuation (Kanwisher 1987). A more detailed account of the judgments or tasks requiring token individuation must be formulated. An argument must be made as to why type activation is insufficient to permit semantic categorization. As already noted, an encoding deficit provides a possible explanation. Difficulty in encoding an orthographic and or phonological lexical representation will cause difficulty in accessing a word's semantic representation (Luo & Caramazza 1995).

Semantic Priming Experiments

The semantic categorization task may demand conscious, explicit access to the category exemplar. Consequently, the results reported above do not discriminate between the refractoriness of encoding and the failure of token individuation explanations of phonological and orthographic repetition blindness. The experiments described below aimed to establish whether semantic information about word 2 is activated in a task that did not require any overt response to word 2. They follow up a paradigm developed by one of my students, Nicole Bateman (1994). She combined an RSVP list (like those of Bavelier & Potter 1992) with a lexical decision semantic priming task. In her first experiment, she presented RSVP lists of lowercase words and symbols followed by an uppercase target word. On some trials, the target was semantically related to the preceding word. The subjects' task was to make a speeded lexical decision about the final uppercase letter string and then to recall

Table 8.7
Mean percentage false alarms for sequences of negative instances, by type of foil

Homophone		
Similar	Dissimilar	Unrelated
24	10	4

the (lowercase) word list. Some lists contained homophone pairs that normally yield repetition blindness, and recall was worse for these pairs of words than it was in the control conditions in which there were no homophone pairs. On some trials, the target word was semantically related to the preceding word, which was the critical word 2.

The question of interest was whether, on the related trials, the critical word 2 could facilitate the decision about the semantically related target following it. Bateman found no evidence of semantic priming for targets following a homophone pair, but no semantic priming occurred in the baseline condition either—that is, when word 2 was not preceded by a homophone, and therefore not subject to repetition blindness. However, lexical decisions were rather slow and variable in this dual task. In a second experiment in which recall was not required, but in which subjects had to monitor list length, she found semantic priming in the control baseline condition and not in the (repetition blindness) homophone condition.

Robyn Landgon and I followed up these experiments using more items, additional controls, and a more homogeneous target word set. We also made the lexical decision item easier to detect by printing it in blue and preceding it with white list words. The following five conditions were included:

1. Repeated semantic
   @@@ &&&& none wade nun \\\\\ PRIEST
2. Semantic control
   @@@ &&&& box wade nun \\\\\ PRIEST
3. Homophone control
   @@@ &&&& none film wade \\\\\ PRIEST
4. Repetition control
   @@@ &&&& some box sum \\\\\ PRIEST
5. Unrelated control
   @@@ &&&& tile box sum \\\\\ PRIEST

The third condition was included as a control for possible phonologically mediated semantic priming by word 1, and the fourth was a control for any possible effect of homophone repetition on subsequent lexical decision. Primes in the conditions above were all homophones, had an average length of 4.6 letters, and were matched on word frequency and orthographic neighborhood size. The lexical decision word and nonword targets were similar in length and orthographic neighborhood size, and the word frequencies of experimental and filler target words were also matched. The lists were preceded by the word READY, and each contained 2 symbol strings, 3 words, another symbol string, and then the target word or nonword. The symbol strings varied in type and length (3–5 symbols) within and between lists. These lists were presented at a rate of approximately 9 items per second (114 msec), and the uppercase lexical decision target printed in blue remained on view for 1141 msec.

Experiment 1: List Recall
In the first experiment, evidence of repetition on list recall was assessed by inclusion of 40 lists of each of types 1 and 2 and 40 lists of fillers with a homophone as word 1. The filler lists were included so as to assess whether subjects adopt a strategy of homophone generation when word 1 is a homophone. Recall levels were low, but the results showed clear evidence of phonological repetition blindness. The mean percentage of trials on which both critical words were recalled was 17% for lists with homophone pairs and 33% for control lists with unrelated word pairs. The filler list recall indicated a very low incidence of intrusions of a second homophone (when none had been presented).

Experiment 2: Semantic Priming
The second experiment investigated the influence of the semantically related prime on lexical decision reaction time (RT) to the final target word in each list. Preceding the prime with a phonologically identical word reduces recall of the prime. The question we asked was Does phonological repetition blindness eliminate or reduce semantic priming of the target? According to a refractoriness-of-encoding account, we would predict a reduction in semantic priming. The token individuation theory assumes that type activation may occur for the repeated word, but that the probability of token individuation is reduced. Thus, this account predicts that semantic priming will occur under conditions invoking phonological repetition blindness.

This experiment consisted of 250 "Yes" and 250 "No" lexical decision trials. There were 40 "Yes" trials of each of the 5 conditions described above, along with 50 filler trials. Mean correct "Yes" lexical decision RTs are shown in table 8.8. Analyses of these results indicated a highly significant (by items as well as by subjects) semantic facilitation effect

Table 8.8
Mean lexical decision "yes" RTs to target words preceded by different types of primes

Type of Prime	Mean RT (msec)
Semantic control	570
Repeated semantic	570
Homophone control	581
Repetition control	589
Unrelated control	583

when related primes preceded the target word. Furthermore, mean decision RTs were virtually identical in the repeated and semantic control conditions. There were no significant differences among the three control conditions. Thus, conditions yielding phonological repetition blindness generated as much priming as did a semantically related prime preceded by unrelated words. These results support a token individuation account of phonological repetition blindness.

The fact that Bateman's (1994) study had obtained no significant priming effect when subjects had been asked to recall the RSVP list, led us to investigate the effect of recall of the prime in a third experiment. In this experiment, for the second half of the trials, subjects were asked to monitor the list because they would periodically have to report the word before the target (which required a lexical decision response). The experiment included 4 conditions (1, 2, 4, and 5 above) in each block of 250 trials. In other respects the task was presented as it had been in the previous experiment. Recall was required on 20% of trials in the second block of 250 trials.

Mean correct "Yes" RTs are shown in table 8.9 for the various types of priming trials in the recall and lexical decision conditions. Once again, significant semantic priming was observed, and its magnitude was very similar in the condition that generates phonological repetition blindness and the condition in which the prime is preceded by unrelated words. The effect of the recall demand was to increase lexical decision RTs by approximately 120 msec, but there was no interaction with the priming conditions.

Recall of Primes
Subjects were significantly less likely to recall the prime *(nun)* when it was preceded by its homophone *(none)* than to recall *nun* preceded by *box;* see table 8.10. The same result was found in the repetition control condition, in which the prime was unrelated to the target *(sum)* but was preceded by its homophone *(some)*. *Sum* was more likely to be

Table 8.9
Mean lexical decision "yes" RTs to words preceded by different types of primes with and without recall of the repeated word (prime) (in msec)

Type of Prime	No Recall	Recall	Mean
Semantic control	562	678	620
Repeated semantic	561	676	618
Repetition control	572	688	630
Unrelated control	569	694	631
Mean	566	684	

recalled when preceded by *tile*. This indicates that some repetition blindness occurred despite the fact that subjects did not have to recall the entire list.

The presence of a semantically related target (PRIEST) appeared to facilitate recall of the preceding prime because there was a significant effect of prime–target relatedness on recall. The interaction between prime–target relationship and repetition was not significant. The results demonstrated that semantic relationships between words presented at fast rates can *enhance* recall, and the results support Potter's (1993) postulation of an early very short-term conceptual STM.

The recall data from this paradigm in which lists of 3 words and 3 symbol strings were presented, provided evidence of phonological repetition blindness: subjects recalled fewer critical word pairs when these were a homophone pair than when the words were unrelated. However, although recall was reduced by homophone repetition, the second homophone's meaning was activated because it facilitated decisions to a semantically related target word that followed 228 msec later. The priming effect was small (10–14 msec) but very reliable. Furthermore, this priming effect was comparable in size to that found when the prime was *not* preceded by its homophone. Thus, phonological repetition blindness does not prevent, or even reduce, access to the form of information that causes semantic priming. Giving that the RT facilitation was manifested at a short SOA of 228 msec, the priming effect can be attributed to an automatic, spreading activation process (Posner & Snyder 1975; Neely 1991).

These results suggest that when a homophone pair is presented in an RSVP list, the second homophone's semantic representation is activated. This is not consistent with an explanation of repetition blindness implying a refractoriness of encoding processes. Instead, it supports Kanwisher's thesis that repetition blindness reflects a failure of token individuation. The results have an interesting similarity to some

Table 8.10
Mean percentage recall of prime words preceding the target lexical decision word

Type of Prime	Mean % Recall
Repeated semantic	64
Semantic control	69
Repetition control	46
Unrelated control	55

reported in chapter 5 in this volume. Words that fail to be reported because of an attentional blink nevertheless generate N400 evoked response potentials (ERPs) that are indicative of semantic processing.

General Conclusions

In this chapter, I have examined research on reading comprehension and short-term memory, and research from paradigms in which visual information is presented at very fast rates of up to 10 words or pictures per second. Phonological similarity of list words has comparable effects on recall for words presented at fast and slow (1 sec) rates, and at both rates, concurrent articulation removes phonological similarity effects. The length of list words also had similar effects for lists shown at fast and slow rates: lists of short words were better recalled than were lists of long words. Likewise, concurrent articulation eliminated the word-length effect. These results indicate that the fleeting memories established at fast rates are at least partly based on phonological coding subject to the same variables as those observed in short-term memory paradigms. It is apparent that phonological encoding occurs rapidly and automatically when lists and sentences are presented at fast RSVP rates.

It has been suggested that the phonological codes that are invoked during written word recognition and comprehension differ from those used by short-term memory. The evidence reviewed at the beginning of the chapter showed that phonological codes play only a limited role in reading comprehension, primarily for low-frequency words, and that phonological effects (manifested as errors) occur only when foils have a high degree of orthographic overlap with their homophonic mate. Under these conditions, phonological codes may partly be due to a nonlexical assembly of phonology, since homophone effects can occur with pseudo homophones.

The phonological (homophone) effects found in sentence comprehension tasks differ from those in the single-word tasks in several ways.

First, they are not restricted to low-frequency words; second, they occur with orthographically dissimilar homophone pairs; and finally, they are confined to real-word homophones. These facts are also true of phonological repetition blindness, which can occur for dissimilar homophones of high frequency, such as *one/won, eight/ate*. As far as the third point is concerned, Robyn Langdon and I have conducted some experiments that indicate that repetition blindness does not occur for repeated nonwords even when these are pseudo homophones. Consequently, at least for written items, phonological repetition blindness is based on lexically derived phonology.

Experiments in which subjects did not have to recall, but had to judge whether a word belonged to a semantic category, showed that performance was still reduced by phonological and orthographic repetition blindness. This task reduced retrieval demands but still is likely to require access to an explicitly available representation of the repeated word. Thus, the reduced detection accuracy could be due to Kanwisher's postulated token individuation failure. The final experiments described in this chapter showed that the repeated word (which was a homophone of word 1) exerted as much facilitatory semantic priming as did an unrepeated semantically related word. These semantic priming results can be explained by Kanwisher's proposal that type activation of the repeated word occurs along with a failure of token individuation. The fact that semantic priming occurred in the RSVP paradigm is, of course, consistent with Potter's theory about fleeting memories being a form of conceptual short-term memory and other evidence indicating the availability of semantic and conceptual information at very early stages of the processing of words, sentences, and scenes.

Acknowledgments

I am grateful to Robyn Langdon, Eleanor Saffran, Molly Potter, and Max Coltheart for their discussion of and comments on this chapter. The research reported was funded by an Australian Research Council grant. The research assistance of Robyn Langdon, Judi Leahy, Jo Millar, and Richard Castles is gratefully acknowledged, as is the computer support and statistical assistance of Alan Taylor.

References

Anderson, R. A. (1982). Speech imagery is not always faster than visual imagery. *Memory & Cognition, 10*, 371–380.

Atkinson, R. C., & Shiffrin, R. M. (1968). Human memory: A proposed system and its control processes. In K. Spence & J. Spence (eds.), *The psychology of learning and motivation* (vol 2, pp. 89–195). New York: Academic Press.

Avons, S. E., Wright, K. L., & Pammer, K. (1994). The word length effect in probed and serial recall. *Quarterly Journal of Experimental Psychology, 47A*, 207–231.

Baddeley, A. D. (1966). Short-term memory for word sequences as a function of acoustic, semantic and formal similarity. *Quarterly Journal of Experimental Psychology, 18*, 362–365.

Baddeley, A. D. (1986). *Working memory.* Oxford: Oxford University Press.

Baddeley, A. D., & Andrade, J. (1994). Reversing the word-length effect: A comment on Caplan, Rochon and Waters. *Quarterly Journal of Experimental Psychology, 47A*, 1047–1054

Baddeley, A. D., & Hitch, G. J. (1974). Working memory. In G. A. Bower (ed.), *The psychology of learning and motivation* (vol. 8, pp. 47–90). New York: Academic Press.

Baddeley, A. D., Thomson, N., & Buchanan, M. (1975). Word length and the structure of short-term memory. *Journal of Verbal Learning and Verbal Behavior, 14*, 575–589.

Banks, W. P., Oka, E., & Shugarman, S. (1981). Recoding of printed words to internal speech: Does recoding come before lexical access? In O. J. L. Tzeng & H. Singer (eds.), *Perception of print* (pp. 137–170). Hillsdale, NJ: Lawrence Erlbaum Associates.

Baron, J. (1973). Phonemic stage not necessary for reading. *Quarterly Journal of Experimental Psychology, 25*, 241–246.

Bateman, N. (1994). Unpublished honors thesis. Macquarie University, Sydney, Australia.

Bavelier, D. (1994). Repetition blindness between visually different items: The case of pictures and words. *Cognition, 51*, 199–236.

Bavelier, D., & Potter, M. C. (1992). Visual and phonological codes in repetition blindness. *Journal of Experimental Psychology: Human Perception and Performance, 18*, 134–147.

Besner, D. (1987). Phonology, lexical access in reading, and articulatory suppression: A critical review. *Quarterly Journal of Experimental Psychology, 39A*, 467–478.

Besner, D., & Davelaar, E. (1982). Basic processes in reading: Two phonological codes. *Canadian Journal of Psychology, 36*, 701–711.

Boyle, R., & Coltheart, V. (1996). Effects of irrelevant sounds on phonological coding in reading comprehension and short-term memory. *Quarterly Journal of Experimental Psychology, 49A*, 398–416.

Caplan, D., & Waters, G. (1994). Articulatory length and phonological similarity in span tasks: A reply to Baddeley and Andrade. *Quarterly Journal of Experimental Psychology, 47A*, 1055–1062.

Coltheart, M. (1978). Lexical access in simple reading tasks. In G. Underwood (ed.), *Strategies of information processing* (pp. 151–216). London: Academic Press.

Coltheart, M., Curtis, B., Atkins, P., & Haller, M. (1993). Models of reading aloud: Dual-route and parallel-distributed-processing approaches. *Psychological Review, 100*, 589–608.

Coltheart, V. (1992). Phonological codes in reading comprehension of rapid serially presented sentences. Paper presented at nineteenth Annual Experimental Psychology Conference, University of New South Wales, Sydney, Australia, April 1992.

Coltheart, V. (1993a). Phonological codes, repetition blindness and printed sentence comprehension. Paper presented at annual meeting of the Psychonomic Society, Washington, DC, November.

Coltheart, V. (1993b). Effects of phonological similarity and concurrent irrelevant articulation on STM recall of repeated and novel word lists. *Memory & Cognition, 21*, 539–545.

Coltheart, V., Avons, S. E., Masterson, J., & Laxon, V. J. (1991). The role of assembled phonology in reading comprehension. *Memory & Cognition, 19*, 387–400.

Coltheart, V., Avons, S. E., & Trollope, J. (1990). Articulatory suppression and phonological codes in reading for meaning. *Quarterly Journal of Experimental Psychology, 42A*, 375–399.

Coltheart, V., & Langdon, R. (1995). Is phonological repetition blindness a recall phenomenon? Paper presented at the 36th annual meeting of the Psychonomic Society, Los Angeles, November.

Coltheart, V., & Langdon, R. (1998). Recall of short word lists presented visually at fast rates: Effects of phonological similarity and word length. *Memory & Cognition, 26,* 330–342.

Coltheart, V., Laxon, V., Rickard, M., & Elton, C. (1988). Phonological recoding in reading for meaning by adults and children. *Journal of Experimental Psychology: Learning, Memory and Cognition, 14,* 387–397.

Coltheart, V., Patterson K., & Leahy, J. (1994). When a ROWS is a ROSE: Phonological effects in written word comprehension. *Quarterly Journal of Experimental Psychology, 47A,* 917–955.

Conrad, R. (1964). Acoustic confusion in immediate memory. *British Journal of Psychology, 55,* 75–84.

Doctor, E. A., & Coltheart, M. (1980). Children's use of phonological encoding when reading for meaning. *Memory & Cognition, 8,* 195–209.

Forster, K. I. (1970). Visual perception of rapidly presented word sequences of varying complexity. *Perception & Psychophysics, 8,* 215–221.

Gupta, P., & MacWhinney, B. (1995). Is the articulatory loop articulatory or auditory? Re-examining the effects of concurrent articulation on immediate serial recall. *Journal of Memory and Language, 34,* 63–88.

Intraub, H. (1979). The role of implicit naming in pictorial encoding. *Journal of Experimental Psychology: Human Learning and Memory, 5,* 78–87.

Jared, D., & Seidenberg, M. S. (1991). Does word identification proceed from spelling to sound to meaning? *Journal of Experimental Psychology: General, 120,* 1–37.

Kanwisher, N. G. (1987). Repetition blindness: Type recognition without token individuation. *Cognition, 27,* 117–143.

Kanwisher, N. G., & Potter, M. C. (1990) Repetition blindness: Levels of processing. *Journal of Experimental Psychology: Human Perception and Performance, 16,* 30–47.

Kolers, P. A. (1966). Reading and talking bilingually. *American Journal of Psychology, 79,* 357–376.

Landauer, T. K. (1962). Rate of implicit speech. *Perceptual and Motor Skills, 15,* 646.

La Point, L. B., & Engle, R. W. (1990). Simple and complex word spans as measures of working memory capacity. *Journal of Experimental Psychology: Learning, Memory and Cognition, 16,* 1118–1133.

Luo, C., & Caramazza, A. (1995). Repetition blindness under minimum memory load: Effects of spatial and temporal proximity and the encoding effectiveness of the first item. *Perception and Psychophysics, 57,* 1053–1064.

MacKay, D. G. (1981). The problem of rehearsal or mental practice. *Journal of Motor Behavior, 13,* 274–285

Marshall, P. H., & Cartwright, S. A. (1978). Failure to replicate a reported implicit/ explicit speech equivalence. *Perceptual and Motor Skills, 46,* 1197–1198.

Marshall, P. H., & Cartwright, S. A. (1980). A final (?) note on implicit/explicit speech equivalence. *Bulletin of the Psychonomic Society, 15,* 409.

Monsell, S. (1987). On the relation between lexical input and output pathways for speech. In A. Allport, D. MacKay, W. Prinz, & E. Scheerer (eds.), *Language perception and production: Relationships between listening, speaking, reading and writing* (pp. 273–311). London: Academic Press.

Murray, D. J. (1968). Articulation and acoustic confusability in short-term memory. *Journal of Experimental Psychology, 78,* 679–684.

Neath, I., & Nairne, J. S. (1995). Word-length effects in immediate memory: Overwriting trace decay theory. *Psychonomic Bulletin and Review, 2,* 429–441.

Neely, J. H. (1991). Semantic priming effects in visual word recognition: A selective review of current findings and theories. In D. Besner & G. W. Humphreys (eds.), *Basic processes in reading: Visual word recognition* (pp. 264–336). Hillsdale, NJ: Lawrence Erlbaum Associates.

Posner, M. I., & Snyder, C. R. R. (1975). Facilitation and inhibition in the processing of signals. In P. M. A. Rabbitt & S. Dornic (eds.), *Attention and performance V* (pp. 669–682). New York: Academic Press.

Potter, M. C. (1976). Short-term conceptual memory for pictures. *Journal of Experimental Psychology: Human Learning and Memory, 2,* 509–522.

Potter, M. C. (1984) Rapid serial visual presentation (RSVP): A method for studying language processing. In D. E. Kieras & Just, M. A. (Eds.). *New Methods in Reading Comprehension Research.* (pp. 91–118). New Jersey: Lawrence Erlbaum Associates.

Potter, M. C. (1993). Very short-term conceptual memory. *Memory & Cognition, 21,* 156–161.

Potter, M. C., & Faulconer, B. A. (1975). Time to understand pictures and words. *Nature, 253,* 437–438.

Potter, M. C., Moryadas, A., Abrams, I., & Noel, A. (1993). Word perception and misperception in context. *Journal of Experimental Psychology: Learning, Memory and Cognition, 19,* 3–22.

Raymond, J. E., Shapiro, K. L., & Arnell, K. M. (1992). Temporary suppression of visual processing in an RSVP task: An attentional blink? *Journal of Experimental Psychology: Human Perception and Performance, 18,* 849–860.

Saffran, E. M., & Marin, O. S. M. (1975). Immediate memory for word lists and sentences in a patient with a deficient auditory short-term memory. *Brain and Language, 2,* 420–433.

Schiano, D. J., & Watkins, M. J. (1981). Speech-like coding of pictures in short-term memory. *Memory and Cognition, 9,* 110–114.

Treiman, R., Freyd, J. J., & Baron, J. (1983). Phonological recoding and use of spelling-sound rules in reading of sentences. *Journal of Verbal Learning and Verbal Behavior, 22,* 682–700.

Van Orden, G. C. (1987). A ROWS is a ROSE: Spelling, sound and reading. *Memory and Cognition, 15,* 181–198.

Van Orden, G. C., Johnston, J. C., & Hale, B. L. (1988). Word identification in reading proceeds from spelling to sound to meaning. *Journal of Experimental Psychology: Learning, Memory and Cognition, 14,* 371–386.

Waters, G., Caplan, D., and Hildebrandt, N. (1987). Working memory and written sentence comprehension. In M. Coltheart (ed.), *Attention and performance XII The psychology of reading.* (pp. 531–555). London: Lawrence Erlbaum Associates.

Watkins, M. J., Watkins, O. C., & Crowder, R. G. (1974). The modality effect in free and serial recall as a function of phonological similarity. *Journal of Verbal Learning and Verbal Behavior, 13,* 430–447.

Waugh, N., & Norman, D. A. (1965). Primary memory. *Psychological Review, 72,* 89–104.

Wickelgren, W. A. (1965). Short-term memory for phonemically similar lists. *American Journal of Psychology, 78,* 567–574.

Chapter 9

Meaning but Not Words: Neuropsychological Evidence for Very Short-Term Conceptual Memory

Eleanor M. Saffran and Nadine Martin

Potter (1993) introduced the term "very short-term conceptual memory" (VSTCM) to designate the transient representations that result from the conceptual processing of scenes or sentences. A discussion of relevant evidence from studies with normal subjects can be found in chapter 2 of this volume. In this chapter, we examine phenomena reported in the neuropsychological literature that bear on VSTCM.

Much of the normal data on VSTCM come from studies in which subjects attempted to report sentences that they read under the constraints of rapid serial visual presentation (RSVP) (Potter & Lombardi 1990; Lombardi & Potter 1992). Under these conditions, words that were synonyms of target words ("lures" presented before or after the sentence) often intruded. The substitution of closely related words indicated that subjects were reconstituting the sentence from a conceptual representation of the input string, as opposed to utilizing a veridical record. Since the sentences contained new information, conceptual representations had to be constructed anew; they could not be retrieved fully formed from long-term memory (LTM). The new representation might subsequently be committed to LTM, but not necessarily; people do not remember the contents of all of the sentences they read or hear. At the very least, the conceptual representation had to be maintained long enough to support regeneration of the input sentence in a form that preserved the gist of the original, if not its exact content. Hence the term VSTCM.

One of the possible consequences of left hemisphere damage is an impairment in the ability to repeat words and/or sentences verbatim. In some instances, the patient succeeds in extracting the conceptual content of the message, although it cannot be reported in the form in which it was heard. In such cases, the repetition response draws on the contents of VSTCM. Our chapter focuses on disorders of this type.

Sentence Repetition in STM Patients

People are capable of reproducing sentences of as many as 20 words, as long as they are semantically coherent (e.g., Miller & Selfridge 1950; Wingfield & Butterworth 1984). This capacity is challenged, under RSVP, by the rapidity with which successive words are presented. Brain damage can produce similar limitations. The sequelae of left hemisphere lesions often include an inability to repeat sentences verbatim. In most cases, the repetition impairment is associated with an evident language disorder. For example, the sentence repetition responses of agrammatic aphasics contain the same morphological and structural errors that occur in their spontaneous speech (e.g., Ostrin & Schwartz 1986). Of most interest to us here is the sentence repetition pattern found in patients who develop verbal short-term memory (STM) deficits following left parietal lesions (for a characterization of this deficit, see Shallice & Vallar 1990). This impairment, which can occur in the absence of significant language impairment,[1] is identified by a digit span of 1 to 4 items—quite a reduction from the normal complement of about 7.

The STM patients' ability to repeat word lists and sentence materials also are limited. But while these individuals are typically unable to repeat sentences of more than 5 or 6 words verbatim, their responses often preserve the gist of the target sentences. Instructed to repeat, they offer paraphrases instead. Examples of this performance pattern can be found in table 9.1. It is evident from these examples that the patients understood the input sentences reasonably well. Why, then, were they unable to reproduce them?

The individuals who generated these responses have reduced auditory verbal short-term memory capacity, as indicated by abbreviated digit and word spans that are not explained by obvious receptive and/or expressive language deficits. The reduction in verbal span is not a manifestation of a general memory disorder. In cases where other memory capacities have been assessed, they appear to be well-preserved. For example, Shallice and Warrington's (1974) patient KF had no difficulty with span tasks involving nonverbal auditory stimuli, and his verbal LTM function, assessed in tasks such as paired associate learning, appeared normal (Warrington & Shallice 1969; see also Vallar & Papagno 1986).[2] Although span performance is seriously impaired with auditory presentation, nearly all of the reported STM patients show an increase in verbal span when the materials are presented visually (Shallice & Vallar 1990). Whether the STM limitation reflects a subtle language impairment remains controversial. Allport (1984) suggested that these patients may have subtle phonological deficits, and noted problems in phoneme discrimination tasks in 2 of 3 patients

Table 9.1
Examples of sentence repetition responses of STM patients

1. The people filed calmly into the ancient cathedral.
   IL:[a] The people went calmly into the old cathedral.
   TI:[b] People calmly went to the cathedral, old cathedral.

2. The residence was located in a peaceful neighborhood.
   IL: The residence was situated in a quiet district
   JB:[c] The residence was in a calm neighborhood.
   IG:[d] The residence was situated in a . . . in a peaceful pla . . . residence area.

3. After searching everywhere, he finally found the keys in his raincoat.
   IL: After searching everywhere, he found the keys in his raincoat pocket.
   JB: After searching everywhere, he at last found the key in the empty pocket of his raincoat.
   IG: After looking all over for it, he finally found the key in the raincoat.

4. The old man sank gratefully into the yellow chair.
   IL: The old man was tired. He wanted to sit in the chair.
   JB: The old man sank thankfully on the yellow chair.
   IG: The old man fell gratefully on the chair.

5. The man's handsome fedora blew away in a gust of wind.
   IL: The man's handsome sombrero sailed away from the man's head.
   IG: The man's fancy fedora got lost.
   DK:[d] The man's handsome hat fell off.

6. The board of directors decided that retiring workers should be encouraged.
   IL: A board director was told that the aged employees should be given permission to retire.
   TI: The board of directors decided that the workers should be compensated.
   DK: The board decided the employees are urged to retire.

7. The women were told that shining floors can be crippling.
   IL: The women were told that it is dangerous to shine slippery floors.
   IG: People were told that shiny floors could be bad for you.
   DK: Shining floors—you will fall.

7. After eating dinner, the man walked the dog.
   EA:[e] After supper, the man took his dog for a walk.

8. Before calling her mother, the girl had a cup of tea.
   EA: The girl drank some hot tea before she went to talk to her mother.

9. Before you mow the lawn, don't forget to trim the shrub.
   DK: Before you mow the lawn, make sure to trim the bushes.

10. Each lesson began with some helpful tips from the driving instructor.
    DK: Each class gave some helpful driving tips.

[a] Saffran & Marin 1975.
[b] Saffran & Martin 1990.
[c] Shallice & Butterworth 1977; Butterworth et al. 1990.
[d] Patient under study in our laboratory.
[e] R. C. Martin 1993; Friedrich et al. 1985.

tested. However, other investigators have failed to obtain evidence of this deficit (Vallar & Baddeley 1984a) or have demonstrated that their patients perform at close to normal levels on such tasks (Shelton, Martin & Yaffee 1992). Most investigators have attributed the reduction in auditory verbal span to an abnormally rapid loss of phonological information (e.g., Shallice & Vallar 1990). Such an impairment could impinge on tasks like phoneme discrimination, where it is necessary to retain information about the first stimulus until the second is presented.

This account is based on several lines of evidence. Consider, for example, the task of repeating nonwords. In the absence of lexical or semantic support for the reproduction of these items, repetition is critically dependent on phonological information. Whereas normal subjects are able to reproduce, on average, strings of 2.5 nonwords (Brener 1940), patients with short-term memory deficits have difficulty reporting more than a single syllable (e.g., R. C. Martin, Shelton, & Yaffee 1994; Saffran & Marin 1975). Other phenomena that are thought to depend on short-term phonological memory are also attenuated in these patients. One is the recency effect in immediate serial recall of digit or word lists—superior recall of items at the end of a list compared with items in the middle. This effect, which normally is greater for auditory than for visual presentation, is thought to depend on the persistence of terminal list items in phonological form (e.g., Crowder & Morton 1969). STM patients do not show a recency effect with auditory presentation (e.g., Basso, Spinnler, Vallar, & Zanobio 1982; Friedrich, Glenn, & Marin 1984; Saffran & Marin 1975). They also show a reduced recency effect in free recall (Shallice & Vallar 1990), an effect that is thought to be supported, at least in part, by phonological information (e.g., Craik 1968; Shallice 1975). Another phenomenon that is reduced or absent in STM cases (e.g., Vallar & Baddeley 1984a) is the detrimental effect of phonological similarity on the retention of visually presented lists (e.g., Conrad 1964). Normal subjects tend to have more difficulty with strings like TZBP than strings like TLHQ, an effect that reflects phonological recoding of the visual materials. As phonological recoding is unlikely to benefit STM patients, they appear to avoid it. Finally, there is evidence that STM patients have difficulty learning new words (e.g., Baddeley, Papagno, & Vallar 1988), a task that appears to depend on phonological memory (Gupta & MacWhinney, 1997).

Like normal subjects, STM patients are able to reproduce longer strings of words when the words are embedded in sentences (e.g., Butterworth, Shallice, & Watson 1990; Vallar & Baddeley 1984b). This pattern presumably reflects syntactic constraints in sentence materials, as well as the conceptual support provided by VSTCM. But the STM patients' sentence span is considerably reduced from the normal span of about 20 items: these individuals are typically unable to repeat sentences longer than 5 or 6 words verbatim, although, as noted earlier, they often generate an acceptable paraphrase instead. Neuropsychologists have attributed the sentence repetition pattern to the same deficit that underlies the impairment in digit and word span tasks (e.g., R. C. Martin 1990; Saffran & Marin 1975). As Butterworth et al. (1990) point out, "the inability to reproduce the full surface representation of a sentence when gist can be retrieved suggests" that the phonological store "is also used in sentence repetition" (p. 188).

Support for this assertion comes from Butterworth, Campbell, and Howard's (1986) case study of a young adult (RE) with a developmental STM disorder. Normal subjects showed a U-shaped function across sentence positions in a sentence repetition task, reflecting more accurate recall of words at the end of the sentence as well as at the beginning. In contrast, RE demonstrated no recency effect in repeating the same sentences; she tended to lose words at the end of the sentence, just as she had in repeating digit and word strings. RE's similar patterns across the two types of materials suggest that they reflect the same underlying disorder.

Potter (1993; Potter & Lombardi 1990), who emphasizes the role of conceptual representations in sentence repetition, has argued that the task does not depend on the retention of phonological information. To account for the STM patients' sentence repetition pattern, she postulates a deficit in lexical retrieval: the patients fail to repeat accurately because they have difficulty accessing the requisite lexical items. It is difficult to exclude this possibility, as word retrieval may not be entirely normal in these patients. However, lexical impairment does not necessarily lead to poor repetition performance. Transcortical sensory aphasics, who have severe word retrieval deficits, perform remarkably well in sentence repetition tasks (e.g., N. Martin & Saffran 1990). These are patients with significant auditory comprehension problems, who are unlikely to be regenerating sentences from conceptual representations. Their ability to repeat sentences presumably reflects the use of syntactic constraints, together with phonologically based activation of lexical items (N. Martin & Saffran 1990). The transcortical patients' dependence on phonological information is evident in word list repetition tasks. In contrast to the STM patients, who have more difficulty with items at the end of the list, the transcortical sensory aphasics tend to retain the recency portion of the list, selectively losing items from the beginning (N. Martin & Saffran 1990). We have recently demonstrated similar effects in other aphasics with semantic impairments (N. Martin & Saffran 1997).

Direct support for a phonological contribution to sentence repetition comes from a study conducted by Butterworth et al. (1990). These authors tested STM patient JB (Shallice & Butterworth 1977), as well as controls, on a sentence repetition task. The materials included sentences in which a set of 4 semantically related words was embedded, either as a single phrase (e.g., The removal firm took a *bed, a cabinet, a wardrobe, and a chair*) or as two separate phrases (e.g., Wash *the sheet and the bedspread* at the same time as *the pillowcase and the napkins*). In an immediate repetition condition, normal subjects repeated 85 percent of the sentences correctly immediately after hearing them; in contrast, JB was unable to reproduce any of the sentences with complete accuracy. Butterworth et al. also tested repetition of these materials after 20 seconds of interpolated arithmetic activity. Under these conditions, the performance of normal subjects declined to 7 percent correct. In terms of the number of words correctly repeated, JB's performance remained stable over the filled delay (.79 content words correct immediately after hearing the sentence and .77 after the delay), while the performance of controls declined significantly (1.0 in the immediate repetition condition, .83 after the delay). Butterworth et al. concluded that these performance patterns reflect the contribution of phonological information to normal performance in the immediate repetition condition. The filled delay would result in the loss of this information, resulting in a decline in performance. As JB lacked phonological support for immediate repetition, she had difficulty in this condition, but her performance was not further affected by the filled delay.

In endorsing this account, we do not wish to imply that sentence repetition depends wholly or even primarily on phonological information. Conceptual representations clearly play an important role in this task. But it is important to note that conceptual information does not uniquely specify the form or the lexical content of an utterance generated from it. As Potter and Lombardi (1990) pointed out, responses in the repetition task are likely to be influenced by priming. Receptive processing of the input string will activate lexical items, and this activation will increase the likelihood of selecting these items in formulating the repetition response. A similar effect should hold for sentence structure, which is also responsive to priming (e.g., Bock 1990; Levelt & Kelter 1982). Potter and Lombardi assume that normal subjects' ability to reproduce the input sentence is based on the conceptual content held in VSTCM, which is filtered through a language system that has been primed by the input sentence; consequently, the response is likely to be faithful to the structure and lexical content of the original. One factor that is not considered in this account is the role of phonological information in priming. The extent to which lexical and structural representations are primed by the input sentence should depend on the amount of activation they receive from phonological-level representations. Where phonological information is subject to rapid decay, lexical and structural elements that correspond to the input string should not be as strongly activated; to the extent that these elements are less-activated, they are less likely to be selected for production. Presumably, this is what happens in STM patients. In the extreme case, the repetition task could reduce to producing a sentence de novo—except that the conceptual content is derived from the input sentence, as opposed to being generated by the speaker.

As noted earlier, it is difficult to rule out lexical retrieval as a contributory factor in the sentence repetition task. Difficulty in retrieving the target words will create discrepancies between the input sentence and the sentence produced in response. But it seems unlikely that this is the primary reason for the STM patients' inability to repeat sentences verbatim. If there is a significant lexical retrieval problem, it should be evident in other production tasks. Analyses of speech samples from two STM patients revealed no evidence of hesitations or decreased rate, 2 possible manifestations of a problem in lexical retrieval (Shallice & Butterworth 1977; Vallar & Baddeley 1984a). In other STM cases, performance on naming tasks was reported as normal (e.g., Saffran & Martin 1990).

We view sentence repetition as dependent on 3 sources of information: a conceptual representation generated from the input sentence; priming of lexical and structural elements by the input sentence; and information held in phonological form. The latter contributes in 2 ways: directly, in the case of words at the end of the sentence, for which a phonological record may still be available as the response is being generated; and indirectly, through the impact of phonology on lexical and structural priming. When a normal subject generates a sentence repetition response, the conceptual representation is filtered through a production system that has been extensively primed by the input string. Hence the response replicates the input sentence, or at most departs from it only slightly. Because the STM patients are receiving less support from phonology, and correspondingly less support from activated lexical and structural representations, their responses will be more discrepant. As these discrepancies reflect the contents of the conceptual representation generated by the input sentence, the sentence repetition responses of STM patients provide a window on the contents of VSTCM.

Impaired Sentence Repetition: A Window on VSTCM

We are not aware of any attempt to use data from STM patients to examine the conceptual representations generated by an input sentence.

For the most part, the repetition paradigm has been used to assess STM patients' ability to process sentences, particularly with respect to syntactic form (Saffran & Marin 1975; Friedrich, Martin, & Kemper 1985). Asked to repeat sentences with complex syntactic constructions (e.g., passives, object relatives), the responses of some STM patients indicate that they failed to comprehend them (Saffran & Marin 1975; Friedrich et al. 1985). Tests of sentence comprehension have confirmed that this is a problem for some (e.g., Caramazza, Basili, Koller, & Berndt 1981; Saffran & Martin 1990; Friedrich et al. 1984), but not all, STM cases (e.g., Butterworth et al. 1986; Vallar & Baddeley 1984b; Waters, Caplan, & Hildebrandt 1991).[3] Other investigators have used the sentence repetition task to examine the contribution of STM capacity to sentence recall (Butterworth et al. 1990, Butterworth et al. 1986).

As an indication of the information that might be derived from an examination of the sentence repetition responses of STM patients, table 9.2 provides examples from IL, the patient studied by Saffran and Marin (1975). Several patterns are evident in these responses. IL's responses to sentences (1)–(5) depart from the input sentence in the use of synonyms or closely related words or phrases, a pattern resembling that of the participants in Potter and Lombardi's (1990) RSVP studies. Note that adjectives, which might be considered less essential, are omitted from these responses. In examples (6) and (7), there is a change in grammatical form; information originally encoded in a single sentence is recoded as two separate sentences. In the remainder of the examples, IL's responses depart further from the input string, in that they include information not present in the original sentence. For example, in (8), the target sentence did not specify the contents of the bottle. Sentence (9) states that the mouse was eaten, but nothing about the events that preceded this act. In (10), the act of hurrying does not necessarily mean that the person was running. In (20), the input sentence contains no mention of clothing. In all of these cases, the response includes information that could reasonably be inferred from the input string but was not explicitly encoded therein. Thus, baby bottles generally contain milk; in order for the cat to eat the mouse, it would first have to catch it; someone who was hurrying was probably running; one of the major items sold in department stores is clothing.

In some cases, the interpretation appears to have gone considerably further. Consider (18), for example: IL evidently inferred from the fact that the mail was heavy that its destination was an office, as opposed to a private residence. IL's response to sentence (23) reflects an inference as to the source of the head injury, and his response to sentence (3) in table 9.1 specifies the place where the key was found. These observations suggest that VSTCM not only contains information drawn directly

Table 9.2
Sentence repetition responses of IL

---

1. The small child hit the large dog.
   The little child hit the big dog.

2. The driver could not locate the package.
   The driver could not find the parcel.

3. Sulphur was put in the empty bottle.
   Sulphur was put into the empty vial.

4. Drinks were generally poured by waiters afterwards.
   Drinks were given by the waiters later.

5. An excellent dinner was prepared for the illustrious guests.
   A dinner was given to the distinguished guests.

6. The dog was brought to the vet already quite sick.
   He brought the dog to the vet. He already had been sick.

7. They were going to the movies and met a dog.
   They were going to the movie. They met a dog.

8. The baby drank his bottle.
   The baby drank his milk.

9. The mouse was eaten by the cat.
   The mouse was caught by a cat.

10. That morning, hurrying to meet him, she soon got lost.
    That morning, hurriedly running to meet him, she lost her way.

11. Terrified of the dark, the child lay awake until dawn.
    Terrified by the dark, the child laid in the bed until dawn.

12. The tiny baby cried because he was very hungry.
    The tiny baby cried because he didn't have anything to eat.

13. Pirates had buried the large treasure chest.
    Pirates hid the large treasure chest.

14. The signal for departure was not given until the boat was fully loaded.
    The boat did not go away; they waited for people to go on the boat.

15. Explosives are used by the Army engineers.
    Explosives are used by the military authorities.

16. Laws are often passed by Congress quickly.
    Laws are adopted fast by the Senate.

17. While sewing, she must have been pricked by the needle.
    While sewing, she pricked her finger.

18. They were astonished at the volume of mail arriving daily.
    They were amazed because heavy mail was brought to the office.

19. This year we will take our holiday at a nearby beach.
    This Christmas we will take our holiday in the nearby vacation resort.

20. Brokers are financing the central department store.
    Brokers are in the fashion business.
21. Rebels have entirely evacuated the area now.
    Rebels have relinquished the town.
22. While going to school, the boy was attacked by bullies on the field.
    While going home from school, a few ruffians fell on the boy.
23. While walking under an elm, the man was hit on the head.
    The people were walking by an elm and were hurt by something dropped
    from the elm.
24. This time, the town was deserted by the people before the storm came.
    Then the town was empty when the storm hit the town.
25. The public was warned about cigarettes, but what about smoking chim-
    neys?
    The people were warned about smoking, but no one has told them about
    the chimneys.

---

from the input sentence but the products of inferential processes as
well. The contents of the sentence, then, serve merely as a point of
departure; the representation generated from the sentence and held
in VSTCM appears to be considerably enriched compared with the
information explicitly encoded in the input sentence. The richness of
these responses is reminiscent of data from studies that have examined
normal sentence memory after a delay. For example, Bransford, Barclay,
and Franks (1972) found that subjects had difficulty discriminating
sentences they had previously read from sentences containing inferences drawn from those sentences. This phenomenon does not necessarily reflect inferences made at the time of recall. There is evidence that
elaborative inferences are generated in the course of normal sentence
processing, although there is debate about the frequency and rapidity
with which they are made (see Sanford & Garrod 1994 for review).
The data from IL suggest that additional information may become
available in the course of processing the sentence, or very soon there-
after.

Other Relevant Phenomena

The STM impairment is not the only disturbance in which the error
patterns generated by patients reflect the contents of VSTCM. Patients
with the disorder termed deep dysphasia make semantic substitutions
in the immediate repetition of single words—*thermometer* "repeated"
as *sick*, for example, or *dinosaur* as *horse* (see N. Martin 1996 for review).

As the patient recovers, the production of semantic errors in single-word repetition may disappear, only to surface again when the task involves word lists rather than single words (N. Martin, Saffran, & Dell 1996). These substitutions are presumably mediated by conceptual representations activated by the target word. However, deep dysphasics are semantically impaired, and we would not want to claim that their errors bear on the contents of normal conceptual representations.

A remarkable example of semantic substitution in list repetition has been reported by Bartha, Lesch, and Martin (1994; R. C. Martin, Lesch, & Bartha, 1998). Their patient, MS, developed a severe naming deficit following a bout with herpes simplex encephalitis, which damaged his left temporal lobe. In repeating word lists, MS produced many errors that were phonologically related to their targets; in addition, he generated semantic descriptions of list items. For example, for the list *lobster, castle, and bagpipe,* he responded "losser—the thing you eat, the place the kings go in, and it comes from the place where men wear the same things as women" (uttered with gestures appropriate for the instrument). These descriptions occurred most frequently with lists of high imageability words; with low imageability lists, MS tended to produce errors that were phonologically related to the target words.

MS did not have an STM deficit; his digit span was 7, and his recall of nonword lists was within normal limits. While there was little evidence of semantic impairment, he did have a severe lexical retrieval problem; for example, he succeeded in naming only 10 of 60 pictures on the Boston Naming Test (Kaplan, Goodglass, Weintraub, & Segal 1983). The vast majority of his naming errors were circumlocutions. For example, for *cane*, he responded, "This is something you use to walk with if you have trouble walking" (R. Martin et al., in 1998). MS's naming performance improved significantly when he was provided with the first phoneme of the target, indicating that he retained the phonological form of the word although he was unable to retrieve it on his own. Data on MS's sentence repetition performance have not been reported, but it is reasonable to assume that he would produce circumlocutory responses similar to those he generated in list repetition tasks.

MS's circumlocutory responses in attempting to repeat word lists clearly depend on the activation of conceptual information related to the target words, and hence on the contents of VSTCM. Of course, his responses are highly abnormal, given the task. However, there is evidence that semantic processes are activated by word lists; for example, semantic priming is demonstrable in tasks that utilize list materials (e.g., Moss, Tyler, Hodges, & Patterson 1995). Where MS clearly differs from normal subjects is that he makes conscious use of this information.

Conclusions

When patients with left hemisphere lesions lose the capacity to repeat words or sentences verbatim, their responses on immediate repetition tasks reflect the contents of conceptual representations generated by the input string. Examination of a set of responses from one such patient indicates that these representations include the products of inferential processes, as well as information retrieved from semantic memory. Data from these cases provide evidence on the nature and extent of elaborative and inferential processes that occur in the course of interpreting a sentence. But while the neuropsychological data testify to the depth and potential richness of these processes, it is necessary to be cautious in drawing implications for normal function. Impaired individuals may attempt to compensate for their deficits by processing sentences more deeply than people typically do in such tasks.

Acknowledgments

Preparation of this chapter was supported by grant DC 00191 from the National Institutes of Health. We are grateful to Tim Shallice for providing unpublished sentence repetition data from JB.

Notes

1. Patients with significant impairments in receptive and/or expressive language function also have STM deficits. We do not consider these clearly language-related STM deficits here.
2. But the capacity to learn new words, which appears to be dependent on phonological memory, is impaired (Baddeley, Papagno, & Vallar 1988).
3. The comprehension problem does not appear to reflect a parsing problem; these patients have proved to be quite sensitive to grammatical violations (Saffran & Martin 1990; Butterworth et al. 1990; R. C. Martin & Romani 1994).

References

Allport, D. A. (1984). Auditory–verbal short-term memory and conduction aphasia. In H. Bouma & D. G. Bouwhuis (eds.), *Attention and performance X: Control of language processes* (pp. 313–325). Hillsdale, NJ: Lawrence Erlbaum Associates.

Baddeley, A. D., Papagno, C., & Vallar, G. (1988). When long-term learning depends on short-term storage. *Journal of Memory and Language, 27,* 586–595.

Bartha, M., Lesch, M., & Martin, R. (1994). Meaning without names: Picture-naming and word-list repetition in anomic aphasia. *Brain and Language, 47,* 332–335.

Basso, A., Spinnler, H., Vallar, G., & Zanobio, M. E. (1982). Left hemisphere damage and selective impairment of auditory–verbal short-term memory. A case study. *Neuropsychologia, 20,* 263–274.

Bock, J. K. (1990). Structure in language: Creating form in talk. *American Psychologist, 45,* 221–236.

Bransford, J. D., Barclay, J. R., & Franks, J. J. (1972). Sentence memory: A constructive vs. interpretive approach. *Cognitive Psychology, 3,* 193–209.

Brener, R. (1940). An experimental investigation of memory span. *Journal of Experimental Psychology, 26,* 467–482.

Butterworth, B., Campbell, R., & Howard, D. (1986). The uses of short-term memory: A case study. *Quarterly Journal of Experimental Psychology, 36A,* 233–252.

Butterworth, B., Shallice, T., & Watson F. L. (1990). Short-term retention without short-term memory. In G. Vallar & T. Shallice (eds.), *Neuropsychological impairments of short-term memory* (pp. 187–214). Cambridge: Cambridge University Press.

Caramazza, A., Basili, A. G., Koller, J. J., & Berndt, R. S. (1981). An investigation of repetition and language processing in a case of conduction aphasia. *Brain and Language, 14,* 235–271.

Conrad, R. (1964). Acoustic confusion in immediate memory. *British Journal of Psychology, 55,* 75–84.

Craik, F. I. M. (1968). Two components in free recall. *Journal of Verbal Learning and Verbal Behavior, 7,* 995–1004.

Crowder, R. G., & Morton, J. (1969). Precategorical acoustic storage. *Perception and Psychophysics, 5,* 365–373.

Friedrich, F., Glenn, C. G., & Marin, O. S. M. (1984). Interruption of phonological coding in conduction aphasia. *Brain and Language, 22,* 266–291.

Friedrich, F., Martin, R., & Kemper, S. J. (1985). Consequences of a phonological coding deficit on sentence processing. *Cognitive Neuropsychology, 2,* 385–412.

Gupta, P., & MacWhinney, B. (1997). Vocabulary acquisition and verbal short-term memory: Computational and neural bases. *Brain and Language, 59,* 267–333.

Kaplan, E. F., Goodglass, H., Weintraub, S., & Segal, O. (1983). *The Boston naming test.* Philadelphia: Lea & Febiger.

Levelt, W., & Kelter, S. (1982). Surface form and memory in question answering. *Cognitive Psychology, 14,* 78–106.

Lombardi, L., & Potter, M. C. (1992). The regeneration of syntax in short-term memory. *Journal of Memory and Language, 31,* 713–733.

Martin, N. (1996). Models of deep dysphasia. *Neurocase, 2,* 73–80.

Martin, N., & Saffran, E. M. (1990). Repetition and verbal STM in transcortical sensory aphasia: A case study. *Brain and Language, 39,* 254–288.

Martin, N., & Saffran, E. M. (1997). Language and auditory verbal short-term memory impairments: Evidence for common underlying processes. *Cognitive Neuropsychology, 14,* 641–682.

Martin, N., Saffran, E. M., & Dell, G. S. (1996). Recovery in deep dysphasia: Evidence for a relationship between auditory–verbal STM capacity and lexical errors in repetition. *Brain and Language, 52,* 83–113.

Martin, R. C. (1990). Neuropsychological evidence on the role of short-term memory in sentence processing. In G. Vallar & T. Shallice (eds.), *Neuropsychological impairments of short-term memory* (pp. 390–427). Cambridge: Cambridge University Press.

Martin, R. C. (1993). Short-term memory and sentence processing: Evidence from neuropsychology. *Memory and Cognition, 21,* 176–181.

Martin, R. C., Lesch, M., & Bartha, M. (1998). Independence of input and output phonology in word processing and short-term memory. Unpublished manuscript.

Martin, R. C., & Romani, C. (1994). Verbal working memory and sentence comprehension: A multiple-components view. *Nerupsychology, 8,* 506–523.

Martin, R. C., Shelton, J., & Yaffee., L. S. (1994). Language processing and working memory: Neuropsychological evidence for separate phonological and semantic capacities. *Journal of Memory and Language, 33,* 83–111.

Miller, G., & Selfridge, J. (1950). Verbal context and the recall of meaningful material. *American Journal of Psychology, 63,* 176–185.

Moss, H. E., Tyler, L. K., Hodges, J., & Patterson, K. (1995). Exploring the loss of semantic memory in semantic dementia: Evidence from a primed monitoring study. *Neuropsychology, 9,* 16–26.

Ostrin, R. K., & Schwartz, M. F. (1986). Reconstructing from a degraded trace: A study of sentence repetition in agrammatism. *Brain and Language, 28,* 328–345.

Potter, M. C. (1993). Very short-term conceptual memory. *Memory & Cognition, 21,* 156–161.

Potter, M. C., & Lombardi, L. (1990). Regeneration in the short-term recall of sentences. *Journal of Memory and Language, 29,* 633—654.

Saffran, E. M., & Marin, O. S. M. (1975). Immediate memory for word lists and sentences in a patient with deficient auditory short-term memory. *Brain and Language, 2,* 420–433.

Saffran, E. M., & Martin, N. (1990). Short-term memory impairment and sentence processing: A case study. In G. Vallar & T. Shallice (eds.), *Neuropsychological impairments of short-term memory* (pp. 428–447). Cambridge: Cambridge University Press.

Sanford, A. J., & Garrod, S. C. (1994). Selective processing in text understanding. In M. A. Gernsbacher (ed.), *Handbook of psycholinguistics* (pp. 699–720). San Diego: Academic Press.

Shallice, T. (1975). On the contents of primary memory. In S. Dornic (ed.), *Attention and performance V* (pp. 269–280). London: Academic Press.

Shallice, T., & Butterworth, B. (1977). Short-term memory impairment and spontaneous speech. *Neuropsychologia, 15,* 729–735.

Shallice, T., & Vallar, G. (1990). The impairment of auditory verbal short-term storage. In G. Vallar & T. Shallice (eds.), *Neuropsychological impairments of short-term memory* (pp. 11–53). Cambridge: Cambridge University Press.

Shallice, T., & Warrington, E. K. (1974). The dissociation between short-term retention of meaningful sounds and verbal material. *Neuropsychologia, 12,* 553–555.

Shelton, J. R., Martin, R. C., & Yaffee, L. S. (1992). Investigating a verbal short-term memory deficit and its consequences for language processing. In D. I. Margolin (Ed.), *Cognitive neuropsychology in clinical practice* (pp. 131–167) New York: Oxford University Press.

Vallar, G., & Baddeley, A. D. (1984a). Fractionation of working memory: Neuropsychological evidence for a phonological short-term store. *Journal of Verbal Learning and Verbal Behavior, 23,* 121–142.

Vallar, G., & Baddeley, A. D. (1984b). Phonological short-term store, phonological processing and sentence comprehension: A neuropsychological case study. *Cognitive Neuropsychology, 1,* 121–141.

Vallar, G., & Papagno, C. (1986). Phonological short-term store and the nature of the recency effect: Evidence from neuropsychology. *Brain and Cognition, 5,* 412–427.

Warrington, E. K., & Shallice, T (1969). The selective impairment of auditory–verbal short-term memory. *Brain, 92,* 885–896.

Waters, G., Caplan, D., & Hildebrandt, N. (1991). On the structure of verbal short-term memory and its functional role in sentence comprehension: Evidence from neuropsychology. *Cognitive Neuropsychology, 8,* 81–126.

Wingfield, A., & Butterworth, B. (1984). Running memory for sentences and parts of sentences: Syntactic parsing as a control function in working memory. In H. Bouma & D. G. Bouwhuis (eds.), Attention and performance X: Control of language processes (pp. 351–364). Hillsdale, NJ: Lawrence Erlbaum Associates.

Chapter 10

Fleeting Memories: A Summary and Conclusion

Veronika Coltheart

This book on fleeting memories has reviewed research on the character-istics of cognition of briefly presented visual stimuli. Thirty years ago, Potter demonstrated that rapidly presented pictures of objects and scenes can be immediately understood although they are not likely to be remembered. Forster (1970), influenced by this work, demonstrated that written sentences shown at a rate of 16 words per second can be understood and reported. Furthermore, even prose passages can be understood when serially presented, word by word, at rates of 10–12 words per second (Potter, Kroll, & Harris 1980).

Potter reviews her research on RSVP sentence processing and evi-dence from scene processing and the other paradigms discussed in this book, and elaborates her theoretical account (Potter 1993) in chapter 2. She argues that most cognitive processing occurs on-line, through the functioning of conceptual short-term memory (CSTM) without effortful, conscious thought. These rapid processes permit comprehen-sion of new sentences and new scenes. Theories of STM cannot provide an adequate account of the immediate, automatic, and effortless nature of most cognitive processing.

Potter's Theory of Conceptual Short-Term Memory

Potter (1993) proposed a theory of conceptual short-term memory that she described as consisting of fleeting conceptual representations that are generated early in perceptual processing and that can be regarded as a form of conceptually structured, very short-term memory "tightly linked to LTM" (p. 156). The instantaneous comprehension manifested in RSVP (rapid serial visual presentation) scene and sentence judgment tasks shows that conceptual information is activated rapidly but fleet-ingly, and the information is lost in less than half a second unless it undergoes further consolidation.

RSVP Sentence Comprehension

Earlier work by Potter (1984; Potter, Kroll, Yachzel, Carpenter, & Sherman 1986) showed good recall of sentences presented at 12 words a second. Thus, individual words can be recognized and understood in under 100 msec, and when a series of words forms a sentence, their meanings can be integrated and the syntactic structure of the sentences can be extracted. In contrast, when words cannot be parsed and represented as propositions, only 2 or 3 words are likely to be recalled.

Potter and her colleagues developed a number of ingenious and novel paradigms to investigate both written and spoken sentence processing. Thus, Potter and Lombardi (1990) proposed that immediate recall of a sentence is based on a conceptual or propositional structure extracted on-line, and that recently activated semantic entries are used to generate appropriate phonological-output lexical entries in recall. They presented distractor words in a list shown either before or after RSVP sentences. If one of the list words was a synonym of a word in the sentence (e.g., *castle* for *palace*), that list word was often substituted in sentence recall. Research using RSVP paragraphs indicated that both discourse analysis and sentence parsing occurred rapidly. However, only gist recall may be possible in the absence of opportunities for further processing.

Potter, Moryadas, Abrams, and Noel (1993) demonstrated that context can determine word perception during RSVP reading at 10 words per second. Their sentences included a nonword that was an orthographic neighbor of a sentence-appropriate word (e.g., *wesp/wasp* or *wisp*). This nonword was very often misperceived as the sentence-inappropriate word. Potter, Stiefbold, and Moryadas (1998) presented a brief double word, one of which was appropriate to the sentence in which the pair appeared. Both paradigms showed that words are comprehended early in processing, but rapid forgetting occurs unless opportunities for further consolidation exist. Selective attention directed by conceptual features of the target, and by semantic and syntactic relationships among stimuli, affect processing early, at least before "late" phonological STM codes are established. Hence, conceptual short-term memory differs from the phonological loop of working memory.

Potter assumed that structuring in conceptual short-term memory is not qualitatively different from normal processes of comprehension required for understanding text or complex pictures, or problem solving in various domains. Conceptual short-term memory is distinguished by the speed with which processing takes place and by a lack of awareness of the processes that have occurred. As stated earlier, consolidation is required if the fleeting memories constructed by conceptual short-term memory are to survive.

Potter considers whether conceptual short-term memory is separable from long-term memory (LTM), and whether conceptual short-term memory is conscious. She concludes that we have no definitive answers to these questions. It seems likely, though, that much of the processing by conceptual short-term memory occurs outside consciousness.

Scene Perception and Memory

Intraub's chapter discusses the considerable body of research that has shown we can comprehend a scene in a brief glance and detect an anomalous object in it, and that we can comprehend a series of scenes shown for about a tenth of a second each in rapid succession. Research by Biederman (1981) on the detection of objects in scenes showed that higher-order knowledge about scenes influences object recognition. Subjects could detect violations in a single glance with a 150 msec presentation of a scene.

Intraub (1981) studied detection of pictures without giving subjects specific information about physical or conceptual features as cues. In some conditions, subjects were asked to detect the picture that did not belong to a general category specified beforehand. The subjects were able to perform these detection tasks even at fast rates of presentation. However, in a memory condition, recognition memory after the list was poor, although all the subjects were able to report that the picture lists contained exemplars of a common category such as furniture or food. Moreover, 83% of subjects noted that the lists had contained an "odd man out," a nonexemplar. Thus, Intraub's research confirmed Potter's earlier conclusion that picture comprehension is possible at fast presentation rates, but that subsequent memory for such rapidly shown pictures is poor.

Intraub's research indicates the use of higher-order information in scene perception and memory. She proposed that the "boundary extension" phenomenon she discovered constitutes evidence of schema activation during perception of pictures of scenes (Intraub & Richardson 1989). Boundary extension refers to the finding that people tend to remember information that was not shown but is likely to have been present outside the picture's boundaries. Although most of the earlier experiments obtained the boundary extension effect with slow presentation rates (4–15 sec), Intraub's more recent research obtained this phenomenon with stimuli shown for 250 msec. She concludes that higher-order knowledge is accessed early in the initial fixation on a scene, and that attention may be allocated quite flexibly during this initial fixation. Thus, conceptual processing of pictures occurs with rapidly presented sequences, but memory for these stimuli is very fleeting.

Failures to Detect Changes in Scenes

Further evidence for the fleeting nature of visual memories is presented in Wolfe's chapter. The striking examples of failure to detect changes in currently viewed scenes discussed there provide a serious challenge to existing theories of memory. For example, in a recent review of research and theorizing about memory, Morton (1997) made the following statements about the current-state buffer.

> If we close our eyes, we still know what room we are in, and if it had changed when we opened our eyes, we would be very surprised. . . . In a group of people, if we close our eyes, we still know where other people in the group are. We keep track of where people are and update who is in the room, where they are, what they are doing; we can manage a number of people in this way. In addition, the location of key objects will be readily to hand. In other words, we have a mental construction of our local environment, where we track objects and individuals around. (p. 936)

The research reviewed by Wolfe's chapter and discussed below suggests that Morton may have overestimated the accuracy and level of detail of the information in the current-state buffer. Wolfe reports that research from a number of laboratories, with a variety of paradigms, has demonstrated that our representations of visual information lack many details. He points out that the failures to report changes in scenes occur after the original scene has been removed and any iconic memory for the stimulus has been replaced by the altered scene. He argues that these failures in detection arise through *inattentional amnesia* rather than *inattentional blindness*.

Thus, research by Simons and Levin (1997), along with the studies by Grimes (1996) and others, suggests that the current-state buffer might represent far less information than Morton, and probably most of the rest of us, envisaged. For example, Grimes (1996) tracked subjects' eye movements while they viewed scenes for 10 sec and tried to remember them, and to report any changes that occurred during the viewing period. Scenes were altered during an eye movement, and the change occurred to one object or region. Objects could change in size, color, or location, or they could disappear. Only 33% of the changes were detected, and some changes were detected by no subjects. For instance, no subjects noticed that a prominent building in a city skyline became 25% larger. These results are surprising, in that the subjects viewing the pictures were trying to remember their contents because they expected a memory test to follow. Blackmore, Nelson, and Trosciansko (1995) used a different technique of forcing subjects to make an eye movement by moving the entire scene after 2 sec to an unpredictable location. Subjects were little better than chance at detecting a change when the scene moved. A static 250 msec gray mask before a scene change also reduced detection.

Simons (1996) examined changes to simple arrays of 5 common objects, such as a cap, keys, and stapler, shown for 2 sec. A scene change occurred after 4.3 sec. An object could be replaced by a new one, 2 objects could switch positions, or an object could be moved to a new (previously empty) location. The subjects were poor at detecting the identity changes and location switches, but were very accurate at detecting the configuration change when an object moved to a previously empty location.

Simons suggested that longer-lasting abstract representations of scenes may be formed through effortful encoding based on serial attentional processing. All subjects reported verbal encoding of the objects in the first array. This should have helped all conditions. Thus, the differences among the conditions must have been based on other factors. If verbal labeling contributes to the encoding of identity, then the object substitution condition should be difficult to detect for stimuli lacking obvious labels. Use of novel shapes devised by DeSchepper and Treisman (1996) reduced identity and location switch detection to chance levels, but configuration changes were still well detected. When subjects had to shadow a spoken story while viewing objects, only configuration change detection remained high (>90%). Thus, memory for layout appeared to be good under all conditions and was unaffected by verbal interference. Little visual information about object properties was preserved across views, whereas layout must have been effortlessly encoded and was retained.

O'Regan, Rensink, and Clark (1996) investigated whether scene changes producing transients were likely to be detected, and whether detection was affected by simultaneously occurring unrelated transients. Their scenes repeatedly changed back and forth every 6.2 sec. Objects changed in color, position, or presence. In a "mud splash" condition, 6 small ovals or squares (0.1 picture width) were "spattered" on the picture for 80 msec but did *not* obscure the scene change. Without the "mud splashes," change detection was immediate; with them, several transitions were needed, and changes in the "center of interest" were more likely to be detected than were other changes.

The role of attention was further explored by Rensink, O'Regan, and Clark (1996), whose subjects had to detect change in alternating (flickering) original and changed pictures (shown for 240 msec) separated by an 80 msec blank field. The large changes were very hard to detect in the flicker condition, with subjects requiring up to 20 sec for some scenes. Verbal cues to the change, or to changing objects, improved performance. Thus, detection of changes in scenes required attention to be directed to the item while it was changing.

A large variety of scenes have been used in these studies. Changes have been made to people, objects, buildings, or landscape features. The parameters that influence change detection have not yet been systematically studied, but the difficulties are not confined to particular classes of objects or types of features. Informal observations suggest that expertise in the domain of the changed object increases the probability of change detection: a colleague who studies animal behavior readily detected the changes in tusks in a picture of elephants, changes missed by the cognitive psychologists viewing the pictures. Likewise, one can only hope that an airline pilot would be better than undergraduates at detecting the 2 disappearing jet engines in one of Rensink et al.'s pair of pictures of a plane.

Changes in Dynamic Scenes

Changes to dynamic videotaped scenes were studied by Simons (1996). As Wolfe notes in his chapter, visual memory for object identity was poor even when the object was central to the event portrayed. Subjects watched a color videotape of a short conversation between two women seated at a table set with food and drinks. One woman poured a Diet Pepsi from a large bottle in view for 6.5 sec. Shortly after, the Diet Pepsi was replaced by a cardboard box. No subject reported the new object or the absence of the bottle. Thus, visual memory for object identity was poor when the object was an integral part of the event.

Further experiments by Levin and Simons (1997) showed poor change detection even when the change involved the sole protagonist in a film, a person who was the focus of attention throughout. Forty subjects were shown a videotape in which a simple action was performed by a single actor, for example, a person seated at a desk got up to answer a phone in the hall. The first actor was replaced between the 2 events shown. The actors were matched on gender, race, hair color, and glasses, and wore similar but not identical clothing. Subjects were asked to write a description of the videotape. Detection of change was reported by 33% of subjects, and only 2 more reported the change when asked.

When subjects were warned about the changed individual and were given a précis of events, few detection errors occurred. Levin and Simons concluded that object features are not automatically used to integrate different views of a scene. Attention seemed to be necessary but *not* sufficient to detect change, and intentional encoding was likely to be required.

Detection of Change in the Real World

People's ability to detect changes in the real world was studied by Simons and Levin (1997), who replaced an attended person in a natural setting. A man with a map approached a person and asked for directions. While the pair were studying the map and discussing the route, 2 men carrying a door walked between them, momentarily obscuring the direction seeker from view. The direction seeker changed places with one of the door carriers, and the former door carrier continued the conversation. Half of the subjects failed to notice the person substitution despite the fact that the 2 men differed in height, clothing, appearance, and voice. Some subjects remarked on the rude behavior of the door carriers. Simons and Levin noted that subjects who were older than the direction seeker were less likely than younger subjects to notice the substitution. This poorer performance was not simply due to aging cognitive processes. Young subjects' performance decreased when the direction seeker was dressed as a workman in uniform. Thus, social variables appear to have influenced the initial attention paid to the direction seeker, and hence the probability of detecting a change in his appearance.

Postattentive Vision and Repeated Search Experiments

In the repeated search task, subjects search for a probe in a display of 3–6 distractors. Surprisingly, even though the display remains the same, subjects' reaction times (RTs) do not improve on this task over hundreds of trials. Over trials, each of the items in the display must have been attended to, yet successive encounters with the previously attended-to objects do not facilitate visual search. In fact, if the task is performed as a *memory search* without the display, performance is actually *faster* than it was with the display present. The subjects can easily *recall* the distractor items (letters) and can perform the task as an STM search.

Wolfe's research has shown that people do not seem to remember postattentive visual representations. Wolfe proposed that the visual representation of an object seems to lapse into its preattentive state.

These and other search experiments indicate that the visual representation created by attention is very short-lived. Experiments using a visual curve-tracing task devised by Jolicoeur, Ullman, and MacKay (1986) yielded similar conclusions. Subjects judged whether a pair of dots was located on the same curve or on different curves when the curves were in close proximity. The locations of the 2 dots varied, but the curves were repeated over trials. There was no improvement in curve-tracing with repetition over a series of 100 trials. Some improvement was possible, and occurred when the curves differed in color.

Thus, the evidence suggests that detailed visual memories are very fleeting and may be available for no more than 100 msec. Wolfe's inattentional amnesia hypothesis claims that the postattentive representation reverts to its preattentive state. However, he argues that attention can prevent amnesia, and can link visual representation with object representations in long-term semantic memory. Wolfe suggests that conceptual STM provides a bridge between the contents of the visual representation and LTM.

The Attentional Blink

Shapiro and Luck's chapter reviewed some of their recent studies of the attentional blink. In these experiments, subjects have to search for 2 targets in a rapidly presented sequences of 8–20 visual stimuli. People are usually very accurate at reporting the first target but are impaired at report of the second target or probe. Probe detection was unaffected when the target immediately preceded the probe, or when a blank interval intervened between target and probe. There has to be at least 1 distractor between target and probe for the blink to occur. Shapiro and Luck review the role of masking and conclude that a number of studies indicate that the attentional blink occurs under conditions of interruption and/or conceptual masking.

Dual-target RSVP experiments show that the allocation of visual attention to an item produces a temporary suppression of visual processing. Raymond, Shapiro, and Arnell (1992) initially argued that target identification mechanisms appear to shut down after use, as if perceptual and attentional mechanisms "blink." More recent research led to a revised interference model proposed by Shapiro, Raymond, and Arnell. (1994).

The operation of the attentional blink was explored in an investigation of unilateral spatial neglect patients by Shapiro, Luck, and their colleagues. These patients suffer from right hemisphere lesions, and neglect has been viewed as a disorder of spatial attention. The patients and control groups were presented the dual-target detection task at a much slower rate of 5.5 items per second because they had difficulty in responding to more rapidly exposed items. In contrast to normal elderly subjects and right hemisphere stroke patients without neglect, the neglect patients showed an attentional blink of greater magnitude and duration (1.6 sec) than did the normal and right hemisphere stroke groups. Thus, patients with an attentional deficit are more susceptible to the conditions producing an attentional blink.

Neurophysiological mechanisms were further studied in experiments using normal subjects and ERP (evoked response potential) recordings. The advantage of the ERP measures is that they have highly accurate temporal resolution, and attentional effects can be reliably recorded within 100 msec after stimulus onset. Recordings taken during the attentional blink interval showed no effects on the early P1 and N1 amplitudes. A second experiment examined the N400 response, which occurs in the presence of semantic incongruity (e.g., a semantically anomalous completion of a sentence). Subjects had to decide whether the first target was an odd or even number and whether the second target (probe word) semantically matched a context word presented at the beginning of the RSVP list. Although the judgment of the probe showed the reduced accuracy characteristic of the attentional blink, the N400 response showed no reduction in amplitude, implying normal semantic processing of the probe word. Shapiro. Driver, Ward, and Sorensen's (1997) results are consistent with this possibility. They found enhanced recall of a third target semantically related to the second target that was subject to an attentional blink. The evidence of semantic processing of the word subject to the attentional blink led Shapiro and Luck to conclude that demands to respond to 2 temporally contiguous stimuli produce very short-lived representations of the second stimulis, which then becomes a "fleeting memory" unavailable for conscious report.

Repetition Blindness for Words and Pictures

Research on the attentional blink and on repetition blindness indicates limits on our ability to detect and register in episodic memory events presented at rates of about 8–12 items per second. Repetition blindness has been reported for letters, digits, and words presented in sentences and as lists.

The Token Individuation Model

Kanwisher argued that visual object recognition and written word recognition involve two processes: recognition of familiar objects or words (types), and distinguishing between different examples of the same type (tokens). Kanwisher's model distinguishes between information about an object's or a word's identity, termed "type" information, and information about visual episodes, termed "token" information. These two forms of information are separately encoded. As each list item is shown, it is recognized through activation of its type node. Episodes are recorded through the establishment of token nodes that represent serial order and other episodic information. Links connect type and token nodes. This process of token assignment was termed "token individuation."

Repetition blindness occurs because of limits on the process of token individuation. When a type node has been token-individuated, it is briefly unavailable for a second token individuation. Recall is possible only after token individuation, so the subject is aware only of the first occurrence of the repeated word. The limit on token individuation of a type must be time-dependent. This assumption explains the fact that repetition blindness does not occur with slower presentation rates, and decreases in magnitude with lag. Kanwisher argued that this limit on processing is a design feature of the visual system, and that it is not specifically linguistic.

Potter proposed, in her chapter, that the structuring process in conceptual short-term memory accesses types and their connections in LTM, but that copies or tokens of types are registered in conceptual short-term memory. Repetition blindness prevents an item from being registered in conceptual short-term memory. Alternatively, Bavelier (1994; Bavelier and Potter 1992) proposed that phonological repetition blindness occurs *after* a token had been opened for the second item, since she viewed token individuation as a gradual process. This explanation implies that items subject to repetition blindness are represented at least partially, and briefly, in conceptual short-term memory.

The lack of synonym repetition blindness suggests that token individuation is concerned with the representation of visual items and their names, but not their meanings. The inability to report a stimulus identical or similar to a recent stimulus indicates the fragility of memory for rapidly presented stimuli. Conceptual short-term memory encodes the two events as one when they are temporally close and have similar visual, orthographic, or phonological codes.

Phonological Repetition Blindness
Bavelier and Potter (1992) demonstrated repetition blindness for stimuli sharing the same name but differing in visual form, such as numbers reported as numbers (9) and written words (*nine*). These examples have the same name and meaning. Bavelier and Potter also found repetition

blindness for words sharing phonology only and differing in meaning (*eight/ate*), implicating a phonological code as the basis for repetition blindness. Subsequent research by Bavelier (1994) showed that repetition blindness can occur between repeated pictures and between a picture and its written name when these are presented in "rebus" sentences (which include pictures in place of some nouns).

Repetition Blindness for Words
Bavelier and Kanwisher's research has shown that some psycholinguistic variables but not others are determinants of repetition blindness. There is a large body of research on written word recognition, and there are detailed theories of the processing systems underlying written (and spoken) word recognition (e.g., M. Coltheart, Curtis, Atkins, & Haller 1993; Plaut, McClelland, Seidenberg, & Patterson 1996). Although there is disagreement between theorists concerning the existence of orthographic lexical-level representations, there is clear evidence of an early influence of orthographic neighborhood density on the recognition of written words. Orthographic neighborhood size was defined by M. Coltheart, Davelaar, Jonasson, and Besner (1977) as the number of real words of the same length as a target word that share all but one letter of the target, and their shared letters are in the same positions within the word (e.g., *like* and *lake*). Written words activate their orthographic neighbors early during the processes of word recognition (M. Coltheart et al. 1977). Bavelier's research discussed in chapter 7 shows that pairs of orthographic neighbors generate as much repetition blindness as do identical words, and that the repetition blindness is maximal at a short interval between the critical words. The finding suggests that for words, type activation involves the orthographic input lexicon (or in parallel distributed processing models, the orthographic units), and that token individuation involves the binding of active orthographic input representations to episodic tokens.

Research on word recognition has shown that phonological information is also activated automatically when words are recognized (e.g., Jared & Seidenberg 1991). Bavelier's research has provided evidence of phonological repetition blindness. Pairs of words sharing the same phonology (homophones such as *won/one*) generate repetition blindness. Thus, orthographic units are not the only form of information represented in tokens. Of course, homophones usually are orthographically very similar. However, Bavelier, Prasada, and Segui (1994) found that phonological similarity, in the absence of much orthographic similarity (*freight/great*), also can cause repetition blindness. Bavelier argues in her chapter that the establishment of tokens is a gradual process, and that orthographic information is represented in the token before phonological information is linked. The phonological units may be sublexical as well as lexical.

Bavelier et al. (1994) examined the relative contributions of orthographic and phonological codes to repetition blindness. Words that are orthographic neighbors (share all but one letter, and all shared letters occupy the same position), such as *reach/react,* yielded as much repetition blindness as did identical word pairs despite the fact that the orthographic neighbors were low in phonological similarity. Phonologically similar but orthographically dissimilar word pairs such as *freight/ great* produced reduced levels of repetition blindness compared with orthographic neighbors. Furthermore, the time course of the repetition blindness effects differed: orthographic effects were greatest at short interstimulus intervals; phonological ones, at longer ones. These results accord with word recognition research that shows early orthographic activation effects by word neighbors and later phonological effects. Bavelier proposes that visual and orthographic repetition blindness occur through failure to instantiate a new token, whereas phonological repetition blindness is produced by difficulty in stabilizing the new token through binding with other codes.

Evidence that orthographic repetition blindness arises at an early stage of word recognition also comes from studies of the role of morphological relationships between similar word pairs. Morphological relatedness (*jump/jumped*) did not increase the level of repetition blindness found for unrelated pairs (*wand/wander*). Word frequency was a determinant of repetition blindness only for the first critical word, with greater repetition blindness for orthographic neighbors of high frequency. This, too, implicates early word recognition processes in repetition blindness.

Phonological codes are activated during word recognition, and their generation is required for oral and written recall. The phonological property of rime agreement appeared not to influence the level of repetition blindness. These orthographic and phonological effects have been simulated by Bavelier and Jordan's (1992) model, which is described in Bavelier's chapter.

That chapter also presents electrophysiological recordings (ERP data) during conditions generating repetition blindness. These recordings showed a reduced negative component at 200 msec after presentation of the repeated word on repetition blindness trials. This effect was observed mainly in recordings over the left fronto-temporal areas, and its occurrence was much earlier than the STM rehearsal effects demonstrated in ERPs at 400–600 msec. Bavelier predicts that token individuation problems should be marked in neuropsychological patients having spatial and temporal deficits. Finally, although the research discussed in the chapter was based mainly on written words, Bavelier argues that the processes postulated are used in establishing object-specific representations in a wider sense.

Semantic and morphological units do not appear to be represented in tokens. Bavelier obtained no evidence for repetition blindness at the morphological level that could not be attributed to orthographic repetition blindness. Kanwisher and Potter (1990) failed to find evidence of semantic repetition blindness between words similar in meaning (*sofa/couch*). Kanwisher, Yin, and Wojciulik's chapter extended these studies and observed a *repetition benefit* or facilitation when a pair of semantically related words occurred in RSVP lists of 3 words. Thus, for written words, tokens represent orthographic and phonological information.

The possibility that semantic information might be represented in tokens was considered in studies of bilinguals required to recall RSVP sequences containing words from both languages (MacKay & Miller 1994; MacKay, Abrams, Pedroza, & Miller 1996; Altarriba & Soltano 1996). The evidence is conflicting concerning the existence of repetition blindness for translations (*horse/cheval*) when these are presented in mixed-language sentences. However with lists of 3 words, Altarriba and Soltano (1996) found a repetition facilitation for translations of English and Spanish words, as did V. Coltheart and Ling (1998) for Chinese–English translations. These results are consistent with the claim that tokens of words represent orthographic and phonological, but not semantic, information, since the Spanish–English and Chinese –English translations were orthographically and phonologically dissimilar.

The semantic facilitation effect, better recall of translations or of words similar in meaning, constitutes further evidence for Potter's theory of very short-term conceptual memory. It indicates the early availability of fleeting semantic, conceptual representations. Given the interactive processing assumptions of current language-processing models, it follows that orthographic and phonological representations are further activated by the semantic activation produced by a pair of words related in meaning. Hence, the activation produced by the meaning of *horse* will increment the activation of the orthographic and phonological representations of both *horse* and *cheval*, and increase the likelihood of token establishment for these two words. Similarly, the semantic activation produced by *sofa* and *couch* will increase the orthographic and phonological activations for these words, and thereby increase the probability of token individuation for both *sofa* and *couch*.

Repetition Blindness for Pictures

In chapter 6, Kanwisher et al. reported research demonstrating that tokens for objects, or pictures of them, appear to differ in content from word tokens. They examined the types of relationships between a pair of objects likely to yield repetition blindness—specifically, transformations, size changes, rotations in the picture plane or in depth. They reasoned that if repetition blindness is present and its magnitude is unaffected by these differences between the critical picture pair, the episodic memory token established within 200–300 msec must be relatively abstract. Their results indicated that repetition blindness occurred for a pair of objects shown in different locations, in different sizes, from different viewing angles, and, to a lesser extent, for different exemplars of the same type of object (piano: upright vs. grand). Unlike repetition blindness for word pairs, pairs of semantically related objects (e.g., *helicopter/plane*) showed significant but weaker repetition blindness. Similarly shaped objects that were taxonomically unrelated (e.g., *pear/guitar*) also generated significant but weaker repetition blindness than did identical objects. Thus, for pictures of objects, repetition blindness can arise from view-independent object representations, but both visual similarity and conceptual/semantic similarity contribute to the deficit. Again, unlike repetition blindness for words, for pictures of two objects, sharing a phonological code (name) was insufficient to generate repetition blindness. Thus, there was no repetition blindness between the visually dissimilar baseball bat and mammalian bat, which share the name *bat*.

The absence of phonological repetition blindness might be due to the fact that the retrieval of object names is a slow process compared with the derivation of phonology for a written word (Potter & Faulconer 1975). Use of the typical RSVP rate of 10 pictures/second does not permit retrieval of phonological (name) representations early enough for the phonological codes to be registered in episodic memory tokens. Furthermore, semantic information about a picture or object is extracted very early, and this information might be represented in the picture's token.

The Role of Phonological Coding in RSVP Picture and Word Recall

Further evidence that phonological codes are unlikely to contribute to recall of rapidly presented pictures, but can play a role in the recall of written words, is provided by some results reported in my chapter 8. Recall of rapidly presented word lists showed a detrimental effect of phonological similarity; this effect was removed by concurrent articulation. Recall of picture lists was unaffected by the similarity of their *names* when the lists were shown at the rate of 8 per second. However, at the slower STM rate of 1 picture per second, pictures with similar names were harder to recall than were pictures with dissimilar names.

When picture *names* were the list items, the lists showed a phonological similarity effect at both fast and slow rates. This latter finding is also consistent with Kanwisher et al.'s work. When they presented picture names in their RSVP task, phonologically identical names generated repetition blindness. Thus, when rapidly presented pictures are shown, these are encoded into episodic memory tokens as abstract visual representations, and the tokens contain some semantic/conceptual information as well. In contrast, as stated earlier, episodic memory tokens for words represent orthographic and phonological information.

Conceptual/semantic information is activated rapidly for written words. However, through processes of interactive activation in the word recognition system, semantic activation can enhance orthographic and phonological activation, resulting in a facilitation effect on recall of written words whose tokens are thereby more readily established. Thus, fleeting memories established at fast presentation rates of up to 10 items per second may be based on phonological codes, but only if item names can be retrieved rapidly. Rapid retrieval of phonological information can occur for monosyllabic written words but not for pictures of common objects.

Chapter 8 reports experiments using RSVP presentation showing that the phonological effects found in sentence evaluation in normal reading tasks also occurred at rates at which repetition blindness is observed. Recall of such RSVP sentences demonstrated phonological repetition blindness when sentences contained homophone pairs. Thus, it seems likely that a common phonological code is generated in STM list presentation, written sentence comprehension, and phonological repetition blindness. However, as Potter has noted in her chapter and elsewhere, recirculation or rehearsal of this phonological code is not likely to be possible at fast RSVP rates. Thus, the phonological code that is generated in sentence comprehension tasks, phonological repetition blindness, and RSVP word lists is not produced through rehearsal, but is the result of automatic processes occurring during reading. The typical repetition blindness paradigm and the list recall task require explicit generation of the phonological codes for the recall task. This explicit generation of the phonological code is possible for no more than 2 or 3 words when presentation rates of 8–10 per second are used. Thus, as Potter argued in her chapter, recall of whole sentences of up to 12 words shown at rates of 10 words per second cannot be based on phonological codes of the individual words. Sentence recall must be based on semantic and conceptual codes activated very early in processing.

When a pair of homophones is presented in close temporal proximity in a rapid sequence of words, it is difficult to establish separate episodic memory representations for them because tokens for words are based on orthographic and phonological information. Experiments reported in chapter 8 showed that phonological repetition blindness reduced access to the repeated word's semantic features in an explicit semantic categorization task (Is it part of the body? NOSE). On the other hand, the repeated word produced as much semantic priming of a lexical decision target as did the same semantic prime when no related word preceded it. Thus, semantic information about the second, critical word is available in phonological repetition blindness, as it is for words that are subject to the attentional blink. The finding of semantic priming in a phonological repetition blindness paradigm supports Potter's theory of early activation of semantic and conceptual representations of words, and can be explained by the 2-stage model of Chun and Potter (1995) described below.

Mechanisms Underlying the Attentional Blink and Repetition Blindness

The attentional blink and repetition blindness are phenomena that occur under similar temporal parameters when visual stimuli are presented at the rate of 8–12 items a second. The attentional blink has been found with lists of 9–20 alphanumeric characters and with word lists. Repetition blindness has been studied with shorter lists of the same types and also with sentences, pictures, and picture–word mixed lists. Both phenomena diminish as a function of increase in a filled temporal lag between 2 critical targets. The response requirements differ in that subjects search for and report 2 targets whose category is prespecified in attentional blink experiments, whereas they usually have to report the entire list or sentence in repetition blindness studies. The report of the first target is usually more accurate than is the report of the second target for both phenomena.

Potter's chapter comments on these phenomena and refers to some of Chun's recent research. Chun (1997) devised an elegant series of experiments aimed at establishing whether limitations at different processing stages underlie the attentional blink and repetition blindness. He investigated the presence of attentional blink and repetition blindness within a single task in which subjects had to report only 2 targets: letters in a sequence containing digit or keyboard distractors. Chun found a double dissociation between variables affecting the attentional blink and repetition blindness. In experiments 1 and 2, the attentional blink did not occur with symbol distractors that are dissimilar to targets (and some of whose names are less familiar than are letter and digit names, e.g., #, <, /), whereas repetition blindness did occur when the repeated letter immediately followed its predecessor (lag 1) or followed after 1 intervening symbol distractor (lag 2). In contrast, increasing the distinctiveness between the two targets (by presentation of each in a different color) eliminated repetition blindness but not the attentional blink in experiment 3. A similar pattern of results occurred in experiments 4A and 4B, but the attentional blink effect appears to have been considerably attenuated in experiment 4B, in which letter targets were colored.

Chun concluded that the 2 deficits are due to limitations at different stages of visual processing. He argued that the visual system constructs episodic representations through the activation of visual types in long-term semantic memory and registers spatiotemporal information. These separate forms of information must be linked, a process termed "binding" that has been assumed to require attention (Kanwisher 1991; Treisman & Gelade 1980). These temporary episodic representations are the basis for conscious visual object recognition. Chun proposed that familiar forms of stimuli such as letters, numbers, words, and objects can activate their entries in the orthographic or object recognition systems very rapidly at presentation rates of 10–15 items per second. Identification or recognition is possible, but conscious report or storage in short-term memory requires additional processing (Chun & Potter 1995).

The attentional blink and repetition blindness occur through failures in the processes of token establishment. The attentional blink arises through difficulties in visual type discrimination when there is a low signal-to-noise ratio between the LTM representations of targets and distractors. Repetition blindness occurs through a failure to individuate separate tokens of the *same* type.

Chun and Potter (1995) proposed that 2 stages were required for target identification and report with rapidly presented sequences of stimuli. Stage 1 involves processes of word or object recognition, specifically, activation of orthographic units, object recognition units, and semantic, phonological, and possibly other forms of representations. Stage 2 involves object token instantiation. Spatiotemporal tokens are set up, and focal attention is used to link the activated recognition units of stage 1 to appropriate spatiotemporal tokens. This second stage is required for conscious report, and the process is rate- and capacity-limited. Chun and Potter (1995) assumed that adjacent targets entered stage 2 together, and the results indicate that subjects have difficulty in discriminating their temporal order. According to the 2-stage model, the attentional blink occurs when the second target arrives while stage 2 processing of the first target is still in progress. Thus, the second target undergoes only stage 1 processing and will be unavailable for report.

Repetition blindness occurs through a different processing limitation, difficulty in setting up a second spatiotemporal token for items that have the same, or very similar, activated representations. Under conditions of close temporal contiguity, the 2 sets of active representations are treated as arising from a single event.

Support for the 2-stage model is provided by the findings of semantic priming in both repetition blindness and attentional blink paradigms. The fact that a word subject to attentional blink or repetition blindness can semantically prime a subsequent word indicates that its semantic representation has been activated, and that the recognition processes hypothesized to occur in stage 1 have taken place.

Sentence Repetition by Patients with STM Deficit

The performance of a subgroup of patients with a short-term memory deficit (termed conduction aphasia) is intriguing. Research with these types of patients was reported by Saffran and Marin (1975), and more recent studies are discussed by Saffran and Martin in chapter 9. Most of these patients are capable of verbal learning and do not have episodic LTM impairments. Their major difficulty appears to be a deficit in phonological encoding and storage. Their deficit is manifested by poor nonword repetition as well as reduced or absent phonological similarity effects in STM tasks. Their poor verbatim recall of sentences has been interpreted as suggesting that phonological coding might contribute to sentence repetition. Potter (1993) questioned the necessity of phonological coding to support sentence recall, arguing that lexical retrieval deficits might also contribute to the patients' performance. Saffran and Martin argue in chapter 9 that there is little evidence of lexical retrieval deficits in these patients. They suggest that for unimpaired adults, sentence repetition is based on conceptual representations (as claimed by Potter), primed lexical and semantic representations, and phonologically coded information. The reduction in use of phonologically coded information implies that sentence repetition will largely reflect conceptual STM in patients with such impairments.

The repetition responses of the STM patients demonstrate that inferences were frequently drawn. Structurally ambiguous sentences are sometimes repeated, with both meanings represented in the paraphrased recall. If these repetitions are indeed overt manifestations of conceptual STM, then these fleeting memories are remarkably elaborated. It would be interesting to discover whether the patients display normal forms of attentional blink and orthographic and object-based repetition blindness. Given their failure to demonstrate phonological similarity effects in STM tasks, will they display phonological repetition blindness? The answers to these questions may be difficult to determine if the patients have a general impairment in processing rapidly presented visual stimuli, and it would then be inappropriate to subject them to the demands of these tasks.

Conclusion

The research reviewed in this book about fleeting visual memory has shown that words, sentences, and scenes rapidly generate a conceptual representation. This ensures that words, sentences, and scenes are almost instantaneously comprehended, on-line, as they are encountered. Thus, we can make immediate sense of the world around us, and respond appropriately to changing situations and verbal communications. Potter's chapter reviewed many examples demonstrating that semantic representations of sentences are very rapidly constructed and that early selection determines the processing of ambiguous elements (e.g., misspelled words). However, the ability to extract the essential meaning of a scene or a statement entails some processing costs.

A variety of processing failures are discussed in this book. Wolfe's research demonstrated failures in retention of postattentive visual representations in repeated visual search tasks. These search experiments suggest that visual memories generated by attention are fleeting. Such processing limits cause failures to detect scene changes if the changes involve scene components that are not of major importance for conceptual representation of the scene. For example, Mondy (1997) found no failures to detect the removal of a baby carried on the back of a woman who was the central figure in a scene. Likewise, we sometimes fail to detect the occurrence of 2 different tokens of the same stimulus, or even of 2 tokens of stimuli with similar visual forms, the phenomenon termed repetition blindness.

Although the processing system that generates conceptual representations operates very rapidly, additional processing stages are required to permit conscious report of designated stimuli. These stages are subject to some processing limits. If they are needed for 2 (or more) stimuli shown in rapid succession, they may not be available for the second stimulus. Such processing limitations are illustrated by the multiple-target report task that has been shown to yield an attentional blink. Additionally, we sometimes fail to detect the occurrence of 2 different tokens of the same stimulus, or even of 2 tokens of stimuli with similar visual forms (repetition blindness).

A good understanding of the short-term memory processes important in memory for slowly presented sequences of items has developed over the past 30 years. As this book shows, however, there are other memory processes highly competent at dealing with very rapidly presented stimulus sequences: memory processes responsible for early cognitions and fleeting memories. A task for future memory theorists is to develop an integrated model of memory that will offer an account of both sets of memory processes.

References

Altarriba, J., & Soltano, E. G. (1996). Repetition blindness and bilingual memory: Token individuation for translation equivalents. *Memory & Cognition, 24* 700–711.

Bavelier, D. (1994). Repetition blindness between visually different items: The case of pictures and words. *Cognition, 51,* 199–236.

Bavelier, D., & Jordan, M. I. (1992). A dynamic model of word recognition. In C. L. Giles, S. J. Hanson, & J. D. Cowan (eds.), *Advances in neural information processing systems* (vol. 5, pp. 879–886). San Mateo, CA: Morgan Kaufman.

Bavelier, D., & Potter, M. C. (1992). Visual and phonological codes in repetition blindness. *Journal of Experimental Psychology: Human Perception and Performance, 18,* 134–147.

Bavelier, D., & Prasada, S., & Segui, J. (1994). Repetition blindness between words: Nature of the orthographic and phonological representations involved. *Journal of Experimental Psychology: Learning, Memory and Cognition, 20,* 1437–1455.

Biederman, I. (1981). On the semantics of a glance at a scene. In M. Kubovy & J. R. Pomerantz (eds.), *Perceptual organization.* Hillsdale, NJ: Lawrence Erlbaum Associates.

Blackmore, G. B. (S. J.), Nelson, K., & Troscianko, T. (1995). Is the richness of our visual world an illusion? Transsaccadic memory for complex scenes. *Perception, 24,* 1075–1081.

Chun, M. M. (1997). Types and tokens in visual processing: A double dissociation between the attentional blink and repetition blindness. *Journal of Experimental Psychology: Human Perception and Performance, 23,* 738–755.

Chun, M. M., & Potter, M. C. (1995). A two-stage model for multiple target detection in rapid serial visual presentation. *Journal of Experimental Psychology: Human Perception and Performance, 21,* 109–127.

Coltheart, M., Curtis, B., Atkins, P., & Haller, M. (1993). Models of reading aloud: Dual-route and parallel-distributed-processing approaches. *Psychological Review, 100,* 589–608.

Coltheart, M., Davelaar, E., Jonasson, J. T., & Besner, D. (1977). Access to the internal lexicon. In S. Dornie (ed.), *Attention and performance IV* (pp. 535–555). Hillsdale, NJ: Lawrence Erlbaum Associates.

Coltheart, V., & Ling Ban Seng, J. (1998). Recall of single and mixed language RSVP lists by Chinese-English bilinguals. Paper presented at the International Workshop on Written Language Processing. Sydney, December.

Currie, C. B., & McConkie, G. W. (1997). Detecting single fixation changes in pictures. Paper presented at 38th annual meeting of the Psychonomic Society, Philadelphia, November.

DeSchepper, B., & Treisman, A. (1996). Visual memory for novel shapes: Implicit coding without attention. *Journal of Experimental Psychology: Learning, Memory and Cognition, 22,* 27–47.

Forster, K. I. (1970). Visual perception of rapidly presented word sequences of varying complexity. *Perception & Psychophysics, 8*, 215–221.

Grimes, J. (1996). On the failure to detect changes in scenes across saccades. In K. Akins (ed.), *Perception* (pp. 89–110). New York: Oxford University Press.

Intraub, H. (1981). Rapid conceptual identification of sequentially presented pictures. *Journal of Experimental Psychology: Human Perception and Performance, 7*, 604–610.

Intraub, H., & Richardson, M. (1989). Wide-angle memories of close-up scenes. *Journal of Experimental Psychology: Learning, Memory and Cognition, 15*, 179–187.

Jared, D., & Seidenberg, M. S. (1991). Does word identification proceed from spelling to sound to meaning? *Journal of Experimental Psychology: General, 120*, 1–37.

Jolicoeur, P., Ullman, S., & MacKay, M. (1986). Curve tracing: A possible basic operation in the perception of spatial relations. *Memory & Cognition, 14*, 129–140.

Kanwisher, N. G. (1991). Repetition blindness and illusory conjunctions: Errors in binding visual types with visual tokens. *Journal of Experimental Psychology: Human Perception and Performance, 17*, 404–421.

Kanwisher, N. G., & Potter, M. C. (1990). Repetition blindness: Levels of processing. *Journal of Experimental Psychology: Human Perception and Performance, 16*, 30–47.

Levin, D. T., & Simons, D. J. (1997). Failure to detect changes to attended objects in motion pictures. *Psychonomic Bulletin and Review, 4*, 501–506.

Luck, S. J., Vogel, E. K., & Shapiro, K. L. (1996). Word meanings can be accessed but not reported during the attentional blink. *Nature, 382*, 616–618.

MacKay, D. G., Abrams, L., Pedroza, M. J., & Miller, M. D. (1996). Cross-language facilitation, semantic blindness, and the relation between language and memory: A reply to Altarriba and Soltano. *Memory & Cognition, 24*, 712–718.

MacKay, D. G., & Miller, M. D. (1994). Semantic blindness: Repeated concepts are difficult to encode and recall under time pressure. *Psychological Science, 5*, 52–55.

Mondy, S. (1997). Unpublished PhD experiments. Macquarie University, NSW, Australia.

Morton, John. (1997). Free associations with EPS and memory. *Quarterly Journal of Experimental Psychology, 50A*, 924–941.

O'Regan, J. K., Rensink, R., & Clark, J. J. (1996). "Mud splashes" render picture changes invisible. *Investigative Ophthalmology and Visual Science, 37*, S213.

Plaut, D. C., McClelland, J. L., Seidenberg, M. S., & Patterson, K. E. (1996). Understanding normal and impaired word reading: Computational principles in quasi-regular domains. *Psychological Review, 103*, 56–115.

Potter, M. C. (1975). Meaning in visual search. *Science, 187*, 965–966.

Potter, M. C. (1976). Short-term conceptual memory for pictures. *Journal of Experimental Psychology: Human Learning and Memory, 2*, 509–522.

Potter, M. C. (1984). Rapid serial visual presentation (RSVP): A method for studying language processing. In D. E. Kieras and M. A. Just (eds.), *New methods in reading comprehension research* (pp. 91–118). Hillsdale, NJ: Lawrence Erlbaum Associates.

Potter, M. C. (1993). Very short-term conceptual memory. *Memory & Cognition, 21*, 156–161.

Potter, M. C., & Faulconer, B. A. (1975). Time to understand pictures and words. *Nature, 253*, 437–438.

Potter, M. C., Kroll, J. F., & Harris, C. (1980). Comprehension and memory in rapid sequential reading. In R. Nickerson (ed.), *Attention and Performance VIII* (pp. 395–418). Hillsdale, NJ: Lawrence Erlbaum Associates.

Potter, M. C., Kroll, J. F., Yachzel, B., Carpenter, E., & Sherman, J. (1986). Pictures in sentences: Understanding without words. *Journal of Experimental Psychology: General, 115*, 281–294.

Potter, M. C., & Lombardi, L. (1990). Regeneration in the short-term recall of sentences. *Journal of Memory and Language, 29*, 633–654.

Potter, M. C., Moryadas, A., Abrams, I., & Noel, A. (1993). Word perception and misperception in context. *Journal of Experimental Psychology: Learning, Memory and Cognition, 19*, 3–22.

Potter, M. C., Stiefbold, D., & Moryadas, A. (1998). Word selection in reading sentences: Preceding versus following contexts. *Journal of Experimental Psychology: Learning, Memory and Cognition, 24*, 68–100.

Raymond, J. E., Shapiro, K. L., & Arnell, K. M. (1992). Temporary suppression of visual processing in an RSVP task: An attentional blink? *Journal of Experimental Psychology: Human Perception and Performance, 18*, 849–860.

Rensink, R. A., O'Regan, J. R., & Clark, J. J. (1996). To see or not to see: The need for attention to perceive changes in scenes. *Psychological Science*, 368–373.

Saffran, E. M., & Marin, O. S. M. (1975). Immediate memory for word lists and sentences in a patient with a deficient auditory short-term memory. *Brain and Language, 2*, 420–433.

Shapiro, K., Driver, J., Ward, R., & Sorenson, R. E. (1997). Priming from the attentional blink: A failure to extract visual tokens but not visual types. *Psychological Science, 8*, 95–100.

Shapiro, K. L., Raymond, J. E., & Arnell, K. M. (1994). Attention to visual pattern information produces the attentional blink in RSVP. *Journal of Experimental Psychology: Human Perception and Performance, 20*, 357–371.

Simons, D. J. (1996). In sight, out of mind: When object representations fail. *Psychological Science, 7*, 301–305.

Simons, D. J., & Levin, D. T. (1997). Change blindness. *Trends in Cognitive Sciences, 1*, 261–267.

Treisman, A. M., & Gelade, G. (1980). A feature-integration theory of attention. *Cognitive Psychology, 12*, 97–136.

Contributors

Daphne Bavelier
Department of Brain and Cognitive Sciences
University of Rochester
Rochester, New York

Veronika Coltheart
Psychology Department
Macquarie University
Sydney, Australia

Helene Intraub
Department of Psychology
University of Delaware
Newark, Delaware

Nancy Kanwisher
Department of Brain and Cognitive Sciences
Massachusetts Institute of Technology
Cambridge, Massachusetts

Stephen J. Luck
Department of Psychology
University of Iowa
Iowa City, Iowa

Nadine Martin
Center for Cognitive Neuroscience
Department of Neurology
Temple University School of Medicine
Philadelphia, Pennsylvania

Mary Potter
Department of Brain and Cognitive Sciences
Massachusetts Institute of Technology
Cambridge, Massachusetts

Eleanor M. Saffran
Center for Cognitive Neuroscience
Department of Neurology
Temple University School of Medicine
Philadelphia, Pennsylvania

Kimron L. Shapiro
School of Psychology
University of Wales
Bangor, Gwynedd
Wales

Ewa Wojciulik
Department of Brain and Cognitive Sciences
Massachusetts Institute of Technology
Cambridge, Massachusetts

Jeremy M. Wolfe
Center for Ophthalmic Research
Brigham and Women's Hospital
Boston, Massachusetts

Carol Yin
Department of Brain and Cognitive Sciences
Massachusetts Institute of Technology
Cambridge, Massachusetts

Index

Abstract representations, 119, 121
Acoustic similarity effect. *See*
Phonological similarity effects
ACT, 15
Agrammatic aphasia, 226
Allport, D. A., 20, 226
Altarriba, J., 9, 24, 251
Armstrong, I. T., 124, 143, 146
Andersen, R. A., 105
Anderson, J., 15
Anderson, R. A., 187
Anllo-Vento, L., 171
Aperture viewing experiment, 60
Arnell, K. M., 20, 21, 95, 98, 99, 103, 143, 144
Articulatory loop, 14, 38–41, 186, 187, 190
Atkinson, R. C., 186
Attention
and change detection, 244–245
in elderly individuals, 105, 107
and electrophysiological responses, 108–109
Attentional blink, 7, 33, 73, 89, 95, 189.
See also Repetition blindness
Chun and Potter's two-stage model of, 8, 18–20, 101, 103, 254, 255–256
and conceptual short-term memory, 16, 17, 18–20
conditions for, 246
and elderly subject data, 247
and evoked response potential, 109, 114–115, 219, 247
and fleeting memories, 115–116, 247
interference model of, 98, 103–104, 246
and masking, 102–105, 246
method, 96, 97, 109

and right hemisphere stroke patient data, 247
in unilateral spatial neglect patients, 8, 105–108, 246–247
and visual stimuli, 254
Attentional deficits, 20–22, 247
Attentional mechanisms in neglect, 105–107
Attentive vision, 74–75
Attig, E., 175
Auditory blink, 20, 25
Auditory verbal span, 226, 228–229
Averbach, E., 1, 2
Awareness, 121, 123, 145, 146

Baddeley, A. D., 10, 14, 38–39, 162, 169, 185, 186, 187, 188, 190, 195, 228, 236
Baillargeon, R., 152
Banks, W. P., 181
Bartha, M., 235
Bartram, D. J., 122
Basic-level objects in memory, 131–132
Basso, A., 228
Bateman, N., 214, 215, 217
Bauer, R. M., 123
Bavelier and Jordan's model of repetition blindness, 165–167, 250
Bavelier, D., 9, 10, 23, 24, 41, 119–147 *passim*, 151–175 *passim*, 181–220 *passim*, 248, 249, 250, 251
Baylis, G. C., 75, 76, 120, 174
Behrmann, M., 151
Benson, R., 175
Berti, A., 123
Besner, D., 190
Biederman, I., 49, 122, 123, 131, 136, 142, 241